The Crypto Launderers

The Crypto Launderers

Crime and Cryptocurrencies from the Dark Web to DeFi and Beyond

David Carlisle

WILEY

Registered Office(s)
John Wiley & Sons Ltd, The Atrium, Southern Gate, Chichester, West Sussex, PO19 8SQ, UK
John Wiley & Sons, Inc., 111 River Street, Hoboken, NJ 07030, USA

Editorial Office
The Atrium, Southern Gate, Chichester, West Sussex, PO19 8SQ, UK

For details of our global editorial offices, customer services, and more information about Wiley products visit us at www.wiley.com.

Library of Congress Cataloging-in-Publication Data:

Names: Carlisle, David (Financial crime consultant), author.
Title: The crypto launderers : crime and cryptocurrencies from the Dark Web to DeFi and beyond / David Carlisle.
Description: Hoboken, NJ : Wiley, 2024. | Includes index.
Identifiers: LCCN 2023040107 (print) | LCCN 2023040108 (ebook) | ISBN 9781394203192 (cloth) | ISBN 9781394203208 (adobe pdf) | ISBN 9781394203215 (epub)
Subjects: LCSH: Cryptocurrencies. | Commercial crimes.
Classification: LCC HG1710.3 .C465 2024 (print) | LCC HG1710.3 (ebook) | DDC 363.25/968—dc23/eng/20231026
LC record available at https://lccn.loc.gov/2023040107
LC ebook record available at https://lccn.loc.gov/2023040108

Cover Design: Wiley
Cover Image: © Oleksandra Klestova/iStock
Author Photo: Nina Assam

Set in 11.5/14pts and STIX Two Text by Straive, Chennai, India
SKY10060328_112223

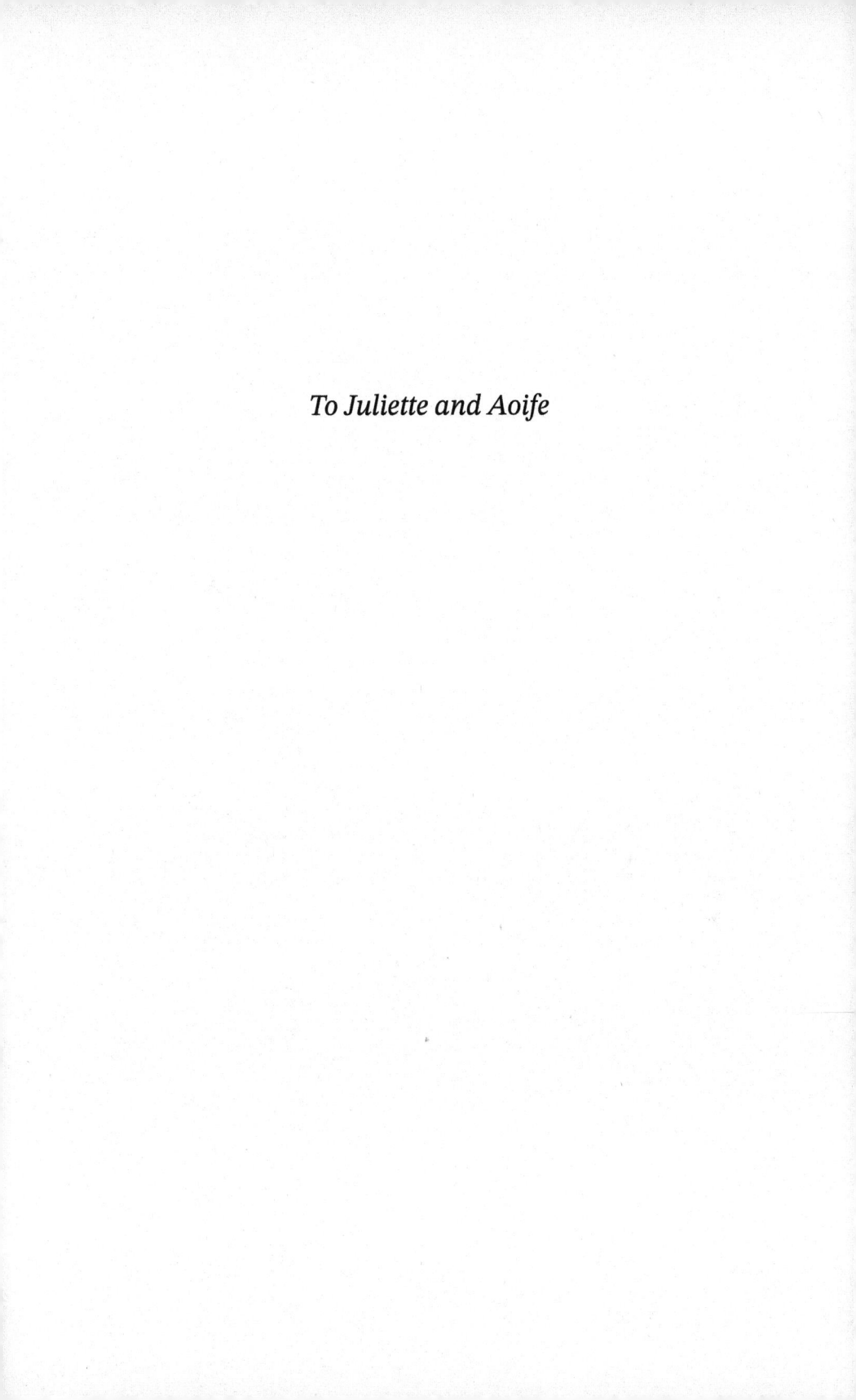

To Juliette and Aoife

Contents

Foreword   ix

Timeline of Key Events   xi

Prologue   xv

Chapter 1: The Dark Web: The Origins of Crypto Laundering   1

Chapter 2: Black Holes: The Rise of the Rogue Exchange   23

Chapter 3: Mixers: Covering Up Their Tracks   39

Chapter 4: Privacy Coins: Going Underground   59

Chapter 5: Bitcoin ATMs: Crypto Hits the Streets   83

Chapter 6: Ransomware: Cybercrime Goes Industrial   97

Chapter 7: Hacked: Crypto Exchange Heists   123

Chapter 8: DeFi: Tornadoes, Bridges, and the Frontiers
                of Regulation   139

Chapter 9: NFTs: Virtual Art, Virtual Crime   163

Chapter 10: Brave New World: The Metaverse, Web 3.0,
               and the Battle for the Future of Finance   177

Afterword: How Much Crime in Crypto?   193
Acknowledgements   199
Glossary   201
List of Figures   207
Bibliography   209
Notes   211
Index   249

Foreword

Money laundering and fraud have threatened our financial systems for thousands of years. Many cite the first recorded instance of financial crime taking place in 300 BC, when a Greek merchant, Hegestratos, took out a large insurance policy on a ship full of grain. Hegestratos proceeded to sink his (empty) ship, keeping both the insurance money and the grain. What is remarkable about this story is that much of the fraud we see taking place today is so similar to what took place over 2,000 years ago.

But what happens to that financial crime when an entirely new form of digital money is introduced, one whose movements are recorded transparently and immutably on a blockchain for all to see? Does the traceability of cryptocurrencies spell the end of money laundering as we know it? Or do the borderless and pseudonymous characteristics of Bitcoin and other cryptocurrencies mean that financial crime will find a place to thrive? These are just some of the important questions that David Carlisle answers for us as he explores the fascinating, and at times unbelievable, history of crypto money laundering in his book, *The Crypto Launderers*.

David has been a committed student of financial crime in cryptocurrencies for a decade, almost as long as cryptocurrencies have existed (Satoshi Nakamoto published the Bitcoin White Paper in 2008). Now turned teacher, David has been educating those of us working in the crypto industry and in the anti-financial crime community on the technologies that enable cryptocurrencies to work and what those innovations mean for how we must fight financial crime in this new world. Crucially, he has been responsible for regularly bringing us together to collaborate on this important topic.

When David authored the world's first guide to the most common typologies in crypto financial crime, which we published at Elliptic in 2018, we were immediately struck by the strong appetite for knowledge about this emerging topic – for a common language to unify our response, and for a collaborative dialogue to align us. The *Elliptic Typologies Report*, which David continues to update annually, is cited by many of our clients as their "bible," and continues to be the definitive reference guide to identifying and understanding the financial crime risk landscape for cryptoassets. David's pioneering thought leadership in this space makes him the authority on money laundering in crypto – the perfect person to tell its story and, critically, to help us understand how to tackle it.

This book is not only a hugely enjoyable and immersive read, but also an incredibly important one. Whether you're a fervent believer in cryptocurrencies, a skeptical onlooker, or somewhere in between, the fact is that the movement of assets on blockchains – from cryptocurrencies such as Bitcoin, to digital artworks known as NFTs, to tokenized real-world assets – is already a reality and becoming more mainstream by the day. We ignore the opportunities and challenges thrown up by the advent of cryptocurrencies at our peril, and *The Crypto Launderers* generously equips its reader with the confidence and wisdom needed to navigate this rapidly evolving world in the months and years ahead.

Simone Maini
CEO, Elliptic

Timeline of Key Events

October 31, 2008: Satoshi Nakamoto releases the Bitcoin White Paper.

January 27, 2011: Ross Ulbricht begins promoting the Silk Road, a drugs market he launched on the dark web.

July 17, 2011: Alexander Vinnik establishes the BTC-e cryptocurrency exchange.

October 21, 2011: The Bitcoin Fog mixing service is launched.

March 18, 2013: The US Treasury's Financial Crimes Enforcement Network (FinCEN) issues guidance on the application of anti-money laundering requirements to virtual currency businesses.

October 1, 2013: The US Federal Bureau of Investigation (FBI) arrests Ross Ulbricht and shuts down the Silk Road.

October 29, 2013: The first Bitcoin ATM begins operating in Vancouver, Canada.

January 23, 2014: Vitalik Buterin announces his plans to launch the Ethereum network.

February 28, 2014: The Mt. Gox cryptocurrency exchange files for bankruptcy in Japan following the theft of more than $350 million in customer funds.

April 18, 2014: The privacy coin Monero is launched.

June 6, 2014: Larry Dean Harmon begins operating the Helix mixing service.

June 27, 2014: The US Marshal's Service undertakes its first auction of bitcoins seized from the Silk Road.

September 4, 2014: Robert Faiella and Charlie Shrem plead guilty to operating unlicensed money transmitting businesses and facilitating transactions on behalf of Silk Road users.

November 19, 2015: The ERC-20 standard is proposed, paving the way for the issuance of new tokens, including stablecoins, on the Ethereum network.

August 2, 2016: The Bitfinex cryptocurrency exchange announces that it was the target of a hack resulting in the loss of bitcoins totaling $72 million.

May 12, 2017: The WannaCry ransomware attack is launched, and later attributed to North Korea's cybercrime outfit, the Lazarus Group.

July 26, 2017: The United States indicts Alexander Vinnik and the BTC-e cryptocurrency exchange on charges of money laundering and operating an unlicensed money service business.

January 24, 2018: The ERC-721 standard is proposed by members of the Ethereum community, providing the basis for the issuance of non-fungible tokens (NFTs) on the Ethereum blockchain.

November 28, 2018: The US Department of the Treasury's Office of Foreign Assets Control (OFAC) issues financial sanctions targeting two Iran-based money launderers and includes their Bitcoin addresses on the Specially Designated Nationals and Blocked Persons List (SDN List).

May 8, 2019: Europol announces the arrest of individuals in Spain allegedly involved in laundering the cash proceeds of drug sales through Bitcoin ATMs.

May 22, 2019: Europol announces the takedown of the Bestmixer mixing service.

June 21, 2019: The Financial Action Task Force (FATF) publishes *Guidance for a Risk-Based Approach to Virtual Assets and Virtual Asset Service Providers.*

March 2, 2020: The US Department of Justice (DOJ) announces the indictment of Tian Yinyin and Li Jaidong, two Chinese nationals alleged to have laundered cryptocurrencies on behalf of North Korea's Lazarus Group.

July 15, 2020: The Twitter accounts of prominent individuals such as Barak Obama and Elon Musk are compromised by hackers, who scam other Twitter users into sending them bitcoins. The hackers launder the fraudulently obtained bitcoins through Wasabi Wallet.

July 31, 2020: The perpetrators of the Twitter hack are arrested.

April 28, 2021: The DOJ announces the arrest of Roman Sterlingov as the alleged operator of the Bitcoin Fog mixing service.

May 7, 2021: The Colonial Pipeline is subject to a ransomware attack perpetrated by the DarkSide ransomware gang.

June 7, 2021: The United States announces the seizure of most of the funds paid to the DarkSide in the Colonial Pipeline attack.

August 18, 2021: Larry Dean Harmon, operator of the Helix mixer, pleads guilty to counts of money laundering and operating an unlicensed money service business.

February 1, 2022: More than 94,000 bitcoins stolen from the Bitfinex exchange in 2016 are transferred from the original wallet that received them.

February 8, 2022: The DOJ announces the arrest of Ilya Lichtenstein and Heather Morgan for allegedly laundering bitcoins from the Bitfinex hack.

March 23, 2022: North Korean cybercriminals steal more than $625 million in cryptocurrencies from Axie Infinity's Ronin Bridge.

June 30, 2022: The DOJ announces fraud and money laundering charges against Le Ahn Tuan, the alleged perpetrator of the Baller Ape Club NFT fraud scheme.

August 4, 2022: Alexander Vinnik, the operator of the BTC-e cryptocurrency exchange, is extradited to the United States to face trial.

August 8, 2022: OFAC sanctions the Tornado Cash mixer for facilitating the laundering of funds on behalf of North Korea's Lazarus Group.

August 10, 2022: Alexey Pertsev, one of the developers of Tornado Cash, is arrested in the Netherlands.

October 20, 2022: INTERPOL announces the launch of the first global police metaverse.

November 11, 2022: The FTX cryptocurrency exchange declares bankruptcy.

November 12, 2022: Cryptocurrencies totaling $477 million are misappropriated from the FTX exchange and subsequently laundered through the decentralized finance (DeFi) ecosystem.

January 18, 2023: FinCEN identifies the Bitzlato cryptocurrency exchange as a "primary money laundering concern" under the Combating Russian Money Laundering Act.

May 3, 2023: A jury convicts Nathaniel Chastain of engaging in fraud and money laundering involving NFTs, in the first ever successfully prosecuted case related to insider trading involving digital assets.

June 9, 2023: The DOJ unseals a criminal indictment alleging that Alexy Bilyuchenko and Aleksandr Verner were the hackers behind the theft of funds from Mt. Gox, and that Bilyuchenko operated BTC-e alongside Alexander Vinnik.

August 3, 2023: Ilya Lichtenstein and Heather Morgan plead guilty to laundering the bitcoins stolen in the Bitfinex hack case.

Prologue

August 2, 2016

Seventy-two million dollars gone – poof! – just like that.

The news rocked Bitcoin trading markets, causing the Bitcoin price to plummet more than 20% overnight, from just above $600 per bitcoin – a near all-time high – to $480 in a matter of hours, resulting in billions of dollars in additional losses to Bitcoin investors around the globe.

Bitfinex, a Hong Kong–headquartered cryptocurrency exchange and one of the ten largest trading platforms in the world, had just announced it had suffered a cybercriminal hack resulting in the loss of 119,756 bitcoins belonging to its customers – losses totaling approximately $72 million, based on the Bitcoin price at the time. The hack occurred after a breach of the infrastructure for securing the credentials of cryptocurrency wallets where Bitfinex held its customers' bitcoins.

News of the Bitfinex hack gave Bitcoin traders everywhere a sinking feeling of déjà vu. The theft was the largest that the cryptocurrency industry had seen since the hack of Mt. Gox, a Japanese exchange that two years earlier had announced the loss of a whopping $350 million in customer funds – an event that, in addition to sending Mt. Gox into bankruptcy and leaving behind a swarm of enraged creditors demanding retribution, had also caused Bitcoin's price to plummet. In the two years since the Mt. Gox implosion, the Bitcoin price had recovered and reached new heights, but this latest hack was a sign that things could change – quite literally – overnight. While Bitfinex was sufficiently capitalized to avoid collapse, and had promised customers they would be able to redeem most of their deposits, the hack was a worrisome sign that cryptocurrency exchanges – the banks of the Bitcoin world – were still vulnerable to major cyberattacks that could imperil traders and thrust Bitcoin markets into chaos. With much of the public still relatively unfamiliar with, and very often skeptical of, cryptocurrencies, headlines screaming about cyber thieves stealing millions of dollars in bitcoins was the last thing that cryptocurrency advocates needed, engaged as they were in a mission to persuade the world of the merits of this new technology, which they believed was the future of money.

Naturally, once Bitfinex announced the hack, speculation turned to the question of who the perpetrators might be. Was it an inside job? Cybercriminals from Russia or Ukraine? Who had the capability, and guts, to steal a haul of bitcoins that big from one of the largest exchanges in the world? And as they pondered these questions, Bitcoin watchers everywhere focused their gaze upon the same spot: a series of numbers and letters recorded on the blockchain – Bitcoin's public transaction ledger – representing the Bitcoin wallet where those 119,756 stolen bitcoins sat.

Immediately after draining the funds from Bitfinex, the attacker, whoever he or she or they were, sent the bitcoins from the exchange's wallets to a separate private Bitcoin wallet – a transaction displayed for all to see on the blockchain. Of the original 119,756 bitcoins stolen from Bitfinex, about 25,000 were transferred sporadically out of this wallet in several separate withdrawals between January 2017 and April 2021, and then laundered onward through the blockchain – possibly, some observers feared, never to be seen again. But about 80% of the stolen funds – approximately

94,000 bitcoins – would sit in that private wallet for the next five-and-a-half years, not moving at all. Over that span, the value of Bitcoin rose dramatically, soaring from approximately $600 per bitcoin at the time of the Bitfinex hack to a high of more than $67,000 in November 2021. This, in turn, caused the value of the stolen bitcoins to skyrocket from $72 million to more than $7 billion.

By late 2021, the wallet with the stolen Bitfinex funds had become one of the highest valued Bitcoin wallets in the world – and its holder, or holders, Bitcoin billionaires. Bitcoin enthusiasts and traders, law enforcement agents and private intelligence firms, watched and wondered for more than five years if the Bitfinex hacker, or hackers, would ever move their enormous virtual pile of bitcoins, and where the trail might lead if they did.

Then, on February 1, 2022, the whole remaining stash moved. To be precise, 94,643.29 bitcoins were transferred from the wallet that had received the stolen Bitfinex funds, driving cryptocurrency watchers into a frenzy. Where would the Bitfinex coins go? Would the perpetrators manage to combine this massive stash with the 25,000 bitcoins they had already laundered, allowing them to get away with billions of dollars in stolen funds? And would the movement of the coins reveal anything about who was behind one of Bitcoin's biggest heists?

The money trail, it turned out, led to some of the most eccentric characters in the relatively short but extremely eventful history of cryptocurrency laundering: a mentalist magician named Dutch, his rapper wife Razzlekhan, and their Bengal cat Clarissa. The virtual trail that the Bitfinex bitcoins followed through the blockchain was one that had been paved across more than a decade – a trail that twisted and turned its way through an ecosystem of rogue cryptocurrency exchanges, digital black markets, anonymizing services, cash-for-Bitcoin trading kiosks, and cryptocurrencies designed to be untraceable – in short, an entire ecosystem available for laundering cryptocurrencies. It was a trail that had been travelled by a long list of characters, from peddlers of opioids to a fugitive Indian entrepreneur to North Korean cybercriminals – a trail over which tens of billions of dollars in bitcoins had flowed, and one that law enforcement agencies, regulators, and private analytics firms had been sniffing around for years, waiting to pounce.

And as that trail grew and grew over the years, accumulating billions of new data points and forming a veritable maze of transactions, it became the focal point for clashes between tech visionaries, entrepreneurs, privacy advocates, lawmakers, and law enforcers over the future of finance, and the potential for disruptive technologies to reshape not only money, but society as a whole.

As we follow that trail, we will in due course meet Dutch, Razzlekhan, and Clarissa. But first we must start at the beginning, 11 years before that giant stash of 94,643.29 bitcoins suddenly moved across the blockchain, back to when the foundations of the crypto laundering trail were laid.

Chapter 1

The Dark Web: The Origins of Crypto Laundering

For Ross Ulbricht, Bitcoin was a godsend. By the time he turned 29 in March 2013, Ulbricht sat atop the largest online drugs market in the world, and Bitcoin was the secret ingredient that made it all possible.

Only two years earlier, in January 2011, Ulbricht had created a marketplace on the dark web called the Silk Road. Launched on The Onion Router (Tor) network, which allows users to obscure their Internet Protocol (IP) addresses and mask information about their whereabouts, the Silk Road was initially a small site for buying magic mushrooms. For several years, Ulbricht had been obsessed with the prospect of launching a marketplace that would allow users to transact with total freedom, beyond the reach of government enforcement. During his studies at Penn State University, Ulbricht had become deeply acquainted with libertarian politics and economics, and it was soon his life's mission to advance the cause of freeing commerce completely from state control. Convinced that the four-decade-long War on Drugs was an exercise in the excessive use of government force that had led to millions of innocent Americans being unjustly incarcerated, Ulbricht wanted to provide a venue where anyone could purchase drugs for recreational use without fear of surveillance or arrest. As Ulbricht wrote in his diary, he sought "to create a website where people could buy anything anonymously, with no trail whatsoever that could lead back to them."[1] Within a year of its launch, the Silk Road had grown into a massive, thriving marketplace, where users could buy all variety of prohibited items – primarily a wide range of narcotics but also fake IDs, hacking tools, and more – generating millions of dollars in monthly sales.

The Silk Road was the first successful, industrial-scale illicit marketplace on the dark web. And the grease in its wheels was Bitcoin, a new form of digital money created only two years before Ulbricht launched his site. Bitcoin was an integral feature of the Silk Road's illicit economy. Purchases for items from Silk Road vendors could only be made using bitcoins, and Ulbricht used the cryptocurrency to pay collaborators who assisted him in running and administering the site. He even, it transpired, paid in bitcoins to arrange the murder-for-hire of people he learned were stealing from the site and threatening to reveal its existence, though those assassinations never took place. The Silk Road quickly became known as the Amazon of the dark web: individual vendors located anywhere around the globe could advertise their goods – whether heroin, LSD, ecstasy, malware, or other prohibited items – and receive reviews from buyers, who settled payment in this new cryptocurrency, which was still essentially unknown to the public. Ulbricht was convinced that in Bitcoin he had found the perfect mechanism for sustaining an online market that no government could ever dismantle. In an interview he held with *Forbes* magazine in August 2013 under his adopted pseudonym Dread Pirate Roberts, Ulbricht would even go so far as to declare, "We've won the State's War on Drugs because of Bitcoin."[2]

What Ulbricht could not have known then was that Bitcoin, which had made him the millionaire kingpin of a new digital underworld, would also contribute to his downfall.

The Birth of Bitcoin and the Rise of the Silk Road

Before Bitcoin, selling drugs online had always been problematic. Just as the rise of websites such as Amazon and eBay in the mid-1990s created a new paradigm for day-to-day commerce that disrupted brick-and-mortar retail businesses, so the global, borderless nature of the Internet offered the prospect of an online trade in illicit items that could allow black markets to thrive beyond the streets. Yet for nearly two decades after the advent of the World Wide Web, payments still could not be conducted in a manner that allowed illicit markets to flourish online.

Before cryptocurrencies, drug dealers faced a dilemma when selling their products on the Internet. A dealer could accept payment through a bank transfer or credit card purchase, but that put them at risk of detection under anti–money laundering laws. They could also arrange to collect payment in cash through a physical meet-up with the buyer, but that risked public detection and capture. Neither presented an attractive or practical option for drug dealers who wanted to leverage the Internet to reach a global clientele. By the time Ross Ulbricht had the idea for the Silk Road, narcotics dealers were desperate for a way to transact with buyers anywhere in the world while maintaining anonymity and avoiding detection.

Bitcoin, it seemed, was the answer. In 2008, a White Paper entitled *Bitcoin: A Peer-to-Peer Electronic Cash System* was published online and distributed to a small mailing list of cryptographers by an author using the pseudonym Satoshi Nakamoto, whose identity remains unknown. Writing amidst the Global Financial Crisis, Nakamoto reflected on the need for a new form of money that would up-end a financial sector beset with rent-seeking behavior and entrenched inefficiencies that served the narrow interests of major financial institutions. What Nakamoto proposed in the Bitcoin White Paper was nothing short of revolutionary: a new form of digital cash that would allow two individuals to transfer funds online, from anywhere in the world, without having to use a bank. Bitcoin offered users one of the main advantages of cash – the ability to interact directly with their counterparties without a bank's involvement (hence the term "peer-to-peer") – while improving on its main weakness, namely, its physical nature, which makes cash impractical to transfer globally and across borders.

Nakamoto was hardly the first to have the idea for a digital cash system. Bitcoin was the culmination of several earlier attempts to create digital money, and it fulfilled a dream long held by a loose collection of libertarian-minded technologists known as the cypherpunks. In *A Cypherpunk's Manifesto*, a treatise published in 1993, Eric Hughes, one of the early proponents of the movement, set out the philosophy behind the quest for digital cash. "Privacy is necessary for an open society in the electronic age," wrote Hughes. "When I purchase a magazine at a store and hand cash to the clerk, there is no need to know who I am. . . An anonymous system empowers individuals to reveal their identity when desired and only when desired; this is the essence of privacy. . . We the Cypherpunks are dedicated to building anonymous systems. We are defending our privacy with cryptography, with anonymous mail forwarding systems, with digital signatures, and with electronic money."[3]

The objective of the cypherpunks was clear: to create a version of electronic cash that would preserve the freedom to transact privately. Several attempted to do just that. The first attempt of real significance came in 1989, when the American computer scientist David Chaum launched DigiCash, which employed cryptography to maintain user privacy. But DigiCash and other early digital currency proposals faced a major limitation: they relied on a central party to issue units of the currency and validate transactions. From a libertarian perspective, a centralized digital cash system was ultimately counterproductive because the issuer could block transactions and be dismantled by the government. For a digital cash system to make good on its true promise of financial freedom, it needed to be decentralized: no single person, authority, or business should own the system, or act as a single point of failure.

Decentralization therefore became pivotal to the cypherpunk ethos and foundational to the ideal of free commerce enabled by anonymizing technology. In 1998, the computer scientist Nick

Szabo put forward a proposal known as BitGold, which envisioned a "trustless" payment settlement mechanism that eliminated middlemen such as banks and other payment intermediaries to allow users to transact directly. The same year, Wei Dei, another American computer scientist, published a paper outlining a concept called B-Money, which envisioned a decentralized payment system much in the vein of Szabo's BitGold, where "participants cannot be linked to their true names or physical locations."[4] However, neither Bit-Gold nor B-Money proved implementable.

It was Nakamoto who eventually made the breakthrough with Bitcoin and was the first to succeed in developing a truly decentralized, peer-to-peer payment mechanism. Critical to achieving this was solving a technical problem that proposals such as BitGold and B-Money had failed to solve, known as "double-spend." One of the main challenges developers had encountered in creating digital cash systems before Bitcoin was that anyone could counterfeit a unit of a given electronic coin. That is, a user could simply create a copy of a coin and repeatedly spend it, jeopardizing the integrity of the system. The simple way to solve this problem is to have a trusted central issuer or authority who can validate the authenticity of transactions. But that centralization runs contrary to the cypherpunk ethos, and undermines the goal of ensuring users' privacy and autonomy.

In Bitcoin, Nakamoto employed a mechanism for establishing consensus about activities of participants in the network without requiring a trusted central authority. This is achieved through a proof-of-work (PoW) algorithm, which requires that network participants devote computing power to solving cryptographic puzzles. This process enables those engaged in the PoW process – known as "miners," who receive bitcoins as a reward for supplying computing power to the network – to validate transactions, and authenticate that no double-spending has occurred. Once validated by miners, Bitcoin transactions are posted on the blockchain, a ledger that provides a complete and chronological history of all transactions and can be viewed publicly as a record of their authenticity. The blockchain is what is known as a distributed ledger technology

(DLT) – a manner of record keeping that enables consensus and validation of information across a disbursed network. Importantly, because no single entity controls Bitcoin, the blockchain is an immutable record. This remarkable innovation ensures that the Bitcoin network remains self-sustaining: no central authority operates Bitcoin, and no central authority can dismantle it. Bitcoin will operate as long as miners remain incentivized to continue validating transactions – and transactions will always be recorded on the blockchain for anyone to see.

In addition to decentralization, Bitcoin possesses another important feature. While all transactions are recorded on the blockchain publicly, the names of the individual users conducting those transactions do not appear on the ledger. Rather, Bitcoin users are pseudonymous: their identities are represented on the blockchain by alphanumeric addresses corresponding to their Bitcoin wallets. No personal identifying information is inherently associated with a Bitcoin transaction. For example, the Bitcoin address 1A1zP1eP-5QGefi2DMPTfTL5SLmv7DivfNa was the address Nakamoto used to receive the first bitcoins ever mined.

With Bitcoin, therefore, the cypherpunk dream seemed fulfilled. Nakamoto had created a technology that was decentralized, couldn't be dismantled by governments, and would allow users to conceal their identities while maintaining control over their wealth. In the eyes of the cypherpunks, the implications of this innovation were nothing short of earth-shattering. Over the course of the next several years, a dedicated global community of enthusiasts emerged among Bitcoin's early adopters, united by a conviction that Nakamoto's invention would change the future of finance, and society at large, by freeing individuals from reliance on a financial system controlled by self-interested, institutional middlemen.

It was also not lost on early adopters that Bitcoin could play a role in facilitating illicit activity. In June 2010, one user on the forum bitcointalk.org – a message board Nakamoto created for the community – discussed the potential to host a "heroin store" on Tor that could accept Bitcoin payments.[5] In June 2011, another bitcointalk.org user speculated about the possibility for Bitcoin to facilitate a prediction market for assassinations, in which users could bet on the probability that politicians might be assassinated, and would then receive bitcoins if those predictions occurred.[6] This assumed that the existence of such a market would incentivize assassinations, drawing in a growing user base that would make the market self-sustaining. Eventually, cryptocurrency-enabled assassination markets would indeed emerge, such as those available on the Augur blockchain.[7]

Before Bitcoin, criminals had sought several ways to engage in illicit transactions and launder funds online. In the early 2000s, one popular option was e-Gold. Established in 1996 by an oncologist and a lawyer in Florida, e-Gold was the first large-scale digital currency-based system that enabled merchant payments and was accessible via mobile phone transfers. By 2000 it had obtained over one million users, but was quickly exploited by criminal actors, especially Russian and Ukrainian cybercriminals. In 2008, e-Gold was shut down by the US government after its founders were charged with money laundering violations, and for failing to register with the federal government under anti–money laundering laws.[8]

Another early digital currency system, Liberty Reserve, met a similar fate. Based in Costa Rica, Liberty Reserve allowed users to access its site without verifying their identities. Users purchased Liberty Reserve Dollars or Liberty Reserve Euros, which they could transfer freely to other users of the site while remaining anonymous. Liberty Reserve's founding, unsurprisingly, was highly problematic. Its founder, Author Budovsky, had been charged in the United States in 2006 with running an illegal e-Gold business known as Gold Age. Budovsky then fled to Costa Rica while still on probation in 2007, and launched Liberty Reserve. The new service rapidly became a favored method for drug dealers, credit card thieves, cybercriminals, vendors of child pornography, and other illicit actors to transfer funds internationally, serving more than one million users globally – nearly a quarter of whom were in the United States.[9] In May 2013, Budovsky was arrested in Spain and indicted alongside his accomplices by the US government, which accused Liberty Reserve of laundering criminal proceeds worth more than $6 billion. Budovsky was eventually extradited to the United States and handed a 20-year prison sentence for operating the service. The US Treasury also drew on a provision in the USA PATRIOT Act to designate Liberty Reserve as a financial institution of "primary money laundering concern," ensuring that it was permanently cut off from any ties to the US financial system.[10]

E-Gold and Liberty Reserve had demonstrated that a demand existed in the online criminal ecosystem for reliable digital payments. Yet both systems had suffered from a major flaw, one familiar to the cypherpunks: they were centralized. The issuers of e-Gold and Liberty Reserve were essential to the ongoing functioning of those systems, which meant that when their founders were arrested, both platforms were seized by the US government and completely dismantled. As Nakamoto commented in an early Bitcoin discussion forum in 2009: "A lot of people automatically dismiss e-currency as a lost cause because of all the companies that failed since the 1990s. I hope it's obvious it was only the centrally controlled nature of those systems that doomed them."[11]

With Bitcoin, however, this would never be a problem. Because no single person or organization ran Bitcoin, it could never be shut down. Law enforcement agencies might arrest individual criminals who traded in bitcoins, but they could never dismantle the Bitcoin network. This made Bitcoin a seemingly trustworthy tool for criminals, who could depend on it to operate around the clock, 24 hours a day, seven days a week – accessible from anywhere on the globe.

The timing of Bitcoin's arrival could not have been more fortuitous for Ross Ulbricht, who was convinced that he had found the secret weapon he needed to liberate markets from the suffocating grip of the state. As he conceived of an anonymous online marketplace, Ulbricht knew he could look to the dark web as a place to host it and hide the identities of users. The Tor network had been developed by the US government in the mid-1990s as part of an effort to encrypt confidential communications by concealing information about users' identities and locations. Because it is an open-source project, Tor is free and accessible to anyone. It therefore offered the ideal home for an anonymous online market.

Having identified where to host his site, which he originally called Underground Brokers, Ulbricht needed a way for buyers and sellers to transact in secret. Earlier attempts to set up illicit markets on Tor had failed, in part due to the inability to anonymize payments, and their reliance on the regulated financial sector. One of the most successful early drug markets on the dark web was Farmer's Market, a site on Tor that generated approximately $1 million in drug sales between 2007 and 2009. But Farmer's Market was ultimately undone owing to its payment methods of choice: users settled their drug trades via services such as PayPal and Western Union, which identified suspicious transactions and reported them to law enforcement, as was demonstrated when the US Drug Enforcement Agency (DEA) shut down Farmer's Market in early 2012.[12] Ulbricht was determined to learn from the failures of other dark web entrepreneurs. Writing in his diary, Ulbricht noted: "I had been studying the technology for a while, but needed a business model and strategy."[13] Bitcoin enabled Ulbricht to develop that business model, allowing him to establish a sustainable economy for his site. Even Satoshi Nakamoto had recognized that combining Bitcoin with the anonymizing capabilities of Tor was prudent for those seeking maximum privacy, writing in 2010: "If you're serious about privacy, TOR is an advisable precaution."[14]

Ulbricht had learned of Bitcoin during his short-lived stint as a financial trader after university, and through online forums frequented by like-minded libertarians.[15] He quickly realized that Bitcoin gave him what he needed: a way for vendors on his site to receive payments from anywhere in the world for the goods they sold without having to transfer money through a bank, while also concealing their identities. The Silk Road even established a payment settlement mechanism that was essential to building trust among buyers and sellers: after a buyer sent bitcoins to a vendor for a purchase, the funds were kept in an escrow wallet held by the Silk Road; once the buyer confirmed receipt of the goods, the bitcoins were released to the seller. The site also allowed vendors to set the sale price in bitcoins at a fixed US dollar figure to protect against volatility from the frequently fluctuating value of Bitcoin.

For facilitating these services, the Silk Road took a commission of 8–15% of the total value of each transaction.[16]

Ulbricht began promoting the Silk Road on Bitcoin chat forums to recruit users. A March 1, 2011, posting under the username "silk-road" on bitcointalk.org declared: "Silk Road is into it's [sic] third week after launch and I am very pleased with the results. There are several sellers and buyers finding mutually agreeable prices, and as of today, 28 transactions have been made! What is missing? What works? What do you want to see created? What obstacles do you see for the future of Silk Road? What opportunities? The general mood of this community is that we are up to something big, something that can really shake things up. Bitcoin and Tor are revolutionary and sites like the Silk road [sic] are just the beginning."[17]

The Silk Road was the first significant testing ground for Bitcoin. Over the course of two and a half years, it hosted more than 100,000 users and processed more than $1 billion worth of drug sales, all executed in bitcoins. Indeed, a substantial portion of Bitcoin's early users were buyers and sellers of illicit items on the Silk Road. At one point, the main Bitcoin address that the Silk Road used contained 5% of all bitcoins in existence, and the site accounted for as much as one-third of Bitcoin transactions that took place during 2012[18] – a statistic that underscores how Ulbricht's site was not only powered by Bitcoin, but also essential to the cryptocurrency's growth. In an ironic twist, the Silk Road also made what must have been one of the first ever Bitcoin-enabled ransomware payments in history when Ulbricht was forced to pay $25,000 in bitcoins to hackers who had disrupted access to the site and demanded a ransom to halt the attack.[19]

By 2013, Ulbricht had become a Bitcoin millionaire – though he continued to live a modest outward lifestyle, motivated primarily by ideology rather than riches. Nonetheless, Ulbricht and others who ran the Silk Road with him were aware of the potential to accumulate significant wealth through this new cryptocurrency. At one stage, Ulbricht confided to another of the Silk Road's administrators that he expected Bitcoin to make him a billionaire before his thirtieth birthday.[20]

The Feds Follow the Trail on the Blockchain

It turned out that Ulbricht and his accomplices weren't the only ones interested in the role of Bitcoin in unlocking new forms of illicit commerce. So was the US government.

US law enforcement agencies first became aware of the Silk Road the old-fashioned way: officers had intercepted packages of drugs in the mail, and upon questioning the intended recipients, learned that they had been purchased on the Silk Road. As they looked into the site, US law enforcement agents were astounded – and terrified – by what they had discovered. A massive illicit marketplace had emerged nearly overnight in the darkest recesses of the Internet. Before long, the US government was running an extensive investigation into the Silk Road, featuring agents from the DEA, Federal Bureau of Investigation (FBI), Internal Revenue Service (IRS), and other agencies.

As they probed the Silk Road, law enforcement investigators quickly came to understand the essential role that Bitcoin played. Undercover agents began to buy Bitcoin on cryptocurrency exchange platforms so that they could make staged purchases of narcotics on the Silk Road. As they became acquainted with Bitcoin, they discovered an important feature of the technology: because all transactions are recorded publicly on the blockchain, government agents could identify the transactions that they had been undertaking with the Silk Road by observing them on the ledger.[21] In making staged payments on the site, agents were instructed to send their bitcoins to addresses the Silk Road used for settling transactions; the agents could then locate these Bitcoin addresses on the blockchain and see as the site's addresses received bitcoins from other buyers and paid bitcoins out to the site's vendors. Soon, the FBI was monitoring hundreds of thousands of transactions going into and out of the Silk Road's Bitcoin addresses in real time. Ilhwan Yum, an FBI agent working on the case, made staged purchases of illicit items on the Silk Road; he could then readily cross-reference transactions he had made by identifying them once they were recorded on the blockchain. Bitcoin's ledger, it turned out, offered the perfect digital money trail for investigators. In a press interview, Yum later described the impact of this transparency by noting: "Cash transactions are hard to track, but imagine if every serial number [on a dollar bill] used in a transaction was recorded and announced to the public."[22]

Indeed, as they investigated the Silk Road, government agents realized that the blockchain offered them a unique source of intelligence that was in many ways more transparent and accessible than the financial intelligence they normally obtained in money laundering cases. When investigating money laundering through banks, investigators had to obtain court-issued subpoenas to access banking records; and if they were investigating cases involving international money flows, they had to navigate a complex and time-consuming process to access information from their law enforcement counterparts overseas by requesting documents through mutual legal assistance treaties (MLATs). But with Bitcoin, because the ledger is global, public, and decentralized, agents did not need to obtain a subpoena when analyzing the blockchain. The ledger was simply open for anyone to view, constantly updating with new transactions, relaying insights about Bitcoin transfers between counterparties located all over the world, and offering a continuous stream of financial intelligence that unfolded in real time.

But merely looking at the blockchain alone didn't reveal who controlled the Silk Road's wallets, since Bitcoin wallets are pseudonymous. For example, the Bitcoin address 1933phfhK3ZgFQN-LGSDXvqCn32k2buXY8a was one that Silk Road utilized to send and receive more than 222,000 bitcoins across 152 transactions that were worth tens of millions of dollars at the time.[23] But knowing this didn't tell investigators who was behind the site. For the evidence trail on the blockchain to lead to arrests and money laundering convictions, investigators needed to link the pseudonymous transactional information on the blockchain to actual identities associated with the operators of the site. It turned out they would get a lucky break.

Though Ulbricht had gone to great lengths to conceal his role in the Silk Road by adopting the Dread Pirate Roberts moniker and deploying various anonymizing methods, his mask was ultimately unveiled by Gary Alford, an agent with the IRS's Criminal Investigation division in New York who had been assigned to investigate money laundering on the Silk Road. After extensive online sleuthing, Alford had managed to identify a post made on January 27, 2011, under the username "altoid" on a site for selling magic mushrooms known as Shroomery that encouraged users to visit the Silk Road – apparently the first reference Ulbricht ever made online about the market. Alford then discovered posts referencing the Silk Road from a user on the bitcointalk.org website also operating with the name "altoid," including a post from October 2011 that encouraged users to email him at rossulbricht@gmail.com for more information.[24] This clue was essential in enabling law enforcement agencies to identify and verify Ulbricht as the administrator of the Silk Road.

Ultimately, on October 1, 2013, the FBI managed to track Ulbricht to a library in San Francisco, where he was arrested with his laptop open, revealing his Silk Road credentials and administrator details. This allowed federal law enforcement to take control of the administration of the Silk Road and shut it down. Also included on Ulbricht's laptop were his personal Bitcoin wallet details, which enabled agents to tie him to payments made to and from the site's wallets.

In 2015, Ulbricht was sentenced to life imprisonment after being convicted of numerous criminal offenses, including money laundering related to his use of Bitcoin to conceal unlawful transactions. At the time of his sentencing, the court held that Ulbricht was ultimately responsible for money laundering related to every Bitcoin transaction that had ever passed through the Silk Road, given that he provided the infrastructure for users of the site to conceal illicit payments. The transparency of the blockchain had provided critical intelligence in building the government's case against him. In bringing laundering charges against Ulbricht, the US government's indictment noted that Ulbricht "designed the Silk Road to include a Bitcoin-based payment system that served to facilitate the illegal commerce conducted on the site, including by concealing the identities and locations of users transmitting and receiving funds through the site."[25] During the investigation, the

FBI analyzed the blockchain to follow more than 700,000 bitcoins through 3,706 transactions as funds moved between Ulbricht's personal Bitcoin wallet and the wallet he used to administer the transactions conducted on the Silk Road site.[26] At trial, government prosecutors explained the mechanics of the blockchain to the jury, and called federal agents to testify and describe how they had used Bitcoin's public ledger to decipher the Silk Road's financial flows and link them directly back to Ulbricht.

In addition to obtaining a wealth of financial intelligence during the Silk Road investigation that had bolstered their case against Ulbricht, US law enforcement scored another coup: the FBI had managed to seize the funds in Ulbricht's personal Bitcoin wallet.[27] In cryptocurrencies, users have a unique private key corresponding to their public wallet addresses that acts like a password. The private key is essential to authenticate and undertake transactions from a particular wallet. But if another party, such as a law enforcement agency, obtains access to a user's private key, they can take direct control of the coins in the associated wallet. When the FBI arrested Ulbricht, they confiscated his laptop, where his Bitcoin wallet credentials were stored – allowing agents to transfer the funds out of his wallet and into the Bitcoin address 1FfmbH-fnpaZjKFvyi1okTjJJusN455paPH that the FBI controlled. Shortly after Ulbricht's arrest, the FBI announced that it had seized more than 173,000 of his bitcoins, worth approximately $33.6 million at that time.[28] The FBI had also succeeded in identifying servers in Iceland where the Silk Road's escrow wallet was hosted, allowing them to confiscate additional funds.[29]

To emphasize the scale of the Silk Road seizure, at the time of Ulbricht's arrest the FBI provided its assessment that "the site generated sales revenue of more than 9.5 million Bitcoins and collected commissions from these sales totaling more than 600,000 Bitcoins. Although the value of Bitcoins has varied over time, these figures are roughly equivalent to approximately $1.2 billion in sales and approximately $80 million in commissions."[30]

* * *

Ulbricht's arrest was not the end of the Silk Road story. There was another twist to the tale that had all the makings of a Hollywood drama. During the Silk Road investigation, the DEA, the US government's drug cops, had sent undercover agents to infiltrate the site. The DEA's lead undercover agent on the case, Carl Force, had been remarkably successful in his sleuthing, forming a close online relationship with Ulbricht without compromising his cover. During extensive interactions with Ulbricht, Force learned an enormous amount about the inner workings of the Silk Road. He shared this information with Shaun Bridges, an agent with the US Secret Service – the agency responsible for protecting the President but also for investigating threats to the US financial system – who had also been brought onto the US government's Silk Road taskforce because of his expertise in Tor and computer forensics. But as they became familiar with the inner workings of the site, Force and Bridges became tempted by the riches they observed Ulbricht amassing, and they decided to get a cut.

Playing on Ulbricht's fear of detection, Force, posing under pseudonyms, offered to provide Ulbricht with information about police activity – tips that were deliberately misleading. In return, Ulbricht paid Force in bitcoins, which the agent hid from his supervisors. For example, in August 2013, Ulbricht paid Force – who was operating under the false moniker "Nob" as part of the investigation – 525 bitcoins for ostensible intelligence on police activity related to the Silk Road. (This sum was worth approximately $50,000 in August 2013, but would have been worth more than $5 million by October 2020, when Force's eventual prison term ended.) Force had informed his bosses at the DEA that he was attempting to convince Ulbricht – whose true identity was still unknown to the US government at the time – to pay him in bitcoins so the agency could get hold of the funds. In filing a report about this activity, however, Force misled his supervisors, claiming that Ulbricht never made the payment. Instead, Force transferred the funds he had received to his personal Bitcoin wallet and hid them from the government.[31] Force then created another false identity – using the online moniker "French Maid" – that he never informed the DEA about. In this guise, Force persuaded Ulbricht to send him additional bitcoins worth more than $100,000 in several transfers in August 2013 (see Figure 1.1).

That was only the tip of the iceberg. In January 2013, $350,000 in bitcoins went missing from the Silk Road, and Ulbricht believed that the funds had been stolen by Curtis Green, a Silk Road administrator whose account had access to the funds in question. In fact, Green had been arrested by federal agents, and Bridges – who by this point was collaborating with Force – had succeeded in taking over Green's administrator account. This allowed Bridges to obtain access to the site's Bitcoin wallet, steal the funds from it, and transfer them to his own Bitcoin wallet.[32] Force then convinced Ulbricht to pay him a bounty worth $80,000 to have Green murdered. Force and Bridges, along with other federal agents, then faked Green's death to convince Ulbricht that Green had been assassinated. Between them, the two federal agents stole bitcoins worth more than $1 million during the investigation.

Once again, however, the US government investigators succeeded in unmasking Bitcoin activity to bring criminals to justice – this time turning their new intelligence capabilities on their own. Agents with the IRS Criminal Investigations division who had reviewed the records from Ulbricht's Silk Road administrator account after seizing his laptop realized that Force and Bridges had been stealing on the job. Force's correspondence with Ulbricht under the Nob and French Maid monikers had included references to Bitcoin addresses where Force had requested Ulbricht transfer funds. Other records Ulbricht had kept enabled investigators to identify the specific Silk Road administrator accounts from which Bridges had stolen funds. Investigators then used the record of funds on the blockchain to document the trail of payments from Ulbricht and the Silk Road to the two agents' personal Bitcoin wallets. Law enforcement ultimately arrested the pair and seized the bitcoins they had stolen. Both pled guilty to charges of money laundering, among other offenses, and were sentenced to prison time. The blockchain had again taken center stage in uncovering a major case of Bitcoin laundering.

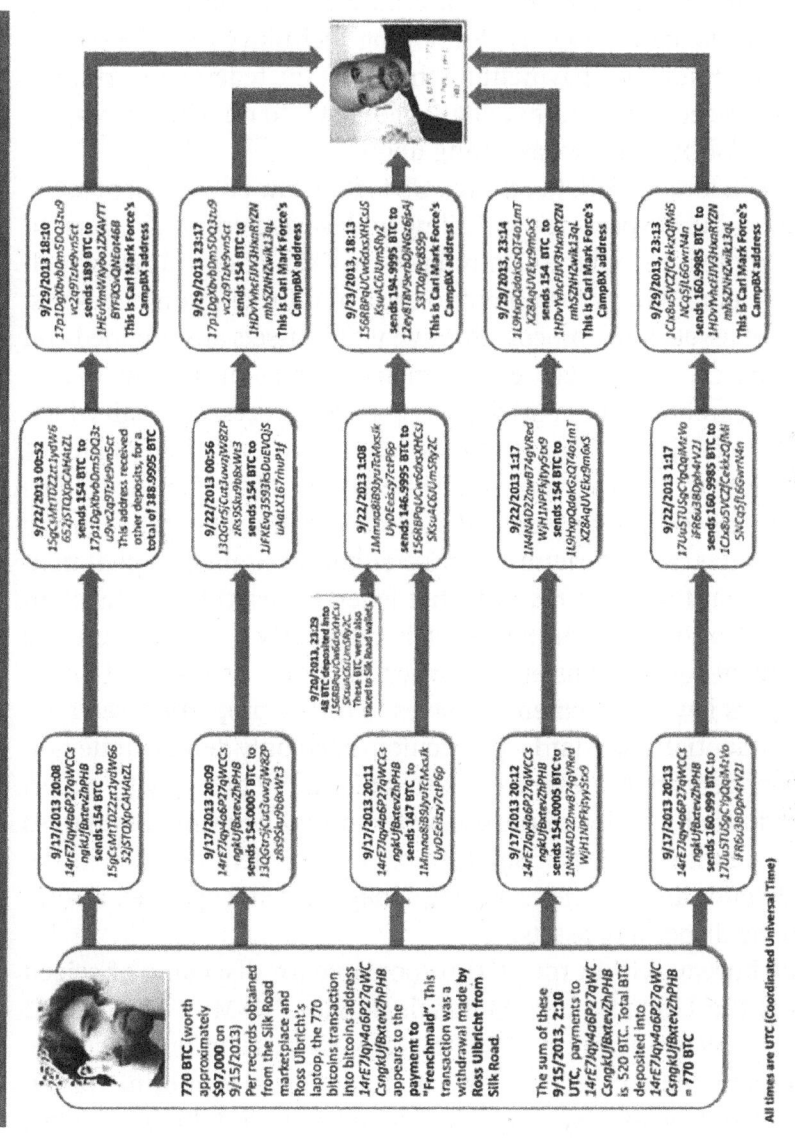

Figure 1.1 Bitcoin payments Ross Ulbricht made to Carl Force, depicted in the US criminal complaint against Force.

SOURCE: US Department of Justice / Public Domain.

The Feds Sell the Silk Road Bitcoins

The US government had brought criminals – including two of its own – to justice by quickly developing techniques for investigating a new, innovative payment method. But the federal government was soon faced with another challenge: what to do with the virtual mountain of bitcoins it was sitting upon.

Long before the Silk Road case, US federal law enforcement agencies had gained experience in dealing with seized criminal assets. In 1984, Congress passed the Comprehensive Crime Control Act, which enables federal law enforcement to seize and forfeit criminal assets. Seizure of assets is the process through which assets are obtained and taken into custody by law enforcement, such as during the execution of a search warrant. Forfeiture is the legal process through which ownership of those assets is transferred from the original holder of the property to the government. The US Department of Justice (DOJ) oversees the federal government's Asset Forfeiture Program. In the United States, asset forfeiture can be either a criminal or civil matter. Criminal forfeiture requires that federal prosecutors convict an individual prior to forfeiting his or her property – which therefore stalls the process of transferring ownership of the assets. Civil forfeiture allows law enforcement agencies to forfeit property based on a lower evidentiary standard – prosecutors need only demonstrate that a "preponderance of evidence" exists linking the property to underlying criminal activity to pursue forfeiture while criminal charges are still pending. Unsurprisingly, most asset forfeiture cases in the United States are civil cases, because they offer an expedited resolution to the disposal of assets.

The bureau within the DOJ responsible for disposing of seized assets is the United States Marshals Service (USMS). Established by George Washington in 1789, the USMS's mission is to facilitate the enforcement of federal laws and support the administration of the federal justice system. This includes undertaking activities such as arresting and transporting criminals (as made famous by the actor Tommy Lee Jones in the film *The Fugitive*), running the federal witness protection program, and "seizing assets gained by illegal means and providing for the custody, management, and disposal of forfeited assets."[33] The USMS routinely manages assets that federal law enforcement agents have seized: homes and yachts belonging to drug kingpins; jewelry, art, and antiques belonging to money launderers; piles of cash, private jets, and much more. The Marshals have managed billions of dollars' worth of criminal assets in the nearly four decades that the United States has had an asset forfeiture program. A critical part of the process of managing these assets is selling them: the USMS holds public auctions to dispose of forfeited property, and it disburses the funds to various payees, including to victims of crime and to state and local governments.

Asset forfeiture cases involving novel and new approaches are handled by the USMS Asset Forfeiture division's Complex Assets Unit. In September 2013, when Ulbricht was indicted, federal prosecutors filed a civil forfeiture claim to confiscate assets belonging to or associated with the Silk Road, including "any and all bitcoins contained in wallet files residing on Silk Road servers."[34] After the FBI seized Ulbricht's Bitcoin wallet at the time of his arrest, it had to transfer the funds to the USMS to arrange for their sale. The USMS suddenly had bitcoins worth tens of millions of dollars in its possession, making it one of the largest Bitcoin holders in the world – and it had to surmount several challenges to deal with seized cryptocurrencies for the first time.

One immediate problem was how to store the seized bitcoins securely until they could be auctioned. When handling seized assets, the USMS has a duty to the public to ensure the safeguarding of those assets until they are liquidated. If the Marshals were to lose any of the seized Silk Road funds (e.g., if an agent were to lose the private keys of the wallet used to hold the funds), or have them stolen (e.g., by a cybercriminal eager to get their hands on a large stash of bitcoins), the Marshals would have failed in their most fundamental mission. The USMS therefore had to surmount the complex challenges of Bitcoin custody to handle the Silk Road funds appropriately. This meant, firstly, transferring the funds from Ulbricht's Bitcoin wallet to a wallet owned by the US government. It meant, secondly, ensuring that wallets the government used were safe from tampering.[35] Securing bitcoins is most effectively achieved by using "cold storage" – which involves keeping the private key to a wallet offline so that the key is less vulnerable to cyber theft. Cold wallets can be maintained as thumb drives, or even by retaining the private key on paper. To ensure the confiscated funds remained secure, the USMS needed access to a cold wallet infrastructure – which required that agents involved in asset forfeiture have access to new technological capabilities, skills, and resources.

Another challenge in the asset forfeiture process is Bitcoin's price volatility. Under asset forfeiture laws, the US government must seek to preserve the value of the assets it seizes. Bitcoin's wild price swings make assessing and setting a suitable value for seized bitcoins problematic. One way of dealing with this challenge where large quantities of bitcoins are seized is to conduct multiple auctions. By selling seized coins across separate auctions, the government can minimize the risk that volatility will reduce the total value of its haul.[36] Another option is for prosecutors to petition a judge to grant a "stipulation for interlocutory sale." This permits the seized assets to be auctioned before the formal forfeiture process has concluded – allowing for the disposal of assets while their value is assessed to be relatively high.

Because US prosecutors pursued civil forfeiture of Ulbricht's bitcoins, the Marshals could auction off his assets even before his criminal conviction and sentencing concluded. In four separate auctions held between June 2014 and November 2015, the USMS sold all 173,998 bitcoins that the FBI had seized from the Silk Road for a total of $65.84 million. The first auction saw 45 potential buyers bid on 29,656 bitcoins from the Silk Road, with the winning bid put in by Tim Draper, a venture capitalist and proponent of cryptocurrencies, who paid more than $17 million.[37] In subsequent auctions for the remaining stash, the impact of Bitcoin's volatility became evident. During its second auction in December 2014, the USMS received $19 million for 50,000 bitcoins from the Silk Road, with Draper purchasing a portion of these bitcoins as well. Only four months later, in March 2015, the USMS received $13.5 million for the same number of bitcoins, reflective of a 30% price dip in the early part of that year.

Though Bitcoin presented the USMS with a novel challenge at the time of the Silk Road case, within less than a decade the agency was routinely handling cryptocurrency forfeiture cases. This arrangement very recently fell through so I have removed reference to it here as it is no longer factual. By late 2021, the USMS was in custody of more than $460 million worth of seized cryptocurrencies obtained through more than 200 law enforcement cases[38] – and ultimately the US government would seize billions more in cryptocurrencies in several high-profile cases. It turned out, in fact, that nearly a decade after the Silk Road case, the US government was not done seizing funds associated with the site. In November 2020, the US government announced that it had seized another haul of bitcoins from the Silk Road worth more than $1 billion, recovered from an individual who had hacked the site back in 2013. In November 2022, the United States announced the seizure of a further $3.36 billion in bitcoins from James Zhong of Athens, Georgia, who pleaded guilty to stealing more than 50,000 bitcoins from the Silk Road by exploiting the site's payment withdrawal system.[39] A portion of the funds confiscated in these actions were used to erase a debt of more than $183 million that Ulbricht owed the US government.[40]

For the US government, selling tainted cryptocurrencies became a routine feature of law enforcement activity in the age of online crime.

The Paradox of Crypto Crime

The Silk Road saga was the opening salvo in an ongoing battle between governments and criminals over cryptocurrencies that has lasted more than a decade. It offered some important lessons that have shaped that conflict over time.

The first lesson was that cryptocurrencies could indeed sustain new criminal environments. Industrial-scale illicit marketplaces on the dark web had not been possible before Bitcoin's creation. A decentralized, peer-to-peer payment mechanism provided the basis for an economic model that could take online crime to new heights. Other marketplaces would soon appear on the dark web that made the Silk Road look tiny by comparison. Even though law enforcement agencies managed to dismantle the Silk Road, the

Bitcoin network was still running unhindered. The Silk Road and its founder were gone, but criminals everywhere realized that they could leverage this new, decentralized payment system. Indeed, within a few months of Ulbricht's arrest, a Silk Road 2.0 successor site was up and running, and accepting Bitcoin payments.

But there was a second lesson that acts as a counterweight to the first. For all its promise of enabling private, anonymous transactions, Bitcoin left its illicit users vulnerable. The transparency of its public ledger, the blockchain, enabled the US government to identify and follow illicit transactions, providing law enforcement with a rich data trail of intelligence to pursue money laundering charges, and to confiscate bitcoins from Ulbricht, as well as from rogue government agents. The US government discovered that if it could identify the holder of a specific Bitcoin wallet, then it could overcome Bitcoin's inherent pseudonymity and study a person's entire transaction history on the blockchain. Law enforcement agencies immediately appreciated that the open nature of this new technology could be a tremendous asset when investigating illicit activity. To demonstrate just how transparent the blockchain is, in 2015 an American computer scientist named Nicholas Weaver published an analysis drawing exclusively from open-source information to show that at least 20% of the bitcoins from Ross Ulbricht's personal wallet could be traced to the Silk Road.[41] It wasn't only the FBI that could trace crypto transactions – it turned out that anyone with access to the Internet could peek into the world of Bitcoin transfers.

It is this paradox – the ability of cryptocurrencies to open new frontiers of criminal finance, and the simultaneous ability of law enforcement agencies to trace cryptocurrency transactions with unprecedented transparency – that has characterized the battle over the technology since the Silk Road. The US government, it turned out, had won the first round in that tussle. But it would hardly be the last. The Silk Road may have been shut down, but Bitcoin had not. It was still there for anyone to use; and those who saw so much potential in it to facilitate illicit payments were more than ready to fight back.

Chapter 2

Black Holes: The Rise of the Rogue Exchange

Despite Bitcoin's revolutionary promise, its early adopters faced a rather mundane problem: the cryptocurrency they had amassed wasn't of much immediate use. Other than purchasing drugs on the dark web, or betting on one of the many Bitcoin gambling sites that had emerged in the few years after Nakamoto's White Paper, Bitcoin was not accepted widely for retail purposes and did not have many practical applications. Anyone who had accumulated a substantial amount of bitcoins needed to turn their holding into fiat currencies such as US dollars, euros, pounds sterling, or yen if they wanted to make use of their new-found wealth.

This need led to the creation of cryptocurrency exchanges – services that are an essential part of the crypto ecosystem's underlying plumbing and have facilitated the astounding growth of cryptocurrency markets. Today, exchange platforms serve as the banks of the cryptocurrency world, processing hundreds of billions of dollars in cumulative trades daily and providing essential liquidity to markets. Exchanges are the primary gateway through which most users access the technology, and have enabled cryptocurrencies to reach a rapidly growing universe of users. The largest

23

exchanges – such as Coinbase, Binance, Gemini, and Kraken – are among the most highly valued financial technology businesses in the world today, with multi-billion-dollar valuations and customers spanning the globe. But the emergence of exchanges had more modest origins, and was inevitably intertwined with the evolving criminal use of cryptocurrencies.

The first cryptocurrency exchange service was called New Liberty Standard, launched by a member of the early Bitcoin community in October 2009. New Liberty Standard allowed users to buy bitcoins with US dollars, with one bitcoin valued at $0.08 – the first such exchange rate ever established.[1] New Liberty Standard never amounted to anything more than a small-scale trading forum for early Bitcoin adopters, but it offered an example that others would look to in developing larger platforms. In March 2010, another exchange named Bitcoin Market launched, allowing users to purchase bitcoins with dollars using their PayPal accounts.[2] Other exchanges would soon sprout up, with their business models based on generating fees from users when processing swaps.

Over the coming years, exchanges would play a vital role in the growth of the crypto ecosystem, particularly as new cryptocurrencies were created as complements and alternatives to Bitcoin. In 2011, the cryptocurrencies Litecoin and Ripple were launched, both seeking to improve upon Bitcoin's initial design by offering more rapid transaction settlement. The launch of the Ethereum blockchain in 2015 was a momentous development in the evolution of the cryptocurrency space, because it enabled innovators to launch new tokens relatively seamlessly, so that by 2017 hundreds of cryptocurrencies existed – a number that would grow to more than 10,000 by 2022. Exchanges where users could swap cryptocurrencies became key drivers, and beneficiaries, of this increasingly rich ecosystem – evolving into highly professionalized services with sleek user interfaces and offering a wide range of products in addition to basic cryptocurrency trading, such as lending products, high-yield accounts, and crypto-based derivatives.

The advent of cryptocurrency exchanges was also critical to the growth of the illicit online ecosystem. Criminals, after all, are motivated by profit. And to put their profits to use, they required a way to turn their ill-gotten cryptocurrencies into dollars and other fiat currencies that they could use to purchase homes, cars, and other luxury items. Criminals soon learned to leverage the emerging global network of cryptocurrency exchanges to their advantage – placing exchanges at the heart of their money laundering schemes, just as banks had sat at the heart of criminals' attempts to launder cash for decades.

The case of Carl Force and Shaun Bridges, the two rogue US government agents who had penetrated the Silk Road, illustrated the role of exchanges in the crypto laundering process. Flush with hundreds of thousands of dollars in bitcoins after the Silk Road investigation, Force needed a way to hide them. Force used his accounts at various exchanges to swap bitcoins from his private wallets into US dollars, which he then transferred to a bank account in Panama, in what the US government described as "an effort to launder and conceal the true source of the ill-gotten proceeds."[3] After convincing Ulbricht to pay him 525 bitcoins in return for false intelligence, Force sent the funds through multiple Bitcoin addresses – a technique designed to try and distance himself from the original source of funds and obfuscate the trail on the blockchain, akin to the practice of breaking up cash transactions into smaller amounts and depositing them into separate bank accounts (a process known as "smurfing" in the banking world). He then swapped the cryptocurrency for dollars at an exchange in the United States called CampBX. The criminal complaint lodged against Force demonstrates how law enforcement agents analyzed information from the blockchain to follow these movements of funds from the time Force received the funds from Ulbricht up to the point he deposited them at CampBX:

> I have performed analysis of the block chain [sic] as it concerns the 525 bitcoin deposit to FORCE's personal CampBX account. The analysis reveals that the 525 bitcoins FORCE received into his own personal CampBX account was directly linked, through a series of transactions, to the 525 bitcoin payment that [Ulbricht] made on August 4, 2013 . . .

Specifically the 525 bitcoin payment was split into 4 smaller payments and made in the following manner:

　　a. On August 4, 2013 at 22:05 a payment of 203 bitcoins
　　b. On August 4, 2013 at 22:05 a payment of 134 bitcoins
　　c. On August 4, 2013 at 22:05 a payment of 61 bitcoins
　　d. On August 4, 2013 at 22:05 a payment of 127 bitcoins

The 525 bitcoin payment went from four addresses and ultimately landed in a single pass-through account on September 1, 2013. The 525 bitcoins remained in the pass-through account from September 1, 2013 until September 27, 2013, when they were transferred into FORCE's personal account at CampBX.[4]

Force also held accounts at other exchanges, including Bitstamp, one of the largest exchange platforms still existing today, which froze Force's account owing to concerns about the unusual nature of his activity.[5] Force didn't stop there: he also invested bitcoins worth $110,000 in a Los Angeles–based exchange known as CoinMKT while he was still working for the DEA, and he even became the company's chief compliance officer – a role he abused to steal funds from CoinMKT's users. Ultimately, Force converted bitcoins worth more than $776,000 into US dollars through swaps at several exchanges over a two-year period.

Like Force, Shaun Bridges relied on exchanges to launder the $820,000 he had stolen from the Silk Road during his time with the US Secret Service. In his case, investigators with the IRS relied on the data trail from the blockchain and identified that Bridges had sent some of the stolen funds to a Bitcoin exchange in Japan. After he swapped his coins at the Japanese exchange for US dollars, he sent the dollars though nine separate wire transfers to a brokerage account he held at Fidelity Investments under the name Quantum International Investments LLC.[6] It was by tying Bridges' account records at Fidelity together with blockchain data related to his Bitcoin transactions that the government managed to build a money laundering case against him (see Figure 2.1). And the Japanese cryptocurrency exchange where his transaction trail led investigators was one whose name became notorious in the world of cryptocurrencies: Mt. Gox.

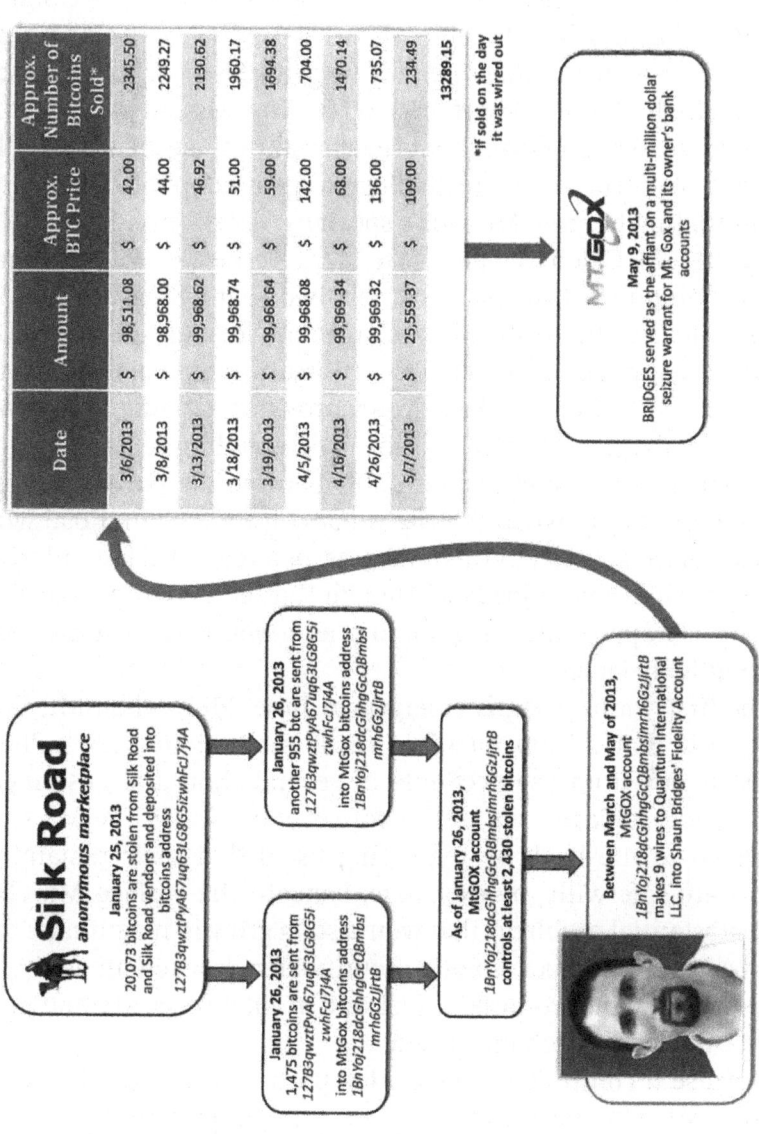

Figure 2.1 Bitcoin transfers Shaun Bridges made to Mt. Gox, depicted in the US criminal complaint against Bridges.

SOURCE: US Department of Justice / Public Domain.

The Mt. Gox Bitcoins Go Missing

Mt. Gox's story is one that features a meteoric rise and an equally stunning fall. It was established in 2006 by Jeb McCaleb, a US programmer who launched the site to serve as a trading venue for digital collectibles from the online role-playing game *Magic: The Gathering Online*, which McCaleb shortened to Mt. Gox. McCaleb learned of Bitcoin in 2010 and realized that the community needed a reliable exchange platform for the technology to gain adoption. That July, Bitcoin trading became Mt. Gox's specialty. A few months later, in March 2011, McCaleb sold the site to Mark Karpeles, a French expatriate residing in Tokyo. Over the next two years, Karpeles turned the site into the largest Bitcoin exchange platform in the world. By mid-2013, as much as 70–80% of all Bitcoin trades globally were processed by Mt. Gox. As the primary provider of liquidity to cryptocurrency markets, Mt. Gox was the logical trading venue for legitimate Bitcoin traders; but it inevitably became the port of call for illicit actors as well, whether drug vendors from the Silk Road who needed a place to cash out their bitcoins, or a rogue US law enforcement agent like Shaun Bridges. Though Karpeles attempted to give Mt. Gox the appearance of a mature and well-run business, that veneer quickly faded.

The first warning signs emerged in June 2011, when Mt. Gox announced that 25,000 bitcoins worth more than $8.5 million had been lost from the accounts of several thousand customers after hackers took the site offline for several days. While Mt. Gox responded to the hack by reassuring users that their remaining funds were safe with the exchange, beneath the surface Mt. Gox faced substantial problems that would soon grow in magnitude: the hack had occurred because of a security breach when an auditor's computer was compromised – just one of many security and governance issues the exchange faced.

Because it controlled a substantial portion of all Bitcoin swaps globally, Mt. Gox periodically halted trading services to prevent rapid Bitcoin price increases, creating frustration among users and the wider Bitcoin community about its concentration and power over the market. In the spring of 2013, the US Department of Homeland Security seized several million dollars in funds from an account belonging to Mt. Gox's US subsidiary during an investigation into its unauthorized activity in the United States. (The federal agent who served the warrant for the seizure of funds from Mt. Gox was none other than Shaun Bridges, whose duplicitous activity still had not been uncovered at that time.[7]) In June 2013, Mt. Gox suspended US dollar withdrawals, leaving US users without access to their funds. In February 2014, it prevented users everywhere from withdrawing their bitcoins as well, and announced that it had lost an additional massive stash of more than 700,000 bitcoins, worth more than $350 million at the time. The funds were lost due to the original June 2011 security breach: the hacker had managed to access the private keys to Mt. Gox's Bitcoin wallet, which gave them control over the exchange's funds. The hacker then slowly drained most of the bitcoins from Mt. Gox's wallet over the course of two years, so that the losses went undetected until it was too late.[8]

Mt. Gox filed for bankruptcy in Japan in February 2014. Traders who had used Mt. Gox lost hundreds of millions of dollars due to the exchange's insolvency – leading to protracted legal battles, and an ongoing debate about who was behind the loss of funds from the exchange. Karpeles was eventually given a suspended two-year prison sentence by a Japanese court, which found that he had manipulated data about the exchange's trading activity. Nearly a decade later, Mt. Gox's creditors would recover a substantial portion of their funds due to the appreciation in the price of more than 200,000 bitcoins that the exchange had managed to keep in reserve despite the hack[9] – but the overall losses Bitcoin investors suffered from the Mt. Gox collapse were nonetheless severe, and the case would continue to dredge up bad memories among the Bitcoin community when other similar episodes eventually occurred.

In addition to the devastation it caused to the many well-intentioned individuals who had traded at Mt. Gox, the exchange's collapse presented a problem for its illicit users, like Shaun Bridges, who could no longer rely on Mt. Gox to launder their ill-gotten cryptocurrencies. Before long, other exchanges emerged to fill the void.

FinCEN Lays Down the Law

While Mt. Gox imploded, US financial regulators were turning their attention to the rapidly growing cryptocurrency exchange industry.

On March 18, 2013, the US Treasury Department's Financial Crimes Enforcement Network (FinCEN) issued a public guidance note that is one of the defining documents in the regulation of cryptocurrencies.[10] FinCEN is the US federal regulator for anti–money laundering and countering the financing of terrorism (AML/CFT), and it administers the Bank Secrecy Act, legislation passed in 1970 that forms the basis of America's AML/CFT efforts. FinCEN is responsible for supervising certain US entities, such as money service businesses (MSBs), which include companies like Western Union and PayPal, and for ensuring that they comply with AML/CFT rules, such as the requirement to gather Know Your Customer (KYC) information about users, and to file suspicious activity reports (SARs) with FinCEN about transactions that feature money laundering red flags.

It was in this capacity that FinCEN issued its March 2013 guidance entitled "Application of FinCEN's Regulations to Persons Administering, Exchanging, or Using Virtual Currencies." The purpose of the guidance was simple: it clarified when services involved in exchanging virtual currencies – a catch-all term that refers not only to cryptocurrencies, but also to centralized digital payment systems such as e-Gold and Liberty Reserve – must comply with AML/CFT requirements. The approach FinCEN outlined would shape how regulators globally treated cryptocurrencies for the ensuing decade. FinCEN used its guidance to explain that its regulations do not apply to individual users of Bitcoin or other virtual currencies. Rather, FinCEN stated that AML/CFT regulation applies to exchanges and other services that enable third parties to buy and sell cryptocurrencies for fiat currencies, or for other cryptocurrencies, or who transmit crypto on behalf of others. This principle – that regulation should not attempt to govern the underlying technology, or individual users of it, but rather should apply to the on-and-off ramps that enable users to trade and move their cryptocurrencies – has been at the heart of all efforts to regulate cryptocurrencies since. The rationale for this approach was straightforward: because criminals need to convert their cryptocurrencies into fiat currencies like the US dollar to realize their illicit profits, regulation should focus on bringing transparency to these touchpoints, since that is where criminals are most likely to be unmasked. In June 2015, the Financial Action Task Force (FATF) – the global AML/CFT standard-setting body associated with the G20 that determines how countries should tackle illicit financial threats – issued guidance recommending that other countries should regulate exchange platforms to address the growing risks of crypto-related money laundering.[11]

Because of FinCEN's stance, cryptocurrency exchange businesses operating from or servicing the US market were suddenly expected to adhere to the same AML/CFT rules that other financial institutions follow. US cryptocurrency exchanges could not allow customers to set up anonymous accounts, and they had to identify when their customers engaged in transactions with high-risk entities, such as dark web markets. Cryptocurrency exchanges that failed to do so would risk fines and other penalties from FinCEN. By extending its rules to the growing exchange sector, FinCEN was making clear that it had no tolerance for exchanges that enable money laundering.

Unsurprisingly, the prospect of regulation initially did not sit well with much of the early Bitcoin community. Government intervention in cryptocurrency markets ran contrary to the ethos of the cypherpunks, who saw Bitcoin as a way of preserving anonymity and undermining government control. Now, to fulfill their regulatory requirements, US cryptocurrency exchange platforms would need to report information about Bitcoin transactions to the government and collect identifying information from users. Diehard Bitcoin enthusiasts worried that any exchanges complying with FinCEN's requirements would allow the government to exert unwanted control in what was intended to be a free space liberated from the state.

Despite some initial reluctance, certain US cryptocurrency exchanges – including many that would go on to become the industry's best-known brands, such as Coinbase, Gemini, and Kraken – ultimately accepted that regulation was a fact they needed to live with if they wanted their businesses to succeed, and if they were to fulfill their mission of driving the widespread adoption of Bitcoin. These exchanges would eventually hire large teams of regulatory compliance specialists and legal professionals to ensure that they could meet their obligations under FinCEN's rules, as well as other rules imposed over the coming years. Indeed, over time, many popular exchanges came to see regulatory compliance as a benefit, in that obtaining approval from regulators conferred legitimacy on startup companies that were relatively young and unknown. As frustrating and intrusive as regulation might have seemed, it was certainly better than the alternative of governments attempting to ban cryptocurrencies altogether. Regulation meant rules, but it also represented an acknowledgment among regulators that they needed to find a way to live with Bitcoin, since they could not shut the network down. Skepticism about regulatory intentions among some in the Bitcoin community also thawed when FinCEN made attempts to engage the industry. Shortly after FinCEN issued its March 2013 guidance, FinCEN Director Jennifer Shasky Calavery held meetings with US cryptocurrency businesses to discuss their concerns about regulation, and to offer FinCEN's perspective on the importance of crime prevention.[12]

But if some Bitcoin exchange operators were willing to play the regulatory game, others, like Charlie Shrem of New York, failed to heed FinCEN's warnings. Shrem was a young entrepreneur and Bitcoin investor who was one of the founding members of the Bitcoin Foundation, an advocacy organization that aimed to promote Bitcoin's use – and which met with FinCEN Director Shasky Calavery in 2013 to discuss regulatory expectations. In addition to his work with the Bitcoin Foundation, in August 2011 Shrem had established a cryptocurrency exchange called BitInstant. Shrem obtained backing for BitInstant from high-profile investors, including Tyler and Cameron Winklevoss, the twin brothers who had once been embroiled in controversy with Facebook founder Mark Zuckerberg but who later founded the cryptocurrency exchange Gemini.[13] Though he had managed to obtain funding from reputable supporters, Shrem soon became entangled with other more problematic connections, including Robert Faiella, a restaurateur from Coral Gables, Florida.

Over the course of two years, BitInstant facilitated trades totaling more than $1 million on behalf of Faiella, who operated a Bitcoin-for-cash swapping service on the Silk Road and advertised his services under the name BTCKing. As part of the laundering scheme, Faiella sold bitcoins to Silk Road users who needed the cryptocurrency to buy drugs on the site. Faiella would then purchase bitcoins from Bit-Instant to fill the orders on behalf of Silk Road users, charging a mark-up and receiving cash from the Silk Road buyers in exchange. According to the US Department of Justice (DOJ), "Shrem was fully aware that Silk Road was a drug-trafficking website, and through his communications with Faiella, Shrem also knew that Faiella was operating a Bitcoin exchange service for Silk Road users. Nevertheless, Shrem knowingly facilitated Faiella's business. . . to maintain Faiella's business as a lucrative source of revenue."[14]

In April 2014, Shrem and Faiella were both indicted on counts of operating unlicensed money transmission services.[15] Because they were in the business of exchanging cryptocurrency for dollars, Shrem and Faiella should have registered their services with FinCEN and adhered to AML/CFT laws. In arresting and charging the pair – who both pled guilty and received fines and prison sentences – the US government was sending a message to anyone running a cryptocurrency exchange that it meant business when it came to preventing money laundering. But the amount of money that Shrem and Faiella had laundered was ultimately a drop in an ocean of bitcoins. Another rogue exchange would soon take Bitcoin laundering to an entirely different level.

The Rise and Fall of BTC-e

During the investigation into Carl Force, federal agents reviewing his financial records had noticed an unusual transfer. In May 2014, Force wired $235,000 to a bank account in Panama. Ownership of the Panama account led to a company called the Canton Business Corporation – an entity registered in the Seychelles and ultimately owned by a Russian national, Alexander Vinnik. Canton Business Corporation was the legal name of a cryptocurrency exchange that Vinnik ran, known as BTC-e.[16]

BTC-e's precise origin and Vinnik's own prior history are murky, but according to the US government, Vinnik founded BTC-e in 2011. The exchange's website claimed it operated in Bulgaria and was registered in Cyprus, but Vinnik actually owned and operated BTC-e through a series of shell companies registered across the globe, including in the Seychelles, Singapore, France, the British Virgin Islands, and New Zealand.[17] BTC-e users could swap Bitcoin and other cryptocurrencies, such as Litecoin, for US dollars, euros, and rubles – enabling the exchange to serve a global customer base of more than 700,000 users.[18] BTC-e customers could also establish accounts without providing any identifying information. Users opened accounts with nothing more than an email address, guaranteeing their anonymity. Some users, however, made no effort to conceal their intentions, registering for the site with usernames such as "CocaineCowboys" and "hacker4hire."[19] Vinnik also allegedly established payment settlement methods designed to facilitate easy money laundering through the site. For example, when users wanted to buy bitcoins from BTC-e, rather than transfer US dollars directly to an account in BTC-e's name, they were instructed to send the funds to offshore bank accounts held in the name of shell companies such as Canton Business Corporation that Vinnik ultimately owned – as in the case of Carl Force. Users of the exchange could also purchase "BTC-e code" – or credits they could trade to other BTC-e users, providing an avenue for anonymous internal transfers on the platform.

BTC-e benefited from the downfall of other platforms and quickly obtained a near monopoly over the market for facilitating illicit cryptocurrency swaps. The US takedown of Liberty Reserve in 2013, and the subsequent collapse of Mt. Gox, led criminal users of those defunct sites to flock to BTC-e. The US government alleges that, before long, BTC-e was acting as the premier money laundering venue for nearly every criminal actor in the world who used cryptocurrencies, facilitating illicit transfers related to a wide range of crimes. Not only was BTC-e the favored portal for Silk Road drug vendors to cash out their Bitcoin proceeds – US law enforcement alleges it also processed swaps for the growing number of criminals who used cryptocurrencies in conjunction with crimes such as identity theft, tax evasion, and hacking.

Overall, BTC-e ran a huge business, processing Bitcoin payments totaling more than $4 billion over six years. Once again, however, the ability of investigators to analyze data on the blockchain proved critical in disrupting a key player in the world of crypto-enabled money laundering.

Most transactions that cryptocurrency exchanges undertake are recorded "off-chain" – that is, many of the trades they process are settled internally and recorded on their own order books, and therefore do not appear on the blockchain. But when customers deposit or withdraw cryptocurrency to or from the exchange using their personal wallets, a record of those inflows and outflows from the exchange remains on the blockchain. The sheer scale of BTC-e's on-chain business meant that the blockchain contained extensive records of Bitcoin transactions flowing to and from it. Among the most significant and visible of these were transfers involving the bitcoins stolen from Mt. Gox. Investigators analyzing the financial trail from Mt. Gox could see on the blockchain that two-thirds of the funds stolen from Mt. Gox's wallet were sent to Bitcoin addresses at BTC-e associated with an administrator account that the US government alleges Vinnik controlled. The US government's analysis of blockchain data also suggested that an account at BTC-e under the name "WME" that Vinnik controlled was linked with wallets used to process transfers to another cryptocurrency exchange that had also received funds stolen from Mt. Gox.

The trail of illicit activity on the blockchain leading to BTC-e resulted in Vinnik becoming one of the most wanted financial criminals in the world. In July 2017, Greek police arrested Vinnik, and the DOJ immediately unveiled criminal charges against him and BTC-e for alleged money laundering and for operating an unlicensed exchange service. At the same time, FinCEN issued enforcement penalties totaling $122 million against Vinnik and BTC-e for failure to register with FinCEN and for noncompliance with US AML/CFT laws. Though BTC-e did not have a corporate or legal presence in the United States, because it served US customers Fin-CEN asserted jurisdiction over the exchange, which it claimed facilitated "at least 21,000 bitcoin transactions worth over $296,000,000 and tens of thousands of transactions in other convertible virtual currencies" involving American users.[20]

For more than two years after Vinnik's arrest, the Russian government attempted unsuccessfully to have him repatriated, and he was reportedly the target of a foiled assassination plot drawn up by Russian criminals while he was still in police custody in Greece.[21] In 2020, Vinnik was extradited to France, where a court convicted him of money laundering charges and sentenced him to five years' imprisonment.[22] That same year, police in New Zealand seized $90 million from bank accounts belonging to the Canton Business Corporation.[23] In August 2022, Vinnik was finally extradited to the United States to stand trial there.[24]

In June 2023, the DOJ revealed a twist in the BTC-e story that illuminated the relationship between the exchange and the funds stolen from Mt. Gox. In a grand jury indictment it unsealed on June 9, the US government alleged that two Russian nationals, Alexy Bilyuchenko and Aleksandr Verner, were the hackers who infiltrated Mt. Gox's IT systems back in 2011 and stole its customers' funds. In addition to outlining how the pair laundered the more than 600,000 bitcoins stolen from Mt. Gox, the US government's allegations claimed that Bilyuchenko had operated BTC-e alongside Vinnik between 2011 and 2017.[25] It was this tie that enabled Bilyuchenko to move a portion of the stolen Mt. Gox bitcoins through BTC-e. According to the US government's allegations, BTC-e was not merely the conduit through which the funds stolen from Mt. Gox flowed, but was in fact controlled by one of the alleged thieves involved in the massive hack.

* * *

In dismantling BTC-e, apprehending Vinnik, and unmasking the individuals allegedly behind the Mt. Gox hack, the US government once again demonstrated that Bitcoin's public ledger could serve as a tremendous asset in the fight against financial crime. The blockchain enabled investigators to follow the flow of funds from wallets belonging to illicit actors to the wallets controlled by BTC-e, providing a critical intelligence trail needed to pursue Vinnik, bring charges against him and the alleged Mt. Gox hackers, and shut down an exchange that was central to the ecosystem of criminal Bitcoin users. Yet the story of BTC-e's takedown was not one of complete triumph. Although the US government had managed to dismantle BTC-e, many of the funds BTC-e had allegedly helped to launder were as good as gone. After sending their bitcoins to BTC-e and converting them into fiat currencies, many criminals who had used it managed to launder their ill-gotten gains onward into the banking system. Because BTC-e allowed users to maintain anonymous accounts, law enforcement agencies in some cases would never be able to identify who the criminal perpetrators were behind those accounts. This was especially true where criminal funds were funneled off from BTC-e to bank accounts in secretive tax havens, or in jurisdictions like Russia, that are not inclined to cooperate with the United States on money laundering cases. The BTC-e case therefore highlighted the critical role that rogue cryptocurrency exchanges could play in facilitating criminal activity at a large scale.

The case also underscored a widening rift between those exchange services – such as Coinbase and Gemini – that had accepted oversight from FinCEN and sought to comply with US AML/CFT requirements, and those that defiantly refused government control. What's more, while the United States had managed to assert regulatory jurisdiction over BTC-e, the exchange's rise reflected a gap in global regulation of the cryptocurrency industry. Countries in Europe and Asia where BTC-e had established a corporate presence had not yet created regulatory regimes for cryptocurrencies – and would not do so for another few years. Consequently, exchanges like BTC-e faced no requirement to comply with AML/CFT measures in most of the world outside the United States. This dynamic made it incredibly easy for alleged criminals like Bilyuchenko and Vinnik to create and operate an exchange through which they could move large sums of ill-gotten cryptocurrencies for several years before the US government identified them.

Regulatory arbitrage – the practice of jurisdiction-hopping with the aim of avoiding scrutiny – was therefore critical to allowing the illicit cryptocurrency underworld to thrive. With few countries enforcing any rules, it was only a matter of time before new exchange services emerged in BTC-e's wake to assist the growing online criminal community in laundering cryptocurrencies. Shortly after Vinnik's arrest, his accomplices reconstituted BTC-e under the name WEX – ostensibly operating out of Singapore[26] – and migrated BTC-e user accounts to the new site, which closed after only a year in operation. Because of the BTC-e case, US regulators also became convinced that aggressively compelling exchanges to comply with AML/CFT laws through enforcement action was the best way to ensure that they played by the rules. In November 2020, FinCEN together with other US regulators issued a $100 million penalty against BitMEX, a Hong Kong–based cryptocurrency exchange that admitted to servicing the US market without approval and failing to comply with AML/CFT measures. Identifying and countering rogue exchanges became a centerpiece of the effort to crack down on illicit cryptocurrency activity.

The BTC-e case also demonstrated a conundrum for criminals. Illicit users of cryptocurrencies required a service like BTC-e to swap their bitcoins for fiat currencies as part of the money laundering process. Yet they had discovered that the exchanges they relied on were vulnerable to law enforcement disruption. Criminals could not count on even apparently complicit exchanges like BTC-e to act as permanent black holes if law enforcement agencies could continue to leverage the blockchain to identify and dismantle those same trading platforms. To avoid disruption, criminals needed to break the money trail on the blockchain between the point of generating their illicit proceeds in bitcoins and the point of cashing them out at an exchange. Put simply, they needed a better way to throw the police off their tracks.

Chapter 3

Mixers: Covering Up Their Tracks

The BTC-e case showed that the US government was determined that cryptocurrencies should not become an easy conduit for money laundering, and that it was committed to leveraging the blockchain's transparency in that fight. When US law enforcement agents seized BTC-e, the Federal Bureau of Investigation (FBI)'s Special Agent in Charge, Amy Hess, stated: "This investigation demonstrates the long-term commitment given to identifying and pursuing criminals world-wide with a whole of government approach. . . We must continue to impose real costs on criminals, no matter who they are or where they attempt to hide."[1] The United States wanted criminal users of cryptocurrencies to know that they were being watched, and that the financial technology they had thought promised them anonymity could in fact be used against them.

The Myth of Bitcoin's Anonymity

Though Bitcoin's early advocates believed that absolute financial privacy was foundational to social and economic freedom, even

Satoshi Nakamoto understood that Bitcoin's traceability could undermine this ideal. In the Bitcoin White Paper, Nakamoto had advised users to create a new Bitcoin wallet for every new transaction, because: "The risk is that if the [wallet] owner is revealed, linking could reveal other transactions that belonged to the same owner."[2]

Bitcoin's traceability is a function of its design. When a Bitcoin user sends funds from her address to another user's wallet, any funds remaining unspent must be accounted for and recorded on the blockchain. The process of recording data about unspent funds on the blockchain mimics the pattern of using cash and coins in the real world. Imagine a scenario where you wish to pay your friend four dollars, but you have a five-dollar bill in your pocket and do not carry exact change. In that case, you will give five dollars to your friend and then receive one dollar as change in return. Bitcoin works with a similar logic. A simple example helps to illustrate the implications for identifying connections between users' Bitcoin addresses.

Suppose a Bitcoin user named Alice wishes to pay her friend Bob four bitcoins. Alice, however, does not have exact change; rather, she has a balance of five bitcoins allocated to a public address beginning with the digits 1Az2kH. Therefore, when Alice generates a transaction using her unique private key, four bitcoins will be deposited in Bob's wallet, while one bitcoin will remain as change. In Bitcoin, this change is referred to as an unspent transaction output (UTXO) and will be deposited in a separate public address that Alice controls, in this case a wallet beginning with the digits 12t9YDP. This process is illustrated in Figure 3.1.

Now, suppose that Alice wishes to undertake a new transaction, this time to send two bitcoins to her friend Carol. Alice can use the UTXO of one bitcoin remaining from her transaction with Bob as an input to generate this new transaction. But because her change is insufficient to cover the amount she owes to Carol, Alice must combine the one bitcoin in her address beginning with 12t9YDP with one bitcoin contained in another address she controls beginning with the digits 115p7UM. To generate the transaction to Carol, Alice signs the transaction with the same private key that she used when transacting with Bob, and a total of two bitcoins is transferred to Carol's wallet. This process is illustrated in Figure 3.2.

Because Alice used the same unique private key to sign her transactions with Bob and Carol, an observer of the blockchain can see that the three public addresses used to create those transactions must be controlled by the same individual. The three addresses that Alice controls comprise her Bitcoin wallet and are also known as her "cluster" of addresses.

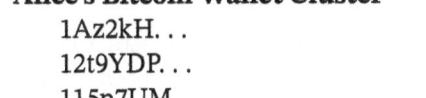

Alice's Bitcoin Wallet Cluster
    1Az2kH...
    12t9YDP...
    115p7UM...

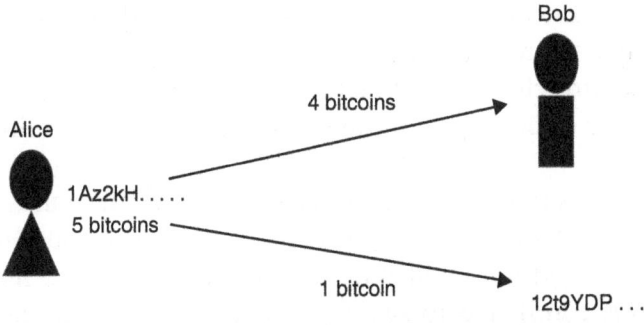

Figure 3.1 Example of an unspent transaction output (UTXO) in a Bitcoin transaction.

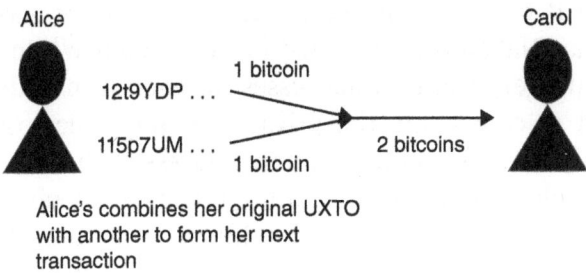

Figure 3.2 Example of UTXOs used to generate a new Bitcoin transaction.

The process described here is one that is constantly unfolding on the blockchain. As Alice undertakes additional transactions in the future, she will generate more and more UTXOs, generating further addresses to hold her change. As she combines these addresses to form new transactions, Alice will leave a growing trail of interconnected addresses on the blockchain – a concept known as "common spend." Therefore, if an outside observer can tie Alice's identity to any of the pseudonymous addresses she uses, her entire Bitcoin transaction history will forever be associated with her cluster on the blockchain, and visible for all to see.

This ability to link addresses and distinguish a user's complete transaction history has important implications for the detection of illicit activity. When law enforcement agents investigate a criminal entity that uses Bitcoin – such as the Silk Road – they need only identify a single address belonging to that entity, and they can then identify the entire cluster of linked addresses that the entity controls, even if the entity uses hundreds, thousands, or even millions of addresses.

Clearly, this is not the complete privacy the cypherpunks had envisioned when dreaming of a world flush with anonymous digital cash. And one need not be ideologically committed to the notion of anonymous commerce to see a problem with the traceability of Bitcoin transactions: it seems unlikely that any reasonable person would be comfortable with having her entire financial history recorded online for anyone else to view.

Bitcoin, many of its early proponents realized, would struggle to gain traction or provide a meaningful alternative to the banking system if privacy could be violated so easily. It was with this in mind that Nakamoto suggested in the Bitcoin White Paper that users should generate new addresses for each transaction, a practice aimed at countering the privacy-busting effects of common spend analysis. By generating a new address with no existing balance for each new transaction undertaken, a Bitcoin user could avoid generating a trail of easily identifiable, interconnected UTXOs that could be linked back to her. This tactic was available to legitimate users of the technology who sought greater confidentiality, but early criminal users were also aware of Bitcoin's traceability and attempted to counteract it using these techniques. Carl Force had heeded Satoshi Nakamoto's advice and attempted to launder his bitcoins by sending them through numerous unused addresses before depositing them at exchanges – though his relatively unsophisticated attempt at this technique was easily unmasked by law enforcement analysts. Ross Ulbricht also understood that Bitcoin transactions could be linked, but he had looked to another method to conceal the Silk Road's transactions: Bitcoin mixing.

Bitcoin mixing does exactly as advertised: it involves co-mingling bitcoins from multiple users to confuse observers of the blockchain about the origin of each user's funds, with the aim of enhancing user privacy. Bitcoin mixers combine funds from multiple users before redistributing the co-mingled bitcoins to users' requested destination addresses. By pooling funds together in this way, a mixer obfuscates the connection between the origin and destination of a user's funds. If a user sends her bitcoins from her address into a mixer, then the funds will be deposited into a new address on the other end without leaving a clear indication that the two addresses are connected. If the user's funds originate from an illicit source, such as a dark web market, then she will have broken the link between the addresses where those funds originated and any transactions she undertakes in the future.

A key factor in determining a Bitcoin mixer's effectiveness is the strength of its "anonymity set" – or the number of transactions passing through the mixer. The more users who transact with a mixer, and the more liquid it is, the more effective it will be in obfuscating the connection between any given user's source and destination of funds. Mixers with a small anonymity set can be vulnerable to "de-mixing" – that is, an observer can potentially establish a direct connection between funds going into the mixer and funds coming out if there are fewer complementary transactions that help to obfuscate a user's attempt to mix her funds. To understand this concept, consider a cash register: if a criminal were to put a $100 bill into the cash register, and there were only ten other $100 bills in the register, you would have a one-in-ten chance of establishing a link between the criminal and her bill. If, however, there were one hundred thousand $100 bills in the cash register, then the chance of identifying the criminal's original bill would be extremely unlikely. Mixers work in a similar fashion. Highly liquid mixers that process large volumes of transactions provide criminals with a valuable service in the money laundering process, enabling them to mask their flows of funds from observers of the blockchain.

To obscure payments related to the Silk Road, Ulbricht had made a mixing service available to the site's users, who could pass funds through the mixer before withdrawing them to their personal wallets. The mixer the Silk Road employed, however, was not particularly effective or consistently employed by users – as demonstrated by the substantial success the FBI had in monitoring the Silk Road's transactions.[3] Ulbricht also did not routinely mix transactions he sent between his personal Bitcoin wallet and the Silk Road administrator wallet – providing investigators with clear indications on the blockchain of his transactional ties to the site.[4]

In the years after the Silk Road takedown, the criminal ecosystem sustained by Bitcoin grew exponentially, producing dark web marketplaces that dwarfed Ulbricht's. Undeterred by Ulbricht's arrest, other dark web entrepreneurs who emerged after Ulbricht were resolved to learn from his mistakes and outdo him. Over the course of the decade following Ulbricht's arrest, more than 100 illicit markets emerged on the dark web – run by individuals both intent on profiting from the trade, as well as pursuing Ulbricht's vision of liberated marketplaces that could defy the unjust and oppressive War on Drugs and enable commerce to thrive beyond the reaches of what they saw as an increasingly pervasive police state set on constant digital surveillance.[5] Some of these markets specialized in selling specific types of illicit items – such as drugs or stolen credit card data – while others functioned as one-stop shops for a variety of illicit goods. Dark web markets such as Agora, Dream Market, Evolution, and Cloud 9 offered users a plentiful supply of narcotics, while sites such as UniCC provided cybercriminals with an endless supply of stolen credit card details to exploit. Law enforcement agencies, building on their success in the Silk Road case, managed to dismantle some of these new dark web markets. In November 2014, the FBI worked with Europol, the European Union's police intelligence agency, to coordinate Operation Onymous – a joint law enforcement action that led to the takedown of some of the largest sites that had emerged after the Silk Road. Despite these successes, law enforcement agencies seemed caught in continuous pursuit of the operators of dark web markets, who remained committed to fulfilling widespread demand and would set up new sites as soon as the police had taken one down.

Of the dark web markets that emerged in the few years after the Silk Road's demise, the one that dwarfed the competition and attracted the most attention from law enforcement was AlphaBay. Established in late 2014 by Alexandre Cazes, a Canadian citizen, AlphaBay quickly achieved a tremendous scale of illegal sales. Benefiting in part from the exodus of users from sites dismantled during Operation Onymous, AlphaBay attracted a user base nearly ten times the size of the Silk Road's, hosting a thriving trade in narcotics, stolen IDs, weapons, counterfeit goods, and more. At its height, AlphaBay generated nearly half a million dollars in sales daily, exceeding the Silk Road by orders of magnitude. Unsurprisingly, this extensive transactional activity left a highly visible imprint on the blockchain associated with AlphaBay's address cluster, which law enforcement agencies in the United States and Europe had begun to monitor.[6]

With investigators lurking, the operators behind this boom in dark web markets were desperate for Bitcoin mixers that could absorb and obfuscate rising volumes of illicit payments. Fortunately for Cazes and other dark web kingpins, there was an ordinary-looking guy from Akron, Ohio, named Larry Dean Harmon, who was prepared to help.

Helix and the Rise of the Industrial-Scale Mixer

According to his social media accounts, Harmon was a Bitcoin enthusiast and operator of a cryptocurrency exchange called Coin

Ninja, whose stated mission was "accelerating the global adoption of Bitcoin."[7] From his online profile alone, the casual observer might have assumed that Harmon was a harmless and moderately successful Bitcoin trader. In fact, Harmon operated a Bitcoin mixing service that was vital to the growth of AlphaBay and other dark web markets.

In April 2014, Harmon launched a search engine on Tor called Grams, and used it to advertise a mixing service for dark web users that he named Helix and began operating that same summer. Harmon pitched the Helix mixer as a way for buyers and sellers on dark web markets to keep their bitcoins clean and evade law enforcement detection (see Figure 3.3). Users of numerous dark web markets – including Agora, Dream Market, Evolution, and Cloud 9 – mixed their coins through Helix, which Harmon made easy to access through an Application Programming Interface (API) that enabled Helix to be implemented directly into the Bitcoin wallet infrastructure on those dark web markets.[8]

Figure 3.3   The Helix mixing service as it was advertised to users of the dark web.

Precisely when Harmon began collaborating with Cazes to launder funds from AlphaBay is unclear, but from at least November 2016 Helix became the official mixing service for AlphaBay. Helix provided the site's users with a ready-made solution for cleaning their coins that they could access through an embedded link on AlphaBay, which was the largest source of Helix's mixing activity.[9] Over a three-year span, Helix mixed over 360,000 bitcoins through more than 1.2 million transactions – processing funds that totaled more than $311 million and yielded Harmon millions of dollars in commissions from the fees he charged.[10]

A mixer like Helix provided users with a vital asset in the money laundering process. After cleaning their bitcoins with Helix, dark web users could send their new, "clean" coins onwards to an exchange service, where they could convert their now ostensibly legitimate bitcoins into US dollars or other fiat currencies. Law enforcement agencies therefore could not see the direct connection between the illicit source of funds where bitcoin proceeds were generated and the exchange platforms where the criminals cashed out. And a compliance team at a US exchange subject to FinCEN regulations in that scenario would be unaware that the funds they had received originated from the dark web. With a service like Helix, the funds trail truly could be broken.

In July 2017, Harmon lost his largest source of revenue when US and European law enforcement agencies announced that they had arrested Alexandre Cazes and shut down AlphaBay. US and European investigators had grown increasingly alarmed over AlphaBay when they discovered that some vendors on the site were peddling fentanyl, the lethal synthetic opioid that was causing a growing wave of overdoses in the United States and had ignited a new crisis of drug addiction. US investigators had managed to link instances of fentanyl deaths directly to specific sales they had observed on AlphaBay – such as the case of an 18-year-old from Vancouver, Washington, who died in November 2016 after buying fentanyl from an AlphaBay vendor who used the name Fentmaster on the site. "Fentmaster" was an individual from New York named Chukwuemeka Okparaeke, who pleaded guilty in July 2021 to charges of fentanyl trafficking and admitted to engaging in more than 7,000 sales of the drug on AlphaBay.[11] With authorities determined to clamp down on the networks enabling fentanyl deaths, AlphaBay soon became the subject of a global law enforcement effort determined to dismantle it.

Despite his attempts to ensure anonymity and avoid Ross Ulbricht's fate by mixing funds through Helix, Cazes committed a similar set of mistakes to the Silk Road founder, which ultimately tipped investigators off to his identity. Like Ulbricht, Cazes had included his personal email in an early post to AlphaBay users – a clue that investigators used to identify other accounts he maintained elsewhere online and eventually track him to Thailand, where he was residing in a mansion he had purchased.[12] Cazes was arrested and taken to a Thai jail, where he was to await extradition to the United States. Cazes, however, committed suicide just one week after he was taken into police custody.[13]

With his biggest client gone, Harmon began to wind down Helix, and by the end of 2017 the mixer was defunct. By that time, Harmon had used the millions of dollars in fees he'd earned from Helix to buy properties in Belize.[14] The loss of Helix, though, didn't stop dark web market operators from mixing their bitcoins elsewhere. Helix was just one among numerous Bitcoin mixing services that had emerged.

Alongside Helix, the most effective and prolific mixing service available to the early crypto laundering ecosystem was Bitcoin Fog, a mixer that the US government alleges was established by Roman Sterlingov, a Russian–Swedish national, in 2011 – making it one of the oldest mixers around. According to the US government, Sterlingov was familiar with the online underworld of illicit digital payments, having allegedly been a frequent user of Liberty Reserve, Mt. Gox, and BTC-e. The US government alleges that Sterlingov, like Harmon, promoted Bitcoin Fog on the dark web, and that he established and administered a social media presence for the mixer, creating a Bitcoin Fog website and Twitter account. The US government claims that Sterlingov originally announced the launch of Bitcoin Fog on the `bitcointalk.org` chat forum where Ross Ulbricht had also promoted the Silk Road. Over the course of the next nine years, according to US prosecutors, Bitcoin Fog laundered 1.2 million bitcoins worth more than $350 million. Investigators from the IRS Criminal Investigations division allege that Bitcoin Fog ultimately served users from at least 51 dark web markets.[15]

Busting the Mixers

The growing criminal use of mixers to launder funds naturally drew concern and scrutiny from law enforcement and regulatory agencies. As early as 2014, Europol had warned – in a report on Internet crime – about the growing use of mixers for money laundering.[16] In guidance it published in June 2019, the Financial Action Task Force – the global AML/CFT standard setter – warned regulators around the world to be alert to the use of mixers or "other technologies that obfuscate the identity of the sender, recipient, holder, or beneficial owner of a [cryptocurrency]."[17]

Police investigators and regulatory officials also became aware of another important fact about mixers: while mixers succeeded in breaking the end-to-end trail of funds on the blockchain so that one could not establish a link between the illicit source of funds and their final destination, the clusters of addresses that mixer operators used to receive and redistribute bitcoins could still be viewed on the blockchain. The blockchain, it turned out, kept a record of funds being sent to a mixing operator's wallet, as well as funds being sent from the mixer to users' recipient addresses. The full funds flow might be broken, but if investigators could identify the operators behind a mixer, they could then use the record of transactions on the blockchain showing funds moving from dark web markets to those mixers as evidence to pursue money laundering charges against the mixers' operators. Investigators could also follow the trail of coins that had been mixed to see where they wound up.

For example, if mixed coins were sent onwards to the account of a user at a regulated crypto exchange that held identifying information and documentation about the holder of those mixed coins, that would allow investigators to link personal identities to the mixing activity. The Financial Action Task Force (FATF) and regulators such as FinCEN therefore began to warn cryptocurrency exchanges that they should be on alert for deposits from customers who received funds into their accounts from mixers. Even if the exchanges could not confirm that the underlying funds originated from an illicit source, they could still treat the receipt of mixed coins as a red flag and report suspicious cases to law enforcement.

In May 2019, European law enforcement agencies struck the first in a series of blows against mixers when they announced the seizure of the Bestmixer.io service, which was the third largest mixer in operation at the time, after Bitcoin Fog and Helix. The law enforcement action against Bestmixer had begun when Dutch police started investigating the service in 2018, after they determined that Bestmixer's operators used computer servers located in the Netherlands and Luxembourg. Dutch police then collaborated with Europol and police in Luxembourg to take the mixer offline by seizing its servers. Bestmixer demonstrated just how prolific an effective mixing service could become in a short span of time. Established in May 2018, Bestmixer enabled users to obfuscate funds in Bitcoin, as well as the cryptocurrencies Bitcoin Cash (a derivative of the original Bitcoin code) and Litecoin. In only a year, the service managed to process more than $200 million in transactions, a substantial portion of which involved dark web markets.[18] Importantly, having obtained data from Bestmixer's servers, Dutch police gleaned information about those individuals who had interacted with it, including their IP addresses, chat messages, and Bitcoin addresses. It turned out that while mixers could obfuscate transaction details on the blockchain, those who dealt with mixers could leave behind other clues available for investigators to follow – just as Alexandre Cazes and Ross Ulbricht had.

Other operators of mixers took the opportunity of Bestmixer's demise to try and consolidate their hold on the market. Larry Harmon had by that point launched Coin Ninja, ostensibly a Bitcoin exchange, but in fact a platform he used as a front to continue mixing using a new service that operated on Tor called DropBit.[19]

In June 2019, the Bitcoin Fog Twitter account started posting messages advising users that Bitcoin Fog was more secure than Bestmixer and could evade law enforcement detection more effectively because it also operated on Tor. By hosting their mixing services on Tor, these operators believed they could keep them beyond the reach of law enforcement and avoid Bestmixer's fate.

They soon learned that their hopes were misplaced. In February 2020, US law enforcement agents arrested Harmon on charges of money laundering and for failing to register Helix as a money transmission business.[20] Harmon entered a guilty plea with US prosecutors in August 2021, and agreed to forfeit $200 million in cryptocurrencies to the federal government. Harmon also received a $60 million fine from FinCEN in October 2021. FinCEN determined that because Harmon was in the business of swapping and transferring cryptocurrencies for a fee, he was operating as an unregistered exchange service that should have registered with FinCEN, which found that he had facilitated mixing on behalf of 39 dark web markets.[21] In a bizarre twist in the Helix story, in January 2023 the US Department of Justice (DOJ) announced that Harmon's brother Gary had pleaded guilty to money laundering charges after stealing more than 712 bitcoins (worth more than $4.8 million) from Harmon's Bitcoin wallet while asset forfeiture proceedings were pending in the Helix case. Gary, it turned out, knew his brother's private key details and managed to transfer funds from Harmon's wallet to his own personal wallets before the forfeiture action commenced. Having obstructed the forfeiture action, Gary then sent the funds from his own Bitcoin wallets through other mixing services, eventually cashing out the funds at exchanges to finance large purchases, including buying a $1.2 million apartment and taking rides on private jets – a highly visible money trail that ultimately led to his arrest alongside that of his brother.[22]

In April 2021, Roman Sterlingov met a similar fate. That month, the US DOJ announced that it had arrested Sterlingov and was pursuing money laundering charges against him for allegedly operating Bitcoin Fog. In the criminal complaint lodged against him, government investigators detailed how they identified Sterlingov as the alleged founder of Bitcoin Fog. Prosecutors claim that Sterlingov had gotten sloppy: law enforcement agents had obtained records of email and IP addresses he allegedly used to register the web domain name and Twitter accounts for Bitcoin Fog. These details matched information from accounts that investigators had uncovered from Liberty Reserve and Mt. Gox, where Sterlingov had used his own name when opening accounts. Investigators also claim that the blockchain shows evidence of Bitcoin payments Sterlingov made to register domain names for Bitcoin Fog, and that among the first transactions Bitcoin Fog ever received were small transfers of bitcoins that Sterlingov made from his Mt. Gox account, in what the US government alleges were likely initial attempts to test the mixer after its creation.[23]

Sterlingov, for his part, denies that he was the founder and operator of Bitcoin Fog, claiming that the government's investigation does not prove he ran the mixer and laundered funds through it, even if he may have administered its social media accounts. In August 2022, Sterlingov's defense team filed motions in court arguing that the US government's reliance on blockchain data was unreliable and demanded that the case be dismissed because transactional information investigators used was entirely circumstantial – offering up the first legal challenge to the analysis of the Bitcoin blockchain as a source of evidence in criminal cases.[24]

Wasabi Wallet: The CoinJoin Alternative

The disruption of the dark web's most prolific mixing services was an important win for US and European law enforcement. Unsurprisingly, however, the illicit online ecosystem had already identified workarounds that criminals hoped would keep them a step ahead.

Mixers such as Bitcoin Fog and Helix had suffered from a flaw that advocates of privacy-enhancing technology had warned about even before Satoshi Nakamoto launched Bitcoin: centralization. The mixers that dark web markets had utilized functioned much like cryptocurrency exchanges by receiving deposits from users, consolidating them in centralized wallets, and taking custody of the underlying funds in the process, before redistributing them to users. This centralization had left those services prone to disruption, and the funds held in them vulnerable to seizure by law enforcement. As with other debates within the Bitcoin community, the preference was for decentralized solutions that would prove less susceptible to disruption. It turned out that a small and obscure company in the British territory of Gibraltar had developed software that offered an alternative.

Founded in 2018 and registered in Gibraltar, the small startup company zkSNACKs makes its mission clear on its website. "We believe that privacy is both a fundamental human right and business need that should be preserved at all times. This is why we focus on your digital financial privacy," the company states. "We live in an Orwellian surveillance society where your information is being used to typecast and manipulate you. Bitcoin projects are being pressured to collect more and more data, if possible. . . Developers can't collect any sensitive information about you. What you do with your bitcoin is your business."[25]

On October 31, 2018, exactly ten years after the launch of the Bitcoin White Paper, zkSNACKs announced the creation of Wasabi Wallet – a wallet software it promised would revolutionize the ability of Bitcoin users to secure their privacy. Wasabi Wallet harnesses an innovation in mixing technology known as CoinJoin, an idea first proposed on the bitcointalk.org forum as early as 2013, but which never took off on a large scale before Wasabi Wallet.[26] CoinJoin involves consolidating funds from multiple Bitcoin users into a single transaction; the funds are then apportioned to output addresses in equal values and reallocated to the original senders based upon the value of the funds they contributed to the consolidated transaction. Consequently, an observer of the blockchain is not able to establish a link between a user's contribution to the original CoinJoin transaction and any wallets where they receive funds. Wasabi Wallet implements CoinJoin capabilities and provides this functionality through a desktop software app that users download to their device. Because Wasabi Wallet does not take possession of user funds in the manner of centralized mixing services and instead provides CoinJoin functionality through an open-source software app, users could continue to access the software even if zkSNACKs were to go out of business – ensuring that there is not a single point of failure as in the case of previous mixing services.

From the perspective of illicit users of Bitcoin, when mixers like Helix and Bestmixer went offline, Wasabi Wallet was there to pick up the slack. In April 2020, a Europol report warned of the growing use of Wasabi Wallet to facilitate money laundering from the dark web, noting that between late 2018 and early 2020, Wasabi Wallet had received more than $500 million in bitcoins, and that in a single week it processed transactions worth more than $50 million – 30% of which had been sent from dark web markets.[27] Other research by the blockchain analytics firm Elliptic indicated that whereas in 2019 only 2% of illicit-origin Bitcoin transactions relied on privacy wallets like Wasabi in the money laundering process, by the end of 2020 that number had risen to 13%.[28]

In July 2020, Wasabi Wallet made headlines in a high-profile cybercrime incident that implicated the social media giant Twitter.[29] On July 15 of that year, hackers managed to take control of the verified Twitter profiles of more than 130 high-profile individuals, including Barak Obama, Joe Biden, Elon Musk, Jeff Bezos, Kim Kardashian, and others. The hackers then used those profiles to post tweets encouraging followers to send money to specific Bitcoin addresses – ostensibly in support of charitable causes, and with the promise that donors would receive rewards in return for their contributions. Hundreds of individuals fell for the scam, which resulted in the hackers receiving bitcoins totaling more than $120,000 into their wallets. Once they obtained the funds, the hackers began to launder them. They sent more than a quarter of the stolen funds through Wasabi Wallet, and another portion through centralized mixers.[30]

While initially it seemed that the hackers had pulled off a daring and clever heist, the scheme quickly backfired. The high-profile nature of the attack meant that law enforcement agencies and regulators were on high alert. The day after the hack, FinCEN issued a notice requesting that regulated cryptocurrency exchanges report transactions they suspected might be related to the attack.[31] After all, upon mixing the coins they had obtained in the hack, the perpetrators would still need to cash them out at an exchange. FinCEN hoped that regulated exchanges that collected information about their users might hold clues about the perpetrators, and could mitigate the damage. This hunch turned out to be correct.

On July 31, just over two weeks after the Twitter hack occurred, law enforcement agencies in the United States and United Kingdom announced the arrests of three individuals they accused of undertaking the hack. The trio were not what many had expected. Far from being experienced criminal masterminds, they were a 19-year-old from the United Kingdom, a 22-year-old from Orlando, Florida, and a juvenile whose identity was not released. In the days before the scam, the three young hackers had used cryptocurrency to purchase the compromised Twitter accounts from vendors on cybercriminal forums – transactions that investigators were able to analyze on the blockchain. US law enforcement agents also discovered that the email addresses the crew used to create profiles on those hacking sites matched email addresses that they had used to create accounts at the cryptocurrency exchanges Coinbase and Binance, both of which supplied investigators with details of the hackers' accounts.[32] Coinbase also announced that it had prevented more than a thousand of its customers from sending funds to the hackers once it was alerted to the scam.[33] Despite their attempt to mask their transactions using Wasabi Wallet, the Twitter hackers were ultimately ensnared by the widening net of government regulation and enforcement. In June 2023, a US federal judge sentenced John O'Connor, the British citizen involved in perpetrating the hack, to five years' imprisonment for his role in the Twitter scam, as well as other instances of crypto-related hacking he undertook that resulted in a total of $1 million in losses for his victims.[34]

Importantly, zkSNACKs and the developers who created Wasabi Wallet have never been accused of crimes, and have not been deemed accountable for the laundering activity that has occurred using their software. There is a critical legal distinction between those who create privacy-enhancing solutions that illicit actors happen to use, and those – such as Larry Dean Harmon – who actively court the business of those engaged in illegal transactions. Amid growing reports of Wasabi Wallet's use by criminals, its creators sought to distance themselves from perceptions that the purpose of the technology was to facilitate crime. In March 2022, zkSNACKs indicated in a blog post that it would begin blacklisting bitcoins used by illicit actors so that they could not be included in Wasabi Wallet's CoinJoin transactions. As the zkSNACKs CEO Bálint Harmat told *Bitcoin Magazine* at the time of the announcement: "People started to identify Wasabi with illicit activities and actors, and we wanted to differentiate ourselves from these players in the space. . . Wasabi is for people to preserve their privacy, and not for hiding illicit activities."[35]

The Privacy Conundrum

Mixing technology fundamentally changed the nature of the game between criminals and law enforcement. US and European law enforcement agencies had come a long way from the early days of the Silk Road investigation, and were increasingly adept at tackling crypto-enabled crime, scoring impressive victories along the way. Mixers, and technologies like Wasabi Wallet, did not make it impossible for law enforcement agencies to identify the perpetrators of crypto-enabled crimes. Criminals were often the victim of their own more basic, careless errors. Mixers, however, added a new dynamic to a cat-and-mouse game that had already been underway for several years, and they provided criminals with an additional avenue for laundering cryptocurrencies that became one more vector demanding law enforcement agents' and regulators' attention and resources.

The rise of mixers and technologies like Wasabi Wallet in the money laundering process was a sign that the online criminal ecosystem was becoming increasingly entrenched and complex – and that it would constantly evolve new, innovative methods for crypto laundering that would test investigators' ability to keep pace. And the desire to find solutions for greater transactional privacy among even legitimate users of cryptocurrencies was one that would not fade away easily – not by a long shot.

Indeed, the next innovation in privacy-enhancing technologies was one that led law enforcement agencies and regulators to worry that crypto laundering could truly become undetectable.

Chapter 4

Privacy Coins: Going Underground

By disrupting the likes of BTC-e, Bitcoin Fog, Bestmixer, and Helix, US and European law enforcement agencies had, within a decade of the Silk Road case, struck important blows against the emerging money laundering infrastructure of the illicit online economy. These successes demonstrated an impressive ability among law enforcement agencies to adapt to a new technology and rapidly evolving criminal behavior. A new generation of law enforcement investigators was honing the skills and expertise needed to combat crypto laundering. Law enforcement agencies such as the Federal Bureau of Investigation, the IRS Criminal Investigations division, and Europol were soon assigning agents to full-time, specialized roles tracking and tracing cryptocurrencies.

Similarly, cases such as the takedown of the Twitter hackers had illustrated that collaboration between public sector agencies and regulated cryptocurrency exchanges could enable the detection and apprehension of criminals in increasingly complex money laundering cases. Regulated cryptocurrency exchanges had begun training staff to identify illicit activity on the blockchain so they could close accounts associated with suspicious payments and report them to law enforcement. Both the cryptocurrency industry and law enforcement agencies had managed to stand up critical defenses aimed at making cryptocurrencies less vulnerable to criminal exploitation.

The development of these defenses was also necessary for cryptocurrencies to gain a perception of legitimacy among the general public. Despite law enforcement successes in disrupting early cases of criminality, in the few years after the Silk Road case much of the public was still largely unfamiliar with cryptocurrencies, and many who were aware of the technology still held a misperception that cryptocurrencies were completely anonymous, untraceable, and served no purpose other than criminal use. Symptomatic of this perception were calls from politicians to ban Bitcoin, as occurred in January 2014, when US Senator Joe Manchin urged regulators to "prohibit this dangerous currency from harming hard-working Americans."[1] If cryptocurrencies were ever to go mainstream and obtain widespread adoption, there would need to be a popular belief that crypto was more than just a form of illicit money, and that the technology offered potential benefits to society. This became true especially as criminal actors beyond dark web merchants adopted cryptocurrencies. As the Twitter hack case had demonstrated, fraudsters and scammers in particular saw the cryptocurrency space as a source of potential income.

Bitcoin's wild price swings and the periods of rampant speculation that occurred as the price per bitcoin rose – from $1,000 to $20,000 to above $67,000 – before crashing back down again offered fraudsters perfect cover to prey on the desire of new entrants to the crypto space to get rich quick. In 2017, when the price of Bitcoin skyrocketed to $20,000 for the first time, market froth led to a proliferation in initial coin offerings (ICOs), or the launch of new cryptocurrencies by teams of developers who sold new coins they had created to investors – much in the manner of issuing shares in a new business venture. The ICO craze led to the creation of thousands of new coins, and while some were legitimate, by at least one estimate as many as 80% of ICOs were fraudulent and fleeced investors of hundreds of millions of dollars.[2] When developers of new coins launched an ICO, they would generally accept Bitcoin or other popular cryptocurrencies as payment for units of the new coin. In many cases, however, the supposed new coin did not actually exist, and the creators of the scheme would disappear with their victims' bitcoins – a type of fraud known in the cryptocurrency space as a "rug pull." In December 2021, the US Securities and Exchange Commission (SEC) filed charges against a Latvian national, Ivars Auzins, for allegedly running two rug pull scams. One of these was a purported token called Innovamine that the SEC alleges Auzins sold to investors for cryptocurrencies, with a promise that they would obtain a stake in a crypto mining business. But according to the SEC's allegations, Auzins simply stole the millions of dollars' worth of cryptocurrencies that defrauded investors had sent to him – a typical rug pull scheme.[3]

Cryptocurrencies also became associated with classic frauds such as Ponzi schemes, in which innocent users are lured into investing in a project with promises of enormous returns, only to have their investments used to settle the claims of previous investors – creating a house of cards that inevitably collapses. (The scams are named after Charles Ponzi, an Italian businessman who pleaded guilty to fraud charges in the United States in 1920.) Over the course of the decade from 2012 through 2022, various Ponzi schemes defrauded investors of cryptocurrencies worth billions of dollars. One of the largest Ponzi schemes of the period involved an investment platform called BitConnect. BitConnect was established in 2016 by Satish Kumbhani, an Indian national who marketed the trading platform to cryptocurrency investors and encouraged them to use bitcoins to purchase another coin he claimed to have created, BitConnect Coin (BCC). Kumbhani claimed to investors that holding BCC tokens would enable them to profit from cryptocurrency price volatility by leveraging purported automated trading bots that could anticipate market movements. In fact, Kumbhani was merely taking bitcoins from new investors and using them to pay early BCC buyers to maintain the appearance that those earlier investors were earning high returns. But BitConnect closed in January 2018, causing the price of BCC to plummet and leaving investors entirely dry.

In less than two years, BitConnect had taken in bitcoins worth more than $2.4 billion from investors – a fact that naturally drew the scrutiny of US regulators and law enforcement agencies. In September 2021, the SEC filed a complaint against BitConnect and Kumbhani, as well as Glenn Arcaro, a US-based BitConnect promoter, alleging that they knowingly stole the funds they had obtained from investors. Arcaro ultimately pleaded guilty to the charges levied against him, and in September 2022 was sentenced to more than three years' imprisonment.[4] The US government also seized cryptocurrencies worth more than $57 million from Arcaro, and used the sale of those seized funds to reimburse victims of the BitConnect scheme.[5] In February 2022, the US Department of Justice (DOJ) announced an indictment charging Kumbhani with allegations of fraud, price manipulation, money laundering, and other crimes. Among the accusations levied against him, the DOJ claims that Kumbhani and BitConnect attempted to launder bitcoins they received from investors by sending them through cryptocurrency exchanges around the world. As of mid-2023, authorities in India and the United States were searching for Kumbhani, who was believed to have fled India but whose whereabouts remained unknown.[6]

The proliferation of fraud demonstrated that innocent and well-intentioned users of cryptocurrencies – often low-knowledge consumers attracted by the latest hype – could easily be scammed and victimized. But the ability of law enforcement agencies to follow the funds trail through the blockchain and unmask the perpetrators of these scams and frauds showed that criminals in the crypto space could be identified and held to account – a precondition for building the general public's confidence in Bitcoin. As Special Agent Ryan Korner of the IRS Criminal Investigation division said about the indictment of BitConnect's founders: "As cryptocurrency gains popularity and attracts investors worldwide, alleged fraudsters. . . are utilizing increasingly complex schemes to defraud investors, oftentimes stealing millions of dollars. . . However, make no mistake, our agency will continue our long tradition of following the money, whether physical or digital, to expose criminal schemes and hold the fraudsters accountable for their illegal acts of trickery and deceit."[7]

The Rise of the Blockchain Analytics Industry

These successes – and those law enforcement actions that preceded them, such as the BTC-e, Helix, and Bitcoin Fog cases – would not have been possible without the emergence of a niche industry devoted to unveiling criminal activity in cryptocurrencies: the blockchain analytics industry. The Silk Road case, and the wave of investigations into its successor dark web markets, had made clear that law enforcement agencies needed sophisticated capabilities to investigate an expanding ecosystem of cryptocurrency-enabled crimes. What's more, FinCEN's March 2013 guidance had clarified that cryptocurrency exchanges needed to be able to detect and report suspicious transactions to meet their regulatory obligations. While the open and transparent nature of the blockchain lent itself to surveilling transactions, it was impractical for both law enforcement investigators and compliance analysts at crypto exchanges to proactively scrutinize billions of cryptocurrency transactions through manual analysis alone. Public and private sector stakeholders required specialist tools that would allow them to comb through an ever-growing trove of data on the blockchain rapidly and seamlessly.

As the number of cryptocurrencies grew to include thousands of new coins, this need became even more pronounced: because each new cryptocurrency comes with a distinct transaction history, analyzing data about the entire ecosystem of all cryptocurrencies in addition to Bitcoin required the ability to trawl through constantly increasing volumes of transactional information across, effectively, thousands of ledgers. Police investigators or compliance analysts sitting at their desks simply could not wade through this vast sea of cryptocurrency transaction data containing records across numerous blockchains without drowning in a swirl of indecipherable noise.

These challenges gave birth to the blockchain analytics industry – a collection of specialized companies that develop software to enable the rapid analysis and detection of illicit activity throughout the cryptocurrency ecosystem. Elliptic, a UK-headquartered firm founded in 2013, launched software to allow cryptocurrency exchanges to meet their AML/CFT regulatory obligations under FinCEN's requirements. The following year, Chainalysis, a company established in Denmark and later based in the United States, developed a software service for investigators that was first deployed to assist in tracking down the stolen Mt. Gox bitcoins.

In developing these capabilities, blockchain analytics companies drew from the pioneering work of academics to apply advanced data analytic techniques to deciphering illicit activity on the blockchain. As early as July 2011, Martin Harrigan and Fergal Reid of University College Dublin published research describing how the public nature of the blockchain could undermine privacy in Bitcoin.[8] In March 2013, a team of computer scientists from George Mason University and the University of California at San Diego, led by Sarah Meiklejohn, published a research paper entitled "A fistful of bitcoins: Characterizing payments among men with no names," in which they described how analysis of common spending patterns among linked UTXO addresses could be used to identify Bitcoin clusters associated with illicit services and develop a map of criminal actors in the ecosystem.[9] That same year, Malte Möser and a team of researchers from the University of Münster published a paper, "An inquiry into money laundering tools in the Bitcoin ecosystem," in which they observed that the transparency of the blockchain meant that the bitcoins illicit actors used could in effect be "blacklisted" – or permanently denoted as tainted by their association with a criminal entity.[10]

Blockchain analytics firms put these academic concepts into practice. The first step in developing blockchain analytics capabilities is to attribute identities to addresses on the blockchain. Blockchain analytics companies employ large teams of researchers and intelligence analysts to investigate dark web markets and other illicit users of cryptocurrencies, collecting their Bitcoin addresses. For example, by opening an account with a dark web market, a blockchain analytics firm can identify the public wallet addresses that marketplace vendors use to send and receive bitcoins. Blockchain analytics firms also deploy web-scraping (or the use of bots to extract data from websites) and other open-source data collection techniques to identify cryptocurrency addresses referenced on social media and elsewhere on the Internet that have been confirmed as controlled by illicit actors.

Having identified an initial set of addresses, the next step is to identify the larger clusters of linked addresses that those actors control. Large entities in the cryptocurrency ecosystem, such as dark web markets or crypto exchanges, may have wallets composed of hundreds of thousands, or even millions, of crypto addresses – connections that can only be identified using complex analytical techniques. This is accomplished by applying heuristics, or data science techniques such as those pioneered by Meiklejohn and her research team regarding common spend analysis, that can be used to obtain a probabilistic view that a given set of pseudonymous addresses is indeed controlled by the same actor. This data analysis results in the assemblage of an extensive map of billions of addresses controlled by illicit actors across the crypto ecosystem, and forms the basis of the software platforms that blockchain analytics firms sell to their clients in the public and private sectors.

These software services enable users – whether law enforcement agents, regulators, or compliance analysts at a cryptocurrency exchange – to visualize and follow the flow of funds through the blockchain and trace a tainted coin from its source to its destination. Over the next decade, blockchain analytics software capabilities would become widely used in identifying illicit activity in crypto, and other blockchain analytics firms joined Elliptic and Chainalysis in providing these services, including the Blockchain Intelligence Group, Ciphertrace, Coinfirm, Merkle Science, and TRM Labs. Regulators also looked to the blockchain analytics industry to provide assurance that cryptocurrency transactions could be carried out in compliance with AML/CFT regulation. In a report in July 2021, the Financial Action Task Force (FATF) noted that blockchain analytics solutions "can be of great potential benefit to law enforcement. . . and the broader private sector in fulfilling their AML/CFT obligations and combating illicit activity."[11] In April 2022, the New York Department of Financial Services (NYDFS) issued guidance indicating its expectation that regulated cryptocurrency exchanges in New York should use blockchain analytics as part of their AML/CFT compliance programs.[12] By this time, jurisdictions beyond the United States had begun to implement AML/CFT regulation for cryptocurrency businesses. This included Japan and Australia, which introduced regulation in 2017 and 2018, respectively, and the European Union, United Kingdom, and Singapore, all of which brought regulation into effect from January 2020. Financial supervisors in these and other jurisdictions began to insist that regulated cryptocurrency businesses use blockchain analytics capabilities to identify suspected criminal transactions.

The blockchain analytics industry played a central role in enabling the public and private sectors to fight back against crime in cryptocurrencies – and assisted in fostering a perception that crypto could be made safer from, if not necessarily free of, crime. Gradually, the perception that cryptocurrencies were nothing more than an anonymous refuge for criminals began to shift, and gave way to a more nuanced view among an increasing number of policymakers – as well as among a growing segment of the public – that cryptocurrencies should not be seen as synonymous with crime. In December 2022, US Senator Pat Toomey offered remarks that reflected this change in attitude, and contrasted markedly with those of Senator Manchin nearly a decade earlier, when he declared that "I hope we are able to separate potentially illegal actions from perfectly lawful and innovative cryptocurrencies. . . It's absolutely essential to investigate any fraud and violations of existing law, and prosecute those who are committing those crimes. . . But let's remember to distinguish between human failure and the instrument with which the failure occurred."[13]

But even as it helped to shift public perceptions of cryptocurrencies, the rise of the blockchain analytics industry reinforced another dynamic: privacy advocates among the cryptocurrency community grew alarmed about the routine surveillance of transactions, and the ease with which identities could be linked to activity on the blockchain. If law enforcement agencies could readily trace and identify the individuals behind dark web markets, privacy advocates worried, what would stop governments from spying on legitimate Bitcoin traders with no ill intent? For example, Bitcoin users in undemocratic dictatorships could have their financial activities watched by police forces intent on monitoring their transactions on the blockchain. What's more, even well-intentioned, legitimate cryptocurrency users in democratic countries could find their financial details revealed all too easily in circumstances where they might seek legitimate anonymity when conducting transactions – for example, when donating to charity, during inheritance proceedings, or if receiving a salary in bitcoins or other cryptocurrencies.

The prospect of easily traceable transactions seemed to herald a dystopia of constant surveillance that would jeopardize the stated aim of cryptocurrencies to make commerce and finance free from predatory behavior. For cryptocurrencies to achieve the cypherpunk ideal, they required truly enhanced privacy. Mixers and Coin-Join transactions were one attempt to address this dilemma, but law enforcement successes in disrupting activity using mixers convinced some crypto users that more robust privacy was essential for free commerce to flourish.

For true privacy to prevail, something stronger was needed. A committed community of privacy advocates therefore set out to defend the right to transact anonymously, with the aim of restoring cryptocurrencies to their cypherpunk roots. And they did it by innovating a new twist on the technology, launching what became popularly known as privacy coins.

The Birth of Privacy Coins

In Bitcoin, privacy is an add-on feature. Services such as mixers are exogenous to Bitcoin's open-source protocol. The same is true of most other crypto assets, which feature inherent pseudonymity but not genuine anonymity. The distinction is an important one. Pseudonymous cryptocurrencies represent identities on the blockchain by displaying alphanumeric wallet addresses as a stand-in for the true names of users. This affords a level of confidentiality, but one that can be routinely undermined. Privacy coins, however, seek to achieve genuine anonymity by eliminating references to users' identities entirely. Privacy coins integrate mixing-like capabilities directly into their protocols as an inherent feature of their design, eliminating the need for third-party privacy-enhancing services like those that exist in the Bitcoin network.

The philosophical and technical foundations of privacy coins were laid down early in the history of cryptocurrencies. In October 2013, a White Paper was published online under the pseudonym Nicolas van Saberhagen, outlining a proposal for CryptoNote, an electronic cash system designed to address "the main deficiencies of Bitcoin."[14] In the CryptoNote White Paper, Saberhagen – whose true identity remains unknown – argued that "Privacy and anonymity are the most important aspects of electronic cash,"[15] and proposed that a truly private cryptocurrency must avoid two inherent features of Bitcoin, or "critical flaws," as Saberhagen described them. Firstly, an anonymous cryptocurrency must be untraceable, so observers cannot follow coins through their entire history of transfers back to their original source. Secondly, transactions should not be linkable; that is, an anonymous cryptocurrency must not enable observers to attribute ownership to users through common spend analysis. Saberhagen therefore proposed that in CryptoNote, transactions should always be sent to an address that is only ever used once – a concept known as "stealth addresses" – ensuring that users do not continuously recycle addresses that can be linked. Saberhagen also proposed using a cryptographic feature known as "ring signatures," which allow for transactions to be authorized by any member of a group, thereby breaking the link between a specific public address and any single individual's private key.

That same year, a group of researchers including Matthew Green, a Professor of Computer Science at the Johns Hopkins University, set out a proposal known as Zerocoin. Like CryptoNote, the Zerocoin White Paper argued that Bitcoin "has significant limitations regarding privacy,"[16] though it offered a different solution for achieving anonymity. Rather than proposing the creation of a separate cryptocurrency, the Zerocoin White Paper proposed an enhancement to the Bitcoin protocol that its authors felt could provide inherent privacy in Bitcoin transactions and obviate the need for third-party services such as mixers. In the Zerocoin proposal, after being used, each individual coin would be destroyed and then re-minted, allowing users to continue spending those coins without revealing the entire past transaction history of a specific coin. The Zerocoin White Paper also proposed the use of a cryptographic technique known as zero-knowledge proofs to enable anonymity. Zero-knowledge proofs use encryption to enable two counterparties to share and validate information about one another without having to reveal their identities during a transaction.

In January 2014, Evan Duffield, an American software developer, released a White Paper for another cryptocurrency called Dash (originally known as XCoin), which is generally considered the first successful privacy coin to launch and obtain meaningful adoption.[17] Dash is a "fork" of the Bitcoin blockchain; that is, it was developed based on the same underlying source code as Bitcoin but utilizes an entirely separate ledger to record transactions. In Dash, Duffield proposed an anonymity-enhancing technique known as "PrivateSend," which allows users to combine their transactions with those of other users who seek to engage in transfers of the same denomination. Because the strength of the anonymizing features increases as more of a user's coins are mixed with others', Dash users must engage in numerous transactions to obtain the full benefits of PrivateSend – but over time they achieve enhanced anonymity as they undertake more transfers.

In April 2014, another privacy coin known as Monero was launched by a community of developers on the bitcointalk.org message board. Drawing inspiration from the CryptoNote White Paper, Monero uses ring signatures, stealth addresses, and other cryptographic techniques to obfuscate information about counterparties and transactions on its blockchain. All Monero transactions are anonymous by default. Unlike Dash users, Monero users do not need to engage in numerous transactions to obtain the benefit of anonymity; rather, obfuscation of all transactions is inherent in the

Monero protocol. The robustness of its privacy features resulted in the initially small developer community who launched Monero, expanding into an extensive, global community of privacy enthusiasts committed to promoting Monero as *the* definitive privacy coin. The public face of the Monero community for several years was Riccardo Spagni, a South African member of the core Monero developer team who acted as an outspoken and at times flamboyant advocate for the project, as well as for the cause of the right to privacy more generally, and who commanded a widespread following on social media under the moniker "Fluffypony." Spagni stepped away from his role as Monero's lead developer in 2019, though he continued to advocate for the Monero community periodically.

In October 2016, a privacy coin known as Zcash entered the scene. Originally developed by Matthew Green, the professor who had proposed Zerocoin, Zcash was launched as a fork of the Bitcoin blockchain. While it was Green and his team who commenced work on Zcash, the remaining work needed to ensure its successful launch was completed with funding from the Zerocash Electric Coin Company (later rebranded as the Electric Coin Company), an enterprise formed by Zooko Wilcox-O'Hearn, a computer scientist and early cypherpunk who had corresponded with Satoshi Nakamoto but later became fully committed to promoting Zcash's development and adoption.

Unlike Monero, Zcash does not feature privacy by default; rather, it enables opt-in anonymity. Zcash users can choose for their transactions to be "shielded" using zero-knowledge proofs, whereby details of counterparties' addresses are not visible on the Zcash blockchain; or they may choose for their transactions to be "unshielded," so that their public addresses are visible on the blockchain, as in Bitcoin. This selective anonymity is one the Electric Coin Company views as a benefit of Zcash's design, arguing that by providing users the ability to choose the level of obfuscation in their transactions, Zcash "ensures transactions remain confidential while allowing people to selectively share address and transaction information for auditing or regulatory compliance."[18] In April 2022, the Zcash team revealed that the famed privacy advocate and US government whistleblower Edward Snowden had participated in test transactions for Zcash in 2016 – an endorsement aimed at bolstering Zcash's own claims of being the premier privacy coin.[19]

Over the next several years, additional privacy coins were launched alongside Dash, Monero, and Zcash – among them Decred, Verge, the Oasis Network, and Horizen. To privacy advocates, these coins were essential to returning cryptocurrencies to their roots. As Riccardo Spagni of Monero said in an interview in October 2020, "You always have to stay alert and remember that there is someone out there trying to break your privacy, and you have to stay ahead of that."[20]

Law Enforcement's Worst Nightmare

Unsurprisingly, the prospect of highly anonymous cryptocurrencies impervious to surveillance raised alarm bells among law enforcement agencies and regulators around the globe.

In September 2016, just weeks before Zcash's launch, Europol issued its annual *Internet Organised Crime Threat Assessment* (IOCTA), in which it warned about the risks of privacy coins and their potential attractiveness to criminals. According to the Europol report: "The philosophy behind many of these projects is the protection of the privacy of those who perhaps need it most, such as activists or those outspoken against oppressive regimes. However, it is not hard to imagine who would be the primary benefactors of a currency which was entirely anonymous and resistant to law enforcement surveillance."[21]

Soon, cases of privacy coins' use in illicit activity emerged that served to reinforce these anxieties. In particular, some dark web market operators looked to Monero as an alternative to Bitcoin, determined to avoid the fate of previous dark web kingpins such as Ross Ulbricht. In the 2017 version of its IOCTA report, issued just a year after its initial warnings, Europol confirmed that Monero "is now accepted on a number of Darknet markets."[22] Dark web adoption of Monero had begun in mid-2016, when a market known as Oasis announced that it was accepting the privacy coin for payments. AlphaBay then announced in August 2016 that it would enable users to undertake Monero payments as well.[23] Other markets, such as Wall Street Market and Valhalla Marketplace, soon began offering users the option to make Monero payments in addition to Bitcoin transactions. Nonetheless, users of these marketplaces mostly continued to transact in bitcoins, despite their inherent traceability. The reason for this was simple: Bitcoin is a much more popular cryptocurrency, which a larger number of users have access to on popular exchange platforms, as well as experience and comfort in using. This continued reliance on Bitcoin, of course, made these dark web markets vulnerable to disruption. In addition to the takedown of AlphaBay in 2017, Europol scored a major double victory in May 2019, when it announced the takedown of both Wall Street Market and Valhalla Marketplace, exploiting their continued use of Bitcoin to trace their activity and seize both markets.[24]

Concerned about the risks of detection, some dark web market operators decided to avoid Bitcoin completely. The largest among these was White House Market, a dark web drug shop that launched in August 2017, just one month after the law enforcement action against AlphaBay. White House required buyers and sellers of illicit items to use Monero exclusively, to ensure an enhanced level of security when transacting; no payments on White House were allowed in Bitcoin. While estimating the exact value of business White House conducted in Monero is challenging, a computer scientist at Carnegie Mellon University, Nicolas Christin, estimated that White House likely facilitated Monero transactions totaling between $35 and $120 million.[25] In October 2021, the administrators of White House announced that they were shutting the site down, noting only that "we have reached our goal now"[26] – a likely reference to their success in generating millions of dollars in commissions from sales on the site. Monero also featured as the sole form of payment on a resurrected version of AlphaBay, which was run by administrators loyal to the original AlphaBay site and had tens of thousands of listings for drugs by the summer of 2022.[27]

In addition to adoption on the dark web, Monero began to feature in other crimes, including "crypto-jacking" campaigns launched by cybercriminals. Crypto-jacking refers to a form of hacking in which an attacker obtains access to a victim's computer and uses it to mine cryptocurrencies and obtain mining rewards for profit. In Bitcoin, mining at scale for profit generally requires specialized hardware known as application-specific integrated circuits (ASICs) stored on "mining farms" – an industrial-scale infrastructure that is necessary to supply the computing power needed to validate transactions and sustain the Bitcoin network as it has grown. In smaller cryptocurrencies, a desktop or laptop PC is all that's required to mine; therefore, if hackers can access a PC, it allows them to generate crypto mining rewards without having to pay for the computing power needed to mine. Where hackers manage to infiltrate hundreds or thousands of computers through concerted campaigns targeting victims' PCs, they can generate substantial cryptocurrency proceeds from mining across a large network of compromised computers – yielding free profits. Crypto-jacking is typically carried out by placing malicious ads on websites, allowing the attacker to mine for cryptocurrencies using the visitor's web browser unbeknownst to them, though it can also occur by attackers tricking victims into downloading malicious files directly onto a PC.[28] Cybercriminals have used crypto-jacking campaigns to obtain stashes of Monero, which they can then handle without fear of being linked to the hacking activity through transactional analysis, as would be possible with Bitcoin. As the security company Symantec has noted: "It's hard to know how much money cyber criminals are making from cryptojacking, but the key to making money in this area is scale. A coinminer running on one computer won't make much money— but a coinminer running on thousands of computers could potentially mine a lot of cryptocurrency."[29]

In late 2017, a case emerged that seemed to offer a warning for law enforcement about the worst-case scenario for privacy coins. In the autumn of that year, a fundraising campaign appeared online under the name of Al Sadaqah – an Arabic word that refers to an act of voluntary charitable giving – seeking donations from supporters.

According to Al Sadaqah's social media accounts, the donations were intended for "benefiting and providing the Mujahidin in Syria with weapons, finical [sic] aid and other projects relating to the jihad."[30] Al Sadaqah's founders – allegedly associated with the terrorist organization al Qaeda, according to the DOJ – made use of Twitter, Telegram, and other social media channels to seek donations from supporters to fund militant activities in Syria.[31] And the payment method they requested for donations was cryptocurrencies.

In a photograph that became infamous in law enforcement and security circles, Al Sadaqah posted an image on social media of two mujahidin fighters holding a banner requesting that donations be sent to a specified Bitcoin address controlled by the group (see Figure 4.1).[32] One of the social media images that Al Sadaqah posted implored supporters to "Donate anonymously with Cryptocurrency" and specifies not only Bitcoin, but also the privacy coins Monero, Dash, and Verge as payment options the organization was willing to accept.

More Than Meets the Eye

As frightening as the prospect of a dystopia of anonymous terrorist payments may have seemed, as with everything in the cryptocurrency space, the reality was far more complex. Several obstacles existed that prevented privacy coins becoming as widely used in illicit payments as some may have feared.

First among these was a realization that not all privacy coins are created equal, or have similar appeal to illicit users. Within a year of Dash's launch, vendors on some dark web markets began using it as a form of payment to facilitate drug sales – but it never obtained widespread adoption across major dark web sites. Zcash, it turned out, held even less appeal to criminals, and with some limited exceptions, featured very rarely on the dark web. In a study that the Electric Coin Company commissioned from the US policy think tank the RAND Corporation, researchers found that "Zcash is seen as a less attractive option to dark web users and is used less

Figure 4.1   An image of the Al Sadaqah fundraising campaign.
SOURCE: US Department of Justice.

often compared to other cryptocurrencies, particularly Bitcoin and Monero."[33] It also turned out that blockchain analytics capabilities could be applied to coins such as Dash and Zcash, at least in certain circumstances. For example, blockchain analytics solutions can monitor "unshielded" Zcash transactions – which does not enable perfect visibility into all transactions on the Zcash blockchain, but provides some insight about users' activity.[34] A similar approach can enable analysis of Dash wallets that have not made extensive use of its PrivateSend features.

The privacy coin that featured most widely among illicit users was Monero, owing to the strength of its anonymity features and the anti-regulatory stance of many members of its community, who largely dismissed the idea of cooperation with authorities. In May 2019, Europol admitted that Monero was undermining its efforts to trace cryptocurrency payments.[35]

But even Monero did not ensure that users could remain perfectly anonymous, or shield their funds completely from law enforcement. Monero wallets, like other crypto wallets, involve the use of private keys to sign transactions. If a law enforcement agency obtains access to the wallet of a Monero user, agents can seize their funds. When Alexandre Cazes was arrested in the July 2017 takedown of AlphaBay, among items law enforcement agents seized when they obtained his belongings were wallets containing his personal holdings of Monero and Zcash.[36]

Because many illicit actors continued to use both Monero and Bitcoin, law enforcement agencies could also identify criminal users of Monero during their Bitcoin investigations – suggesting that not all Monero users had truly gone completely underground. In August 2020, the DOJ announced that the Al Sadaqah terrorist financing campaign had been subject to an asset forfeiture action involving its associated Bitcoin addresses,[37] which law enforcement agencies had been able to trace readily using blockchain analytics capabilities – demonstrating that a nightmare scenario of totally anonymous terrorist payments beyond the full reach of the law had not yet become a reality. At the same time, the DOJ announced actions disrupting other terrorist financing campaigns using cryptocurrencies, including a Bitcoin fundraising campaign undertaken by the military wing of the Palestinian group Hamas – and in subsequent years there were other successful actions to disrupt extremists' cryptocurrency crowdfunding activities. Though terrorist and extremist use of cryptocurrencies was a risk authorities would never take lightly – given the ability of terrorists to wreak extensive damage with even small amounts of funds – the fact that these groups continued to rely heavily on Bitcoin and other transparent cryptocurrencies, despite their apparent willingness to experiment with privacy coins, made their crypto fundraising campaigns vulnerable to detection and disruption.

Another factor worked against privacy coin users. Though Monero payments were highly anonymous, Monero users often left behind other digital breadcrumbs that left them vulnerable, such as their IP address history if they failed to use the Tor network or other anonymizing techniques to cover up their online footprints – just as Ross Ulbricht and Alexandre Cazes had. Monero users, if not careful, could also leave clues in the physical world that clever police work could uncover. In June 2021, a US grand jury indicted Paul Engstrom and his associates, who federal prosecutors allege sold cocaine on the White House dark web market for Monero under the user name "Insta."[38] One clue that tipped off investigators to Engstrom's identity was the use of priority postage stamps that he and his associates used for their personal mail. The stamps were identical to priority postage stamps investigators had seen on packages of cocaine sent to undercover agents who had made staged purchases from "Insta" on White House using Monero.[39]

What's more, in 2018, researchers from Princeton University, the Massachusetts Institute of Technology, and other universities published a paper identifying potential weaknesses in Monero's privacy features that enabled the traceability of a limited set of transactions. While the techniques deployed could not offer the substantial level of visibility that exists in Bitcoin, the analysis suggested that some limited de-anonymization of Monero payments would be possible without continued upgrades to Monero's protocol.[40] As Vitalik Buterin, the creator of the Ethereum blockchain network, noted in a 2016 essay on privacy in blockchains: "Statistical analyses will always be able to figure out *something*; at the least, they will be able to fish for patterns of *when* transactions take place, and in many cases they will be able to narrow down identities and figure out who interacts with whom."[41] Nonetheless, there is no commercially available software that enables the routine monitoring of Monero transactions, which remain largely impervious to blockchain analytics, despite some successful attempts at limited de-anonymization.

Another factor also complicated the use of privacy coins for illicit actors: regulation. As law enforcement concerns about privacy coins mounted, financial sector watchdogs responded by clarifying how AML/CFT rules should apply to this new iteration on cryptocurrencies. As the global AML/CFT standard-setter, the FATF directed its attention to privacy coins, which it dubbed "anonymity-enhanced cryptocurrencies" (or AECs). In guidance it issued in June 2019, and subsequently updated in October 2021, the FATF warned that AECs "may further obfuscate transactions or undermine" the application of AML/CFT compliance measures by regulated cryptocurrency businesses.[42] In a report it issued on red flags of money laundering and terrorist financing in September 2020, the FATF warned that the use of AECs is a risk factor that regulated businesses should consider when deciding if they should report activity to law enforcement.[43]

In response to the FATF's stance, regulators around the world began clarifying rules around privacy coins. In 2019, FinCEN issued guidance stating that regulated cryptocurrency exchanges have an obligation to manage financial crime risks of any privacy coins they allow their users to trade – including by tracking information about transactions in the blockchain.[44] FinCEN's position did not explicitly prohibit regulated businesses from allowing their customers to trade in privacy coins, but it presented a major challenge for any business that wished to do so: given the inability to readily trace payments in Monero, a regulated business would struggle to explain to regulators how it managed to comply with its AML/CFT obligations while allowing users to trade in a highly anonymous cryptocurrency. Indeed, in October 2022, FinCEN imposed a penalty of $29 million on Bittrex, a US cryptocurrency exchange, and cited Bittrex's offering of Monero on its trading platform – despite never implementing controls to manage the related anonymity risks – as one reason for the penalty.[45]

Other regulators took a more overtly hostile approach to privacy coins than FinCEN. In Japan, the Financial Services Agency (JFSA), the regulator responsible for oversight of crypto exchanges, announced in May 2018 that exchanges would not be allowed to offer trading in privacy coins.[46] Instead, Japanese exchanges could only offer trading in pre-approved cryptocurrencies maintained on a JFSA-vetted whitelist of acceptable tokens, all of which feature high levels of traceability.

Regulators in New York state adopted a similar approach to the JFSA. Since June 2015, the NYDFS had administered a regulatory regime for cryptocurrency businesses in New York state known as the BitLicense framework, which imposed stringent compliance requirements on exchanges wanting to offer services to or from New York. In August 2020, the NYDFS announced the creation of a coin listing process, which limited exchanges with a BitLicense to offering trading services only in NYDFS-approved coins.[47] Like the Japanese approach, the NYDFS largely prevents trading in privacy coins. But in May 2018, the NYDFS made a limited exception by authorizing the Gemini exchange platform to offer Zcash trading services to its clients – on the condition that Gemini limit its customers' withdrawals of Zcash to transactions with "unshielded" addresses that do not employ zero-knowledge proofs, so that payments could be traced.[48] The regulatory approach to privacy coins therefore remained consistent with the previous approach of financial supervisors toward cryptocurrencies by avoiding attempts to regulate the technology directly, and instead imposing obligations on gatekeepers such as exchanges to apply AML/CFT controls on dealings with their users.

This approach presented a problem for the illicit users of privacy coins. Like other cryptocurrency users, privacy coin users need exchanges to turn their crypto into fiat currencies that they can use to purchase most goods and services. If a criminal holding privacy coins wished to trade them at a regulated cryptocurrency exchange, they would have to supply identifying documents and other information needed to satisfy AML/CFT requirements – thereby undermining the anonymity that they sought from privacy coins. Additionally, because regulation discouraged – if not always outright prohibited – cryptocurrency exchanges from offering trading in privacy coins, markets for privacy coins lacked the liquidity needed to help them scale in usage. With most of the largest,

reputable cryptocurrency exchanges unwilling to offer trading services in privacy coins, those coins simply would never achieve the
scale of transactions that a highly liquid and widely traded cryptocurrency such as Bitcoin could.

This dynamic forced those criminals who were committed to
using privacy coins, and especially Monero, to seek out unregulated
exchange services where they could swap their privacy coins. Sometimes referred to as "coinswaps," these small, unregulated exchange
services frequently operate out of high-risk jurisdictions such as
Russia and, according to research by Elliptic, are often "dedicated
to an exclusively criminal clientele."[49] These services often advertise
their non-compliance with AML/CFT measures as a perk to attract
clients, offering users the ability to access crypto swapping services
anonymously, and without having to provide ID documents. Where
criminals obtain Monero on the dark web or through crimes such as
crypto-jacking, they will often trade it for bitcoins at these swapping
services. Having obtained new "clean" bitcoins from the swapping
service, the criminal can then send those bitcoins to a larger, more
liquid exchange platform and obtain US dollars or other fiat currencies. The larger exchange platform may be able to use blockchain
analytics software to identify that the funds came from a coinswapping service, but they will not be able to identify the ultimate source
of funds beyond that point – given the previous use of Monero in the
transaction trail. This money laundering methodology is one that
the FATF and other watchdogs have dubbed "chain-hopping" – or
the process of swapping a variety of cryptocurrencies with the aim
of concealing their illicit origin.

These coinswapping services, while valuable for criminal users
of privacy coins, were not large enough to power an entire online
criminal ecosystem the way an exchange like BTC-e had underpinned an entire global underworld of Bitcoin transactions. Privacy
coins might prove useful for illicit actors in some instances, but without robust liquidity and ready trading access via major exchanges,
they would never supplant Bitcoin as the primary cryptocurrency of
use for criminal activity. In a report on cryptocurrencies it released
in December 2021, Europol acknowledged that its worst fears about

privacy coins had not been realized. According to Europol, "While Monero has gained great popularity in the past years, it is still far from overtaking Bitcoin. . . Many exchanges have now delisted privacy coins following guidance from regulators. Nevertheless, these coins have not become as popular as expected, probably because they are not as liquid as Bitcoin and. . . thus more impractical."[50]

* * *

Privacy coins caused governments to worry about a nightmare scenario they had always dreaded: the potential for criminals and terrorists to transfer funds across borders and completely out of sight. But the practicalities of sustaining an online criminal ecosystem proved far more complex – and the pressures of regulation prevented widespread, fully anonymous payments from becoming a reality.

Though privacy coins did not gain the scale of illicit use that some had feared, governments would not dare become complacent. The emergence of privacy coins underscored that new technologies aimed at enhancing anonymity in payments would not simply fizzle out. What's more, their existence demonstrated that a demand for greater transactional privacy among cryptocurrency users was not merely a fringe concern, but also reflected a desire among those interested in expanding the use of cryptocurrencies for legitimate purposes to enhance confidentiality.

For example, as cryptocurrency markets grew across the late 2010s and into the 2020s, some major financial institutions began to explore how they could leverage cryptocurrencies and blockchain technology to offer new services to their clients. One precondition that some financial institutions expressed as essential for undertaking widespread transactions on the blockchain was confidentiality: institutional players simply would not broadcast large amounts of transactional data on shared ledgers without guarantees that their activity could be shielded from their competitors. In what seemed an unlikely pairing aimed at addressing this need, in May 2017, banking giant J.P. Morgan partnered with the Electric Coin Company to implement zero-knowledge proofs on a blockchain-based platform that the bank had developed, featuring confidential transactions that could be undertaken in a manner consistent with regulatory requirements.[51]

This tension between traceability and anonymity, and the intersection with regulatory expectations, was a theme that would persist throughout the evolution of cryptocurrencies. Privacy coins also underscored the ability of continuous innovations in the crypto space to create challenges for law enforcement agencies, adding to the pressure to keep pace and adapt rapidly in this still relatively new environment of online crime.

It therefore must have struck some in the law enforcement world as a surprise when cryptocurrencies turned up in an environment where the police had far more experience operating: the streets.

Chapter 5

Bitcoin ATMs: Crypto Hits the Streets

E ven with the growth and expansion of cryptocurrency markets in the few years after Satoshi Nakamoto launched Bitcoin, direct touchpoints between the cryptocurrency ecosystem and other forms of financial activity remained limited.

For example, turning hard cash into Bitcoin, or vice versa, required several steps and wasn't always straightforward. If you wanted to turn dollar bills into bitcoins, you would need to go to the bank, deposit the cash into your bank account, access your online banking services, transfer the funds to a Bitcoin exchange platform, and then swap the dollars on the exchange for bitcoins. This required having two accounts at two separate regulated businesses – a bank and an exchange – and undergoing identification checks at each, which added friction to the transfer process. In Bitcoin's early years, when many people were not as attached to their mobile devices or as thoroughly integrated with online financial services as they are today, getting access to cryptocurrencies presented practical challenges for the average user. If you were someone who relied heavily on cash in your financial affairs, these challenges were magnified.

That all changed with the advent of Bitcoin ATMs, a technology that eliminated barriers between the cash-based and crypto-based economies and enabled the frictionless movement of funds across the worlds of digital and paper money.

Bitcoin ATMs work much like other ATMs: users can withdraw cash from machines, or deposit cash into them. However, unlike a traditional ATM kiosk, where funds are drawn against the user's bank balance, with a crypto ATM, funds are drawn from, or deposited to, a crypto wallet. When a Bitcoin ATM user deposits $100 of cash into a machine, the ATM will provide her with a Bitcoin wallet in the form of a QR code where an equivalent amount of bitcoins (minus service fees) will have been deposited, and from which she can then transfer the funds. The actual settlement is conducted by a Bitcoin ATM operator who owns – and may franchise out – the machines. Operators generally charge high fees for the use of ATMs, sometimes ranging from as much as 7% to 20%.[1] Despite the common moniker "Bitcoin ATMs," these kiosks often enable cash-for-crypto trading in other popular cryptocurrencies, such as ether, Tether, and Litecoin, with a relatively small number also enabling users to access privacy coins such as Monero, Dash, and Zcash. Bitcoin ATMs can be "one-way" kiosks, only allowing users to buy crypto by depositing cash, but many are "two-way," allowing users to either buy crypto or sell it, so they can withdraw cash from the machine.

The first Bitcoin ATM was set up in a shopping mall in Vancouver, Canada, in October 2013. Over the coming years, Bitcoin ATMs would sprout up at shopping centers, grocery stores, coffee shops, liquor stores, gas stations, and vape shops – among other locations – with the number of ATMs rising substantially. By late 2017, there were more than 1,000 Bitcoin ATMs located globally.[2] By mid-2023, that number had grown more than thirty-fold to over 34,000, with the United States accounting for approximately 29,000 of that total.[3]

To advocates of the societal benefits of cryptocurrencies, the rise of Bitcoin ATMs represented a crucial development because they offered the promise of making crypto more accessible to new users. In particular, advocates touted the potential for Bitcoin ATMs to facilitate financial inclusion – or the expansion of financial services to those underserved by the banking sector and living in so-called "financial deserts," devoid of banking access. Because crypto ATMs allow individuals who are heavily reliant on cash, such as lower-income workers or those in developing economies, to obtain access to a world of digital payments that might otherwise be unavailable to them, advocates believe they could expand access to digital financial services. As Mark Grens, President of the Bitcoin ATM operator Digital Mint, stated in an editorial in *American Banker*: "Although most people would like to think that financial deserts are not very common and the underbanked population is small, the truth is that approximately 25% of all households in the U.S. fall in this category. A significant portion of the community in financial deserts deal almost entirely with cash. . . However, with bitcoin ATMs and point-of-sale teller services, these individuals can instantly take their paper money to the machine and exchange it for a different payment source: bitcoin. And like that, the underbanked have a new tool in their toolkit."

Bridging the Cash and Crypto Underworlds

Inevitably, the same features of Bitcoin ATMs that offered potential benefits to society also provided a mechanism for their use in illicit payments. Indeed, even before the creation of Bitcoin ATMs, criminals had sought ways to bridge the gap between the cryptocurrency and cash economies.

Robert Faiella, the operator of the BTCKing cash-for-crypto swapping service on the Silk Road, who was arrested alongside Charlie Shrem in 2014, had catered to this need. In the ensuing years, other crypto-for-cash traders, or peer-to-peer exchangers (as they became known), emerged as conduits for money laundering. In July 2018, a US court sentenced Theresa Lynn Tetley, a former stockbroker who lived in California, to a year in prison after she pled guilty to running a Bitcoin-for-cash service.[4] According to the US government, between January 2014 and March 2017, Tetley operated under the name "Bitcoin Maven" to provide her swapping services, including to vendors of dark web markets.[5] Tetley advertised her services on LocalBitcoins, a crypto trading site headquartered in Finland that allowed users to post ads for trading cash for crypto. In her guilty plea, Tetley admitted to processing Bitcoin trades through the site totaling between $6 and $9.5 million. Under the scheme, Tetley received bitcoins from her clients and paid them in cash. If the bitcoins she received came from illicit sources, she would then take steps to launder the funds on her clients' behalf. One such client was William Farber, a vendor on AlphaBay from Los Angeles, who was arrested in August 2017 and who operated under the name "Pirate Shit."[6] According to court documents, Tetley "conducted numerous, high-level transactions with him (ultimately amounting to over $6 million)," meeting Farber in coffee shops and restaurants, and providing him wads of cash in envelopes.[7] Undercover agents from the US Drug Enforcement Agency (DEA) eventually learned of the scheme and staged interactions with Tetley, asking her to swap bitcoins they claimed to have obtained from sales on the dark web. When Tetley brought $300,000 in cash in paper grocery bags to a meeting with an undercover DEA agent, she was promptly arrested.[8]

Cash-for-crypto laundering sometimes took on an incredible dimension. One especially creative scheme emerged on a dark web market known as Hydra, a Russian site that will make further appearances in this story. Hydra, like other dark web markets, hosted advertisements from peer-to-peer crypto exchangers offering their laundering services. In March 2021, the blockchain analytics firm Elliptic identified an advertisement on Hydra for a self-described "buried treasure" service. Under the arrangement, the exchanger offered to receive "dirty" bitcoins from users and pledged to help with laundering their funds. In return for a commission paid in bitcoins, the exchanger provided cash – in this case Russian rubles – to their clients. The cash, however, wasn't handed over in a grocery bag. Instead, clients were directed to find the cash in hidden locations, buried in holes up to 20 centimeters deep, with the clients provided GPS coordinates to help them locate the cash underground.[9]

These schemes showed that a demand existed in the criminal underworld for combining cash and crypto in a seamless flow of transactions to enable money laundering. Theoretically, this offered criminals the perfect solution to hiding their funds. Cash, after all, is truly anonymous: cash transactions cannot readily be traced and users cannot be linked to the specific bills they have handled, except perhaps in circumstances where marked bills are used as part of a police investigation. Bitcoin, while lacking true anonymity, possesses a key feature that cash lacks: the ability to transfer funds cross-border. By combining the anonymizing aspects of cash with the global, digital nature of Bitcoin, criminals might have thought they had hit upon a way to evade law enforcement detection.

But in-person swapping services created significant risks of detection and disruption by law enforcement, as the Bitcoin Maven case had revealed. In-person swaps also ran up against the reality of geography: swapping large amounts of cash for crypto required that both parties have physical proximity to one another, which made transferring funds across distances more challenging. Bitcoin ATMs helped to surmount these issues by offering a ready mechanism for one party in a transaction to turn cash into bitcoins and transfer the funds to another person who could cash them out at another kiosk located on the other side of the world.

The growth in the number of Bitcoin ATMs coincided with another development: the increasing adoption of Bitcoin by established organized criminal networks. In the early years of cryptocurrencies, illicit users were drawn almost exclusively from an online underworld – operators of dark web markets and online scammers who found utility in a digital payment method that supported their Internet-based crimes. Cryptocurrencies did not initially see meaningful adoption by organized criminal networks engaged in crimes in the physical world, such as street drug dealing or human trafficking – crimes that frequently involve large amounts of cash.

Over time, however, evidence emerged that organized criminals were increasingly integrating cryptocurrencies into their pre-existing money laundering schemes. International drug gangs had long used a variety of methods to launder cash through the banking system.

This included "smurfing," or repeatedly depositing cash into different bank accounts in small sums to avoid generating suspicion over large cash transactions. Drug gangs had for decades also relied on complex trade-based money laundering techniques, such as the infamous "Black Market Peso Exchange," a money laundering method that enabled drug dealers in South America to move cash from drug deals across international borders by purchasing goods with drug proceeds that they later resold to realize their profits.

As Bitcoin ATMs became more widespread, organized crime groups found opportunities to merge these long-standing money laundering techniques with the new technology. In the summer of 2018, police in Spain, working with Europol in an investigation known as Operation Guatuzo, uncovered a scheme to launder the proceeds of drug sales. The scheme involved cocaine dealers in Spain who imported their product from Colombia. After selling the cocaine on the streets of Spain, the dealers generated large amounts of cash, and needed to transfer the proceeds to cartel members in Colombia. During Operation Guatuzo, Spanish police and Europol discovered that this network of drug dealers had devised an innovative method for money laundering: they used Bitcoin ATMs to convert cash into bitcoins, which they transferred back to South America.

The arrangement worked like this: drug dealers in Spain would deposit cash from street sales into Bitcoin ATMs owned by members of a local money laundering ring. At the ATMs, the cash was converted into bitcoins and transferred to a wallet controlled by the cartel. Members of the cartel in Colombia then swapped these bitcoins for pesos at a local exchange service – and laundered the funds through the local banking system.[10] In total, authorities arrested 23 members of the gang in both Spain and Colombia during the summer of 2018.[11] In May 2019, Spanish police arrested an additional eight individuals involved in the scheme and seized two Bitcoin ATMs belonging to the alleged launderers at the time of their arrest.[12]

US and UK investigators also began identifying organized crime groups using Bitcoin ATMs. In 2017, the London Metropolitan

Police acknowledged that they were seeing increasing cases of drug dealers laundering funds through Bitcoin ATMs in the UK capital (numbering around fifty at that time).[13] A report issued by the US Government Accountability Office (GAO) indicated that US law enforcement agencies had seen "evidence of Mexican and Colombian transnational criminal organizations using virtual currencies to transfer proceeds internationally. . . For example, money couriers deposit large volumes of cash from illegal drug proceeds into a kiosk to convert the value to virtual currency. Once the illicit proceeds are in this form, the funds can easily be transferred to another virtual currency user's wallet, reducing the risk associated with transporting bulk currency."[14]

The same GAO report revealed that the US government had observed Bitcoin ATMs in another cash-intensive criminal enterprise: human trafficking, especially trafficking related to prostitution.

The FATF and other AML/CFT watchdogs had for years studied money laundering related to human trafficking. In July 2018, the FATF published a report entitled *The Financial Flows of Human Trafficking*, describing how traffickers generate profits from crimes such as migrant smuggling and prostitution, and then launder those funds through the financial system. While the FATF's report confirmed that most money laundering related to human trafficking still occurred, overwhelmingly, through the banking system or other established money laundering channels, the report suggested that some human trafficking networks had begun to use cryptocurrencies. For example, the FATF noted that in cases of sexual exploitation, clients of sex workers who have been coerced into the trade may purchase bitcoins to pay for their services, by engaging in "[f]requent purchases in multiples of small amounts of Bitcoin. . . ."[15] Victims who have been coerced into the sex trade may also use cryptocurrencies to pay for advertisements on illegal prostitution sites. This occurred on the website Backpage.com, which was seized in April 2018 by US law enforcement.[16]

Established in 2004, Backpage.com was a site that the United States alleges acted as a market for illegal prostitution, though its founders – indicted by the United States when the website was shut down – attempted to portray it as a site for purely legitimate escort services. US prosecutors also allege that Backpage.com included advertisements for child prostitution. From about 2015, after banks and credit card companies started refusing to do business with Backpage.com, prosecutors claim that it "pursued an array of money laundering strategies," including "converting customer payments, and the proceeds of Backpage's business, into and out of cryptocurrencies."[17] In addition to the founders' use of crypto to launder their earnings, Backpage also allowed sex workers and their exploiters to purchase ads on the site using Bitcoin.[18]

Other organizations have documented ways that Bitcoin ATMs specifically can be used to facilitate payments related to sexual exploitation. The Cryptocurrency Compliance Cooperative, a group of Bitcoin ATM operators dedicated to ensuring that operators adhere to regulations, has published information about how sex traffickers may attempt to use Bitcoin ATMs to exploit their victims. For example, a woman who has been trafficked for prostitution may make small cash deposits into a Bitcoin ATM and then transfer the funds, once converted into bitcoins, to her exploiter – who may also receive funds into their Bitcoin wallet from other women they have trafficked and who have loaded cash they've earned into other Bitcoin ATMs.[19]

In addition to perpetrators of crimes such as drug dealing and sexual exploitation, Bitcoin ATMs attracted fraudsters, who saw in them a useful conduit for extracting cash from their victims. Bitcoin ATM scams often involve fraudsters posing as tax collectors, representatives of a public utility company, or operating under a similar guise, and insisting that the target of the scam pay them to clear any unpaid debts. Victims are instructed to withdraw cash from their bank accounts, deposit the cash in a Bitcoin ATM, and transfer the funds to a specified wallet – which is, of course, controlled by the scammers. The unsuspecting victims, having drained their bank accounts of cash to fund the purchase of bitcoins at the ATM, then discover that their money is gone.

An early version of this scam emerged in 2018, when fraud-sters targeted customers of electric companies in Hawaii. The scam involved fraudsters posing as representatives of the electric com-panies and threatening to disconnect customers' electricity if they failed to settle outstanding payments. The targets of the scam were instructed to convert cash to bitcoins at local ATMs to avoid hav-ing their electricity cut off – only to realize afterward that they had been defrauded.[20] Around the same time in 2018, scammers in Mel-bourne, Australia, posed as tax collectors demanding payment from taxpayers via Bitcoin ATMs on threat of being arrested for failure to settle their tax debts. The fraudsters targeted immigrants as part of the scheme, preying on the migrants' fear of deportation to coerce them into making payments.[21]

Similar scams emerged elsewhere, leading to stories of victims who had their life savings wiped out from Bitcoin ATM frauds – such as a woman in Buffalo, New York, who transferred her retire-ment funds to Bitcoin ATM fraudsters.[22] A commission convened by the state of New Jersey to investigate Bitcoin ATMs described an elaborate hoax that fraudsters had devised:

> In April 2019, a caller identifying himself as both an agent with the Federal Trade Commission and a U.S. Marshal informed the victim that her identity had been stolen. The caller claimed two properties in Texas that authorities suspected were linked to money laundering activity and drug trafficking were purchased in the victim's name. In addition, the caller told the victim her Social Security number was used to open four bank accounts. The scammer warned the victim that all her bank accounts would be frozen pending further investigation, but she could "prove her innocence" if she moved money from her bank accounts, converted it to cryptocurrency and transferred it to an allegedly secure federal account already set up. The victim had 40 minutes to drain her accounts and visit seven different cryptocurrency kiosks in Bergen, Essex and Passaic coun-ties to deposit the money into a secured "federal account." After completing the final transaction at an ATM in Clifton, a store asso-ciate approached the victim and asked where she was sending the money. . . In total, the woman lost $12,000 in the scam.[23]

Bitcoin ATM fraud became so pervasive that US government agencies began sounding the alarm. In November 2021, the Federal Bureau of Investigation (FBI) issued an alert warning the public of Bitcoin ATM scams and offering tips on how to avoid becoming a victim.[24] Two months later, the US Federal Trade Commission (FTC) reinforced this warning, stressing that "nobody from the government, law enforcement, utility company, or prize promoter will ever tell you to pay them with cryptocurrency. If someone does, it's a scam, every time. Any unexpected tweet, text, email, call, or social media message – particularly from someone you don't know – asking you to pay them in advance for something, including with cryptocurrency, is a scam."[25]

In October 2022, the FBI issued a further warning about the growing use of Bitcoin ATMs in an especially insidious form of fraud known as "pig butchering," which originated in Asia and refers to scammers luring their victims in the manner of fattening and leading an animal to slaughter. In so-called pig butchering schemes, victims are targeted through social media by scammers, who sometimes pose as a potential romantic interest, or who cultivate a friendship with victims online. The fraudsters claim to be successful cryptocurrency investors, and they establish fake websites mimicking legitimate cryptocurrency exchanges where the victims are directed to transfer funds. After the victim has sent the funds, often slowly, over the course of weeks or months, the perpetrator ends contact, leaving the victims robbed of their money, and often completely ruined.

In 2021 alone, cases of pig butchering in the United States resulted in victims suffering fraud losses totaling an estimated $429 million – though the actual number may very well be much higher, potentially into the low billions, given the number of unreported cases.[26] According to the FBI, individual pig butchering cases can total in the "tens of thousands to millions of dollars" worth of cryptocurrencies, which are sometimes purchased by the victim using cash at Bitcoin ATMs, and then transferred to a wallet belonging to the scammers.[27]

Pig butchering also has a devastating impact beyond the financial catastrophe its defrauded targets suffer: many of the scams are carried out by individuals in countries such as Laos and Cambodia, who themselves are the victims of human trafficking and are forced to perpetrate the scams by their captors in criminal gangs, who reap the ultimate profits.[28]

The Law Steps In

The rise in Bitcoin ATM crime inevitably attracted attention from FinCEN and other regulators around the world determined to counter the exploitation of cryptocurrency kiosks. In May 2019, FinCEN issued guidance clarifying that its AML/CFT requirements apply to operators of Bitcoin ATMs.[29] Consequently, any Bitcoin ATM operator in the United States needed to require users to provide identifying information, and had to report transactions of concern to FinCEN. But even before FinCEN's guidance of 2019, some US Bitcoin ATM operators had concluded that they would eventually be captured by the regulations and took steps to comply.

Coinsource, a Bitcoin ATM provider founded in February 2015 that operates a network of hundreds of ATMs around the United States, began complying with AML/CFT regulations even ahead of FinCEN's guidance.[30] In November 2018, Coinsource received a BitLicense from the New York Department of Financial Services (NYDFS), allowing it to operate ATMs in New York state.[31] Other ATM providers, determined to maintain a positive reputation and counter misperceptions that Bitcoin ATMs had no legitimate users, also made public commitments to complying with AML/CFT regulations. In August 2021, Digital Mint, another US-headquartered ATM provider, partnered with Coinsource and other providers, as well as with blockchain analytics companies, to form the Cryptocurrency Compliance Cooperative, a non-profit group whose mission is to enhance regulatory compliance standards among the cash-for-cryptocurrency industry.[32]

Despite these responsible actors in the industry, some Bitcoin ATM operators tried to skirt regulations and keep their activity out of sight. In July 2020, the US Department of Justice (DOJ) announced the arrest of a California man, Kaish Mohammad, for operating a network of unregistered Bitcoin ATMs that processed over $25 million in Bitcoin-for-cash swaps.[33] According to the DOJ, Mohammad ran a cash-for-crypto exchange service known as Herocoin and operated a network of Bitcoin ATMs that he failed to register with FinCEN. After entering a guilty plea for running an unregistered service, Mohammad agreed to forfeit over to the US government 17 Bitcoin ATMs that he owned (see Figure 5.1).[34]

In another case, in April 2022, the Manhattan District Attorney (DA)'s office announced an indictment involving a network of

Figure 5.1   A Bitcoin ATM the US government seized in the Herocoin case.
SOURCE: US Department of Justice.

illegal ATMs across New York City. Prosecutors allege that a man from New York, Robert Taylor, operated 46 Bitcoin ATMs across New York that he used to process transfers totaling more than $5 million on behalf of clients – who allegedly included convicted drug dealers and credit card thieves – with the promise of helping them to keep their transactions anonymous.[35] The New York DA's office also alleges that Taylor failed to pay taxes on fees he earned from his unregistered Bitcoin ATM services.

The biggest bust of a non-compliant Bitcoin ATM operator came in March 2023, when prosecutors in Ohio announced an indictment against Bitcoin of America, an operator of more than 2,500 kiosks across the United States. In an operation that law enforcement in Ohio coordinated with the US Secret Service, Bitcoin of America's founders were arrested and over 50 of their ATMs seized, based on allegations that they knew scammers were directing victims of crimes such as pig butchering to deposit cash into their kiosks. Bitcoin of America's founders allegedly earned millions of dollars in fees from those fraudulent transactions and made no effort to stop them.[36]

These cases – as well as the earlier Operation Guatuzo case in Spain – demonstrated that despite the perception that the combination of cash and crypto offered anonymity, the physical nature of Bitcoin ATMs left illicit users vulnerable to detection through old-fashioned police work. In Taylor's case, police surveilled the kiosks he allegedly owned and watched as known criminals accessed the machines across New York.

Outside the United States, some regulators took especially drastic steps to reduce the risks from Bitcoin ATMs. In January 2022, the Monetary Authority of Singapore (MAS) announced a ban on placing Bitcoin ATMs in public spaces in Singapore – a step MAS said was essential to protect consumers.[37] In March 2022, the UK Financial Conduct Authority (FCA) warned that no Bitcoin ATM operators had received approval to operate in the United Kingdom – and it demanded that all operators in the country shut down their ATMs or risk enforcement action.[38]

* * *

Bitcoin ATMs offered a bridge between the worlds of cash and cryptocurrencies, which criminals abused to launder money in new ways. But the physical nature of Bitcoin ATMs meant that boots-on-the-ground police work and surveillance could still help detect criminals who exploited the machines on the streets, and dismantle those ATM operators that refused to comply with regulation. While Bitcoin ATMs featured in some substantial cases of drug dealing and fraud, most criminal activity that involved cryptocurrencies would persist in an exclusively online realm.

And in that digital environment, a form of crime was spreading that would send alarm bells ringing at the highest levels of governments throughout the world.

Chapter 6

Ransomware: Cybercrime Goes Industrial

O n May 12, 2017, around 200,000 people sitting in front of computers across the world were greeted by an ominous message. Presented in a red pop-up box with a header reading "Ooops, your files have been encrypted!," the message stated: "Many of your documents, photos, videos, databases and other files are no longer accessible because they have been encrypted. Maybe you are busy looking for your files, but do not waste your time. Nobody can recover your files without our decryption service" (see Figure 6.1).

Befuddled readers initially may not have understood the full significance of the message, assuming it was a gag or harmless hoax. But reading further along, the message explained: "If you want to decrypt all your files, you need to pay. You have only 3 days to submit the payment. After that the price will be doubled. Also, if you don't pay in 7 days, you won't be able to recover your files forever."

Increasingly panicked readers would by now have realized that they were the victims of some sort of cyber hack. Frantic, and scrolling through the message, they found a section in the pop-up box entitled "How Do I Pay?," which made the hackers' expectations clear. "Payment is accepted in Bitcoin only," it read. Then in

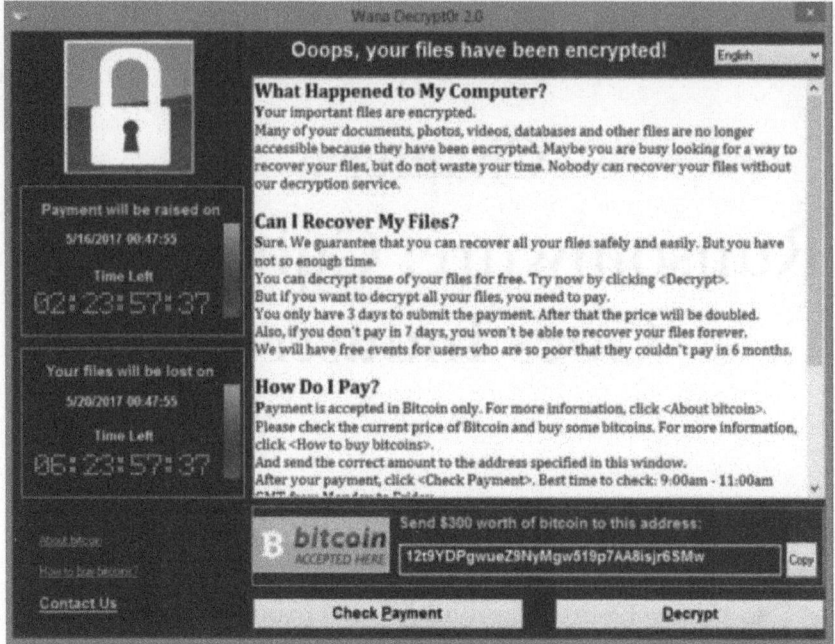

Figure 6.1   Image of the WannaCry ransomware message.

bold yellow letters there appeared an instruction: "Send $300 worth of bitcoin to this address," with a specified Bitcoin address where payment could be transferred.

This message was displayed on computer screens across the globe – from Taiwan to India to Russia to Spain to the United Kingdom to Brazil to the United States, ultimately impacting users in an estimated 150 countries. Those reading it were victims of a ransomware attack – a form of cybercrime in which attackers encrypt sensitive data or restrict access to computer systems and demand payment to restore access. This particular attack involved a strain of ransomware known as WannaCry, the most disruptive and high-profile ransomware attack the world had seen until then.

Over the next half-decade, what emerged in WannaCry's wake was a full-blown epidemic of ransomware that put Bitcoin center stage in policy debates over cybersecurity, and led governments to look for additional tools in the regulatory and legal arsenal for combating crypto-enabled crime.

Bitcoin Transforms the Ransomware Ecosystem

Ransomware existed long before WannaCry, and, indeed, long before Bitcoin. The first known ransomware attack dates to 1989 and was carried out by Joseph Popp, an English biologist who had been educated at Harvard. Popp created a malware known as the AIDS Trojan Horse, which he used to target members of subscriber lists of the World Health Organization AIDS Conference and *PC Business World* magazine. Popp sent a floppy disk infected with the malware to the lists' subscribers, and when recipients inserted the disk into their computers, their files were encrypted. A message on their screens instructed them to mail $189 to a P.O. Box in Panama, in the name of the PC Cyborg Corporation.[1]

During the two decades after the AIDS Trojan Horse, cybercriminals' experiments with ransomware grew increasingly sophisticated, evolving from the distribution of malware via floppy disks to using "phishing" campaigns to infect victims' computers with malicious email links. In 2007, Russian cybercriminals developed a ransomware variant known as WinLock, which was innovative in that it locked users completely out of their PCs, showing pornographic images on the screen until the victim made payment in Russian rubles via a text message link.[2] In 2012, a ransomware strain emerged known as Reveton that was spread by malicious links in email spam. Reveton locked the victim's PC and presented a message designed to look like a website run by the FBI or other law enforcement agency – promising that if the victim transferred their funds to law enforcement, their PC would unlock. Reveton victims were instructed to transfer funds from their bank accounts and onto prepaid cards, which the attackers could then use to spend the funds.[3]

These early ransomware variants had mixed levels of success. Popp's AIDS Trojan Horse seems to have yielded him limited profits, and he was eventually deemed mentally unfit to stand trial in the face of blackmail charges in the United Kingdom. Later variants such as WinLock and Reveton were more successful owing to their greater sophistication, with some distributors of the Reveton ransomware earning as much as $400,000 per month.[4] But these early attempts at ransomware paled in comparison to the profits that the next generation of ransomware attackers would reap. What early ransomware attackers lacked, just like the early pioneers of online drugs markets, was a reliable payment method that would allow them to grow their business to an industrial scale. Because they had to accept ransom payments primarily through methods that involved touchpoints with the banking system, early ransomware attackers were exposed to risks of detection by financial institutions; or, as in the case of Joseph Popp, the risk of having cash or checks seized through the post. Bitcoin, however, would forever alter the economics of ransomware. By demanding that victims send ransom payments to private, pseudonymous Bitcoin wallets, attackers could extort funds from victims located anywhere in the world without the initial ransom payment arriving in an account controlled by a regulated financial institution. The ability of cybercriminals to use peer-to-peer cryptocurrency payments to receive funds paved the way for ransomware to become a truly lucrative enterprise.

The ransomware variant that brought Bitcoin to the fore was CryptoLocker, which featured in a campaign of attacks from September 2013 through the spring of 2014. The CryptoLocker malware was developed by Russian cybercriminals and distributed to businesses through infected email attachments. It received its name not from its use of cryptocurrencies, but rather because of the strength of encryption techniques it employed to lock victims' files.[5] CryptoLocker's reach was widespread because its distributors leveraged a botnet – or network of infected computers – known as GameOver Zeus to infiltrate thousands of businesses around the world. Once their computers were infected, victims were instructed to pay in bitcoins to obtain the keys needed to decrypt their files, with the requested payments ranging between $100 and $460 worth of bitcoins (the fee increasing if payment was not received by a specified deadline). Cybersecurity researchers estimate that CryptoLocker infected more than 250,000 computers around the world in just the first few months of its deployment.[6] By one estimate, between October and December 2013 alone this yielded the distributors of CryptoLocker at least $27 million that they received through four Bitcoin addresses where they had instructed victims to pay the funds.[7]

This major haul of bitcoins in just three months demonstrated that ransomware could earn hefty profits if deployed effectively. CryptoLocker, in fact, had allowed victims the option of paying with prepaid cards in fiat currencies, as in the Reveton campaign, but the overwhelming haul for the CryptoLocker attackers came through payment in bitcoins. Going forward, most ransomware campaigns would rely exclusively on cryptocurrencies to extract payments from their victims – and would rake in increasingly staggering sums. A successor ransomware strain to CryptoLocker was CryptoWall, which is believed to have launched in November 2013 but spread more widely across early 2014 and into 2015. CryptoWall infected as many as 400,000 computers worldwide and, according to one estimate, yielded its distributors $325 million in revenue through bitcoin payments.[8]

The rise of Bitcoin-enabled ransomware in the period across 2013 to 2015 was bolstered by a parallel set of developments: the maturation of the money laundering ecosystem dedicated to cleaning ill-gotten cryptocurrencies. After all, once they received ransom payments from victims, attackers needed to swap the funds into fiat currencies – and fortunately for them, they could count on a network of non-compliant exchange services to launder their proceeds. According to the US Department of Justice (DOJ), the perpetrators of the CryptoWall attacks swapped bitcoins worth hundreds of thousands of dollars at the BTC-e exchange before BTC-e was taken down by US law enforcement in 2017.[9] Ransomware attackers could also rely on mixing services to launder their proceeds. According to FinCEN, the Helix mixer had processed transactions from ransomware attacks – demonstrating that attackers had a selection of complicit services they could choose from to try and hide their bitcoins.[10]

By the time of the WannaCry attack in May 2017, ransomware attackers had a well-developed set of typologies for reaping substantial cryptocurrency profits and laundering them. Unlike CryptoWall and CryptoLocker, WannaCry did not spread via email links; rather, it used a "worm" – or a form of malware that spreads across corporate computer networks searching for vulnerabilities to exploit. The WannaCry malware was designed to identify security gaps in PCs running the Microsoft Windows operating system. Its delivery method allowed WannaCry to slither across enterprise computer networks rapidly, exploiting weaknesses in those that had failed to implement a security patch that Microsoft had released two months before the attack took place. WannaCry wreaked enormous pain on impacted organizations, which suffered ongoing disruption to their operations, as well as substantial costs to repair the damage. The UK National Health Service estimated that the WannaCry attack inflicted £92 million in damages to its IT systems, but the disruption also came with severe human costs: around 19,000 medical appointments were canceled during the attack, including appointments and operations related to cancer diagnoses and other serious conditions.[11] The security firm Symantec estimated that the costs to organizations globally from disrupted operations from WannaCry were approximately $4 billion[12] – an astonishing trail of damage for an attack that only lasted about two days before a British security researcher named Marcus Hutchins discovered a kill switch in the malware that halted WannaCry's spread.

WannaCry, however, while significant in terms of the damage it inflicted on affected businesses and organizations, was not a highly profitable ransomware campaign for its attackers. Despite infecting some quarter of a million computers globally in less than 48 hours, the WannaCry attack suffered from a flaw: as part of its code, victims were instructed to send funds to one of three Bitcoin addresses. Because the attack was so high-profile and disruptive, the attention of the whole world focused on watching the blockchain, waiting for payments to be made into those three addresses. This, consequently, discouraged victims from making payments in the public eye. The three Bitcoin addresses belonging to the perpetrators of the WannaCry attack ultimately only received around $142,000 worth of bitcoins from victims seeking to have their files decrypted – a tiny sum when compared to the earlier CryptoLocker and CryptoWall campaigns.

For more than two months, the WannaCry bitcoins merely sat in the three wallets belonging to the attackers, not moving. As the funds sat there, observers began to wonder, "Would the perpetrators dare to move the funds with the whole world watching?" For a time, it seemed the answer was no. But on July 24, the attackers began withdrawing funds – at first slowly over the course of a few days. But then, on August 3, they emptied their wallet completely.

Blockchain analytics companies and law enforcement agencies began following the WannaCry funds as they were transferred through additional wallets. Analysis of the blockchain indicated that most of the bitcoins were ultimately moved to ShapeShift, a coinswap service founded by Bitcoin enthusiast and investor Erik Voorhees that operated out of Switzerland at the time. Notably, ShapeShift did not require users to provide identifying information.[13] Another portion of the funds was sent to Changelly, a coinswap service located in the Czech Republic that, like ShapeShift, did not require identifying information of users. Upon sending the bitcoins to ShapeShift and Changelly, the attackers engaged in "chain-hopping" – swapping the bitcoins for the privacy coin Monero, in an apparent attempt to make their funds untraceable. While neither ShapeShift nor Changelly required users to provide identification, both exchanges acknowledged publicly that they provided other information about the WannaCry transactions at the request of law enforcement agencies.

Inevitably, another key question that had cybersecurity researchers preoccupied was "Who did it?" And within days of the attack, consensus pointed to a culprit: North Korea. Desperate for funds in the face of sweeping international sanctions targeting its nuclear weapons proliferation activities, North Korea had for years launched daring and sophisticated cybercrime attacks on the global financial system to drum up cash. This included hacking bank ATM networks, as well as audacious cyberattacks like the attempted heist of more than $1 billion from the Bangladeshi Central Bank in 2016. At the center of North Korea's cybercrime activity is the Lazarus Group, the state-sponsored cybercrime unit that has been operating from around 2009. It is unclear precisely when the Lazarus Group began to contemplate undertaking cryptocurrency-enabled cybercrime, but certainly a group with its sophistication would have been aware of the successful CryptoLocker and CryptoWall campaigns. It is unsurprising that the Lazarus Group attempted to emulate those attacks with the hope of generating funds for which the North Korean state was desperate.

By May 15, just five days after the WannaCry attack, cybersecurity researchers at Google, as well as the cybersecurity firms Kaspersky and Symantec, determined that the code used in the WannaCry malware resembled code that the Lazarus Group had deployed in other cyberattacks.[14] Researchers also suggested that the sheer scale of the attack pointed to a state-affiliated actor, rather than the actions of a lone criminal. On December 19, 2017, the US government – joined by the governments of the United Kingdom, Japan, Australia, Canada, and New Zealand – officially attributed the WannaCry attack to North Korea.[15] Ten months later, in September 2018, the DOJ announced a criminal complaint against Park Jin Hyok, a member of the Lazarus Group it accused of perpetrating the WannaCry attack, but who remained elusive from US custody.[16]

OFAC Enters the Crypto Space

The involvement of North Korea in a major ransomware campaign upped the stakes, causing the US government to view crypto-related crime in a new light. It was one thing when drug dealers sold their products on the dark web using bitcoins. That was a matter of serious concern, and one that law enforcement agencies saw as warranting major attention. But when a country like North Korea started using crypto to circumvent sanctions, it was no longer just a police matter – it was an issue of national and international security that required a response equal to the scale of the threat.

In the United States, a small but powerful office within the US Department of the Treasury featured at the heart of that response.

Established in 1950 during the Korean War to freeze Chinese and North Korean assets, the Treasury's Office of Foreign Assets Control (OFAC) is the US agency responsible for the administration and enforcement of US sanctions – which include embargoes on countries such as North Korea, Iran, and Cuba, as well as asset freezes targeting businesses and individuals around the world involved in activities ranging from terrorism to narcotics trafficking to weapons smuggling.

A relatively small office within the Treasury including approximately 200 employees, OFAC packs an outsized punch. At the core of OFAC's efforts to further US national security objectives through economic and financial sanctions is a document known as the Specially Designated Nationals and Blocked Persons List. The SDN List, as it is known, is a blacklist OFAC maintains with the names of thousands of individuals and entities, including members of Colombian drug cartels and their front companies, supporters of terrorist organizations such as al Qaeda and the Islamic State, members of the junta in Myanmar and their cronies, and others on what ultimately forms a who's-who of some of the world's most unsavory actors. When an entity or individual is placed on the SDN List, US citizens and businesses are prohibited from engaging in any dealings with them – subjecting the targets of the sanctions to asset freezes that make it effectively impossible for them to access the US financial system. Penalties for violating these prohibitions can be severe: financial institutions found to have violated US sanctions have been the targets of massive fines reaching into the billions. OFAC's sanctions also have extraterritorial reach: OFAC can punish non-US businesses for engaging in conduct that results in sanctions violations, a fact that leads many non-US companies around the world to adhere to OFAC sanctions for fear of running afoul of its enforcement powers.

OFAC had long been focused on how to combat security threats such as drug trafficking, terrorism, and weapons proliferation, and in the few years preceding the WannaCry attack, the United States was already taking steps to wield OFAC's sanctions hammer at the growing problem of cybercrime. In April 2015, President Barak

Obama signed an Executive Order entitled *Blocking the Property of Certain Persons Engaging in Significant Malicious Cyber-Enabled Activities*. The order provided OFAC with the authority to implement asset freezes on cybercriminals and their support networks. Thus, just as ransomware was becoming a lucrative business, OFAC was granted the power to sanction ransomware perpetrators and their support networks. But it was only after WannaCry that OFAC directed these new powers at the ransomware ecosystem.

In November 2018, OFAC took its first action to hit crypto-enabled ransomware networks with sanctions – though, interestingly, it looked initially not to North Korea, but to another sanctioned country. That month, OFAC added two Iranian nationals, Ali Khorashadizadeh and Mohammad Ghorbaniyan, to the SDN List. OFAC alleged that the pair were involved in laundering the proceeds from a disruptive ransomware strain known as SamSam, whose distributors were also believed to be in Iran and targeted hospitals, government agencies, and corporations in the United States.[17] OFAC claims that Khorashadizadeh and Ghorbaniyan "helped exchange digital currency (bitcoin) ransom payments into Iranian rial on behalf of Iranian malicious cyber actors involved with the SamSam ransomware scheme."[18]

As part of the action against Khorashadizadeh and Ghorbaniyan, OFAC took an unprecedented step: it included on the SDN List two Bitcoin addresses controlled by the accused Iranian crypto launderers. When placing individuals and entities on the SDN List, OFAC routinely includes identifiers about them – indicators such as residential and business addresses, dates of birth, or other data points that can assist financial institutions and others in identifying whether they are interacting with blacklisted parties. By including Bitcoin addresses belonging to Khorashadizadeh and Ghorbaniyan on the SDN List, OFAC was offering cryptocurrency users a way to ensure that they did not transact with the two accused crypto launderers. Because of the action, US individuals and businesses, including cryptocurrency exchanges, were prohibited from dealing with cryptocurrency addresses that Khorashadizadeh and Ghorbaniyan controlled.

In April 2019, OFAC followed this action by sanctioning the Lazarus Group and other branches of North Korea's cybercriminal apparatus – a further stab at the ransomware ecosystem.[19] Over the next several years, OFAC would add to the SDN List hundreds of cryptocurrency addresses belonging to sanctioned individuals and entities – including additional ransomware perpetrators – to prevent crypto from becoming a financial lifeline for threat actors.

But even as US government officials were targeting the assets of ransomware perpetrators, attackers were busy exploring new techniques to make their crimes even more profitable, and more dangerous.

The Rise of Ransomware-as-a-Service and Big Game Hunting

The period of attacks from 2013 to 2017 demonstrated that ransomware could yield huge profits. But during that span, certain problems facing attackers had become evident.

The WannaCry attack had exposed one of these: by broadcasting their Bitcoin addresses across such a large network of computers, the Lazarus Group had made their financial details highly visible, and vulnerable to tracing on the blockchain. For the ransomware economy to scale further, new methods of extracting ransoms from victims were needed to account for Bitcoin's inherent traceability.

A second problem was in the distribution method of ransomware. The early generations of ransomware attacks had operated with a single line of production and distribution: the cybercriminals who developed malware were generally also those – or were closely associated with those – who distributed the malware. This meant that anyone who wanted to distribute malware also had to be relatively technically sophisticated, and those developing the malware had to devote time and energy to other components of the ransomware activity chain, such as distributing malware, negotiating with victims, and laundering profits. This dynamic prevented ransomware from scaling to its full potential. To grow even larger, the ransomware ecosystem needed a more efficient and scalable division of labor – one that eliminated technical barriers to entry so that nearly anyone could launch a ransomware attack.

Out of this need rose the development of ransomware-as-a-service (RaaS), a new business model that enabled the ransomware underworld to achieve new heights of financial success. Like the notion of software-as-a-service (SaaS) in the business world (from which it derives its name, and which allows software companies to achieve economies of scale in the distribution of their products), RaaS utilizes a subscription model to facilitate the distribution of malicious code at scale.

RaaS networks involve two primary parties: ransomware operators and ransomware affiliates. Operators are those who develop the malware and who provide "how-to" kits that offer instruction on how to distribute the malware. Affiliates buy the malware from operators and undertake the distribution of it, including by targeting victims, setting the ransom demands, communicating with victims during any ransom negotiation, and decrypting files on receipt of payment from victims.[20] Affiliates purchase the ransomware kits from operators using bitcoins – often for a small fee, even as low as $50. RaaS operators allow affiliates to pay based on a variety of subscription models – ranging from a flat monthly fee for continued access to ransomware kits, to using profit-sharing models where the affiliate and operator split the profits from attacks. This arrangement allows affiliates who lack the know-how to create malware to engage in lucrative ransomware campaigns while operators can rake in money by cultivating extensive networks of affiliates equipped with high-quality malware. The result is an industrial-scale machinery of ransomware development and deployment.

Along with this evolution in ransomware distribution, attackers also altered their approach to receiving payments from victims. Because of the efficiencies the RaaS model created, affiliates distributing the malware no longer needed to target hundreds of thousands of computers simultaneously to extract small ransoms from each victim. Rather, individual affiliates could focus energy on negotiating bigger ransom payments directly from targets capable of paying large sums. This dynamic incentivized attackers to focus on targets with the means and incentives to pay huge ransoms – such as private hospitals, large corporations, transport networks, providers of public utilities, and other components of critical infrastructure. Consequently, the average size of individual ransomware payments rose dramatically, from $540 in 2017 to approximately $6 million extracted per payment in 2021.[21] This also forced attackers to change the way they interacted with victims. Rather than blasting their cryptocurrency addresses across a large network of computers, affiliates set up dedicated, encrypted chat rooms for negotiating payments directly with victims, and would only share the specific Bitcoin address for receiving funds directly with the target of the attack – an approach designed to make their addresses less vulnerable to detection by investigators and blockchain analytics firms. Additionally, some RaaS affiliates began to demand that victims settle ransoms in the privacy coin Monero with the aim of concealing the funds trail. In these cases, affiliates provided victims the choice of paying in Bitcoin or Monero, offering discounts for those willing to make Monero payments – though most victims continued to pay in Bitcoin because of its wider availability.[22]

The result of these shifting dynamics was an ecosystem of ransomware affiliates and operators who were reaping growing profits, and who were increasingly emboldened in carrying out attacks on targets they suspected would pay the largest ransoms – a technique known as Big Game Hunting. What emerged was an epidemic of ransomware attacks that carried grave implications.

One of the first major RaaS campaigns involved the Dharma ransomware strain. Originally launched in late 2016, the Dharma campaign took off aggressively across 2018 and beyond.[23] Dharma was created by Russian operators, but the RaaS model enabled a network of affiliates outside Russia to utilize Dharma, including affiliates based in Iran.[24] Dharma affiliates attacked financial institutions, hospitals, and government agencies, demanding ever-larger ransoms. In November 2018, a hospital in Baytown, Texas, a suburb of Houston, was hit by a Dharma ransomware attack that encrypted sensitive data from patient files. While the hospital chose not to pay the ransom and instead hired security experts to decrypt the patient files, many organizations targeted in similar ransomware attacks would choose to pay their attackers to decrypt sensitive data as rapidly as possible. Studies suggest that most ransomware victims in the period between 2016 and 2022 chose to pay ransoms to their attackers to have data decrypted, rather than looking to other methods for decrypting their data or restoring systems.[25]

Another ransomware variant that began spreading alongside Dharma was the Ryuk ransomware, distributed by a Russian cyber-criminal group known as Wizard Spider. Ryuk ransomware attacks followed the Big Game Hunting approach, focusing on targeting large corporations. By one estimate, Ryuk attackers generated as much as $3.7 million in Bitcoin proceeds in their first four months of operation between August 2018 and January 2019 – though the actual figure may be higher.[26]

The rise of RaaS business models and Big Game Hunting techniques culminated in a ransomware attack so severe it set the US government on high alert. On May 7, 2021, staff at the Colonial Pipeline Company, which is headquartered in Alpharetta, Georgia, and operates a pipeline system for carrying refined oil between Texas and New York, discovered that the company had been hit by ransomware. The attack targeted the company's billing system, preventing it from receiving payments from purchasers. Consequently, the company closed the pipeline, halting the flow of oil along the East Coast of the United States for a six-day period before it managed to bring operations back online on May 12. By then, the damage was done. The closure resulted in widespread shortages at filling stations along the entire East Coast, with as many as 70–80% of filling stations in some states running out of fuel that week. The shortages triggered panic buying, causing the price of gas to rise temporarily to over $3 per gallon. The crisis was so grave that it became a priority issue in the Oval Office at the White House. On May 9, President Joe Biden declared a state of emergency, and the US State Department issued a $10 million reward for information leading to the perpetrators' arrest.

As this major disruption to the United States' energy infrastructure unfolded, Bitcoin took center stage. Within hours of the attack, the Colonial Pipeline determined that it needed to obtain the decryption key from the attackers to restore access urgently to its billing systems. The company therefore paid the requested ransom by transferring 75 bitcoins – worth approximately $4.4 million at the time – to Bitcoin wallets controlled by the attackers. Even after receiving the decryption key, the decryption process worked very slowly, which contributed to the delay in restoring the flow of oil through the pipeline. Several days later, the US government attributed the attack to affiliates of the DarkSide, a Russia-based ransomware operation that the US State Department claimed had begun launching attacks globally in August 2020, and which, according to blockchain data compiled by Elliptic, had already obtained ransom payments totaling more than $90 million by the time of the Colonial Pipeline attack.[27] The DarkSide affiliates now faced the same dilemma the Lazarus Group had faced during WannaCry: how to move a stash of bitcoins from their wallets with the entire world watching the blockchain.

Blockchain analysis showed that after receiving the bitcoins from Colonial Pipeline on May 7, the DarkSide affiliate moved the funds to other wallets they controlled on May 9. An investigation undertaken by Elliptic indicated that a portion of these funds – about 18% of the original ransom payment – was sent to cryptocurrency exchanges, while another portion – about 4% – was sent to the Hydra dark web marketplace, where the perpetrators may have attempted to use a money laundering service such as the "hidden treasure" cash-for-crypto service to turn their bitcoins into Russian rubles.[28]

But the DarkSide affiliates had made a mistake: while they had managed within a matter of days to launder approximately 20% of the ransom payment from the Colonial Pipeline, they did not move the remaining 80% of the funds fast enough. Consequently, those funds remained vulnerable to law enforcement seizure. Sure enough, on June 7, exactly one month after the attack on Colonial Pipeline, the DOJ announced that it had seized 63.7 bitcoins from a wallet controlled by the DarkSide.[29] While the DOJ did not divulge exactly how it obtained access to the DarkSide's funds, it confirmed that the bitcoins had been transferred to a separate wallet fully under the control of the US government.[30] The seizure had been made possible, of course, by the ability of federal investigators to trace funds through the blockchain and identify the Bitcoin addresses where the DarkSide held the funds from the attack.

Despite the successful recovery of funds from the Colonial Pipeline attack, the aggressive wave of Big Game Hunting persisted. The total value of reported ransomware payments made in the first half of 2021 was $590 million, versus $416 million across the whole of 2020, though the actual figure for both years is likely substantially higher given the extent of unreported attacks and undisclosed payments.[31] In addition to the DarkSide, other RaaS variants featured in major attacks, including the REvil and Conti ransomware campaigns, which also operated out of Russia and collectively obtained hundreds of millions of dollars from victims. Indeed, some attacks took on even bigger targets, and grew even more audacious in scale. In the spring of 2022, the Conti ransomware was targeted at the government of Costa Rica – infecting systems controlled by the country's Ministry of Finance, as well as its Social Security Fund. The attacks disrupted the country's imports and exports, costing tens of millions of dollars per day in terms of lost trade, and also severely impacting Costa Rica's healthcare system, leading to thousands of disrupted medical appointments. The scale of the attacks led the Costa Rican government to declare a national emergency as it worked to restore access to critical systems.[32]

The FATF Responds and Sparks Debate

The growing severity of ransomware attacks prompted governments at their highest levels to formulate increasingly urgent responses. In October 2020, the G7 countries issued a joint statement warning of the rising threat. The G7 advocated for two key elements of a policy response to ransomware. Firstly, it discouraged victims of attacks from paying ransoms, arguing that "The payment of ransoms demanded by these criminals can incentivize further malicious cyber activity; benefit malign actors and fund illicit activities; and present a risk of money laundering, terrorist financing, and proliferation financing (ML/TF/PF), and other illicit financial activity."[33] Secondly, it urged countries around the world to implement the AML/CFT standards developed by the Financial Action Task Force (FATF) aimed at reducing illicit activity in cryptocurrencies. As the ransomware threat accelerated, the FATF took on rapidly increasing influence in the world of crypto.

Established by the G7 in 1989, the FATF is a global standard-setting body that aims to protect the international financial system from illicit finance threats. Originally focused on combating money laundering, over its three-and-a-half-decade history, the FATF's mandate has expanded to include curtailing terrorist funding and the financing of weapons proliferation. Its membership has also grown substantially over the years: the full membership of the FATF now includes 37 countries plus the European Commission and Gulf Cooperation Council, and nearly all countries around the world are affiliate members of the FATF through associated regional bodies. The FATF publishes and periodically updates its Standards – a series of recommendations setting out high-level AML/CFT measures that member countries commit to implementing. While the FATF is not a law-making body or regulator, and cannot penalize non-compliance with its Standards in the form of fines, if countries fail to implement the Standards sufficiently, they can wind up on the FATF "Grey List" – where they are called-out for failing to meet the FATF's expectations.

Its mandate prompted the FATF to begin researching the impact of cryptocurrencies – which it now refers to as "virtual assets" – as far back as 2014, but its preoccupation with the technology would go into overdrive in 2018, when the United States assumed the FATF's rotating presidency. That October, the FATF issued a statement declaring that "there is an urgent need for all countries to take coordinated action to prevent the use of virtual assets for crime and terrorism," which reflected growing concern about the use of mixing technology and other techniques to launder cryptocurrencies, as well as anxiety over North Korea's involvement in crypto-enabled cybercrime.[34] Then, in June 2019, the FATF published extensive guidance entitled *Guidance for a Risk Based Approach: Virtual Assets and Virtual Asset Service Providers*, outlining its expectations for how countries should apply AML/CFT measures to cryptocurrencies (which in FATF parlance are included in the term "virtual assets").

The FATF's guidance made clear that all countries should subject virtual asset service providers (VASPs) – a term that includes cryptocurrency exchanges, coinswap services, Bitcoin ATMs, and a range of other participants in the crypto ecosystem – to AML/ CFT regulation. In practice, this meant that VASPs everywhere should be required by their regulators to obtain a license to operate, and should face obligations to collect identifying information from users and detect high-risk transactions. In advocating for this approach, the FATF as the global AML/CFT watchdog was making clear that combating money laundering in the cryptocurrency space was a growing international concern, demanding increasing regulatory oversight worldwide.

By and large, the FATF's application of its Standards to VASPs was uncontroversial. But one aspect of the FATF's proposed approach did spark significant controversy: a concept known as the Travel Rule. Established as part of the FATF's standards in the wake of the September 11, 2001, terrorist attacks, the Travel Rule has a simple aim: to prevent anonymity in international funds transfers. Under the Travel Rule, financial institutions must retain and share information about both the originator and beneficiaries of payments when their customers send wire transfers to one another. This requirement ensures that criminals and terrorists cannot send funds to anonymous, numbered bank accounts, as was once common practice for decades, for example, by using private accounts at banks in Switzerland or other historical secrecy havens. The Travel Rule put an end to that practice. Under the Travel Rule, if a customer of a bank in the United States wishes to send funds to a Swiss bank, the US bank must obtain the name of the intended recipient of the payment, and must transmit this information to the Swiss bank, which must also retain information about the actual identities of the respective counterparties to the transactions.

In the June 2019 updates to its Standards, the FATF determined that VASPs everywhere should be required to comply with the Travel Rule. In other words, cryptocurrency exchanges everywhere would need to share information with other exchanges about their respective customers. This proposal, however, ran into a problem. In the world of fiat currencies such as the US dollar and Swiss franc, all digital payments must pass through a bank – which means that the Travel Rule can apply to all wire transfers that banks undertake globally. It is not possible to transfer fiat currencies digitally without the presence of a regulated intermediary. In crypto, conversely, users can send payments to one another without relying on a regulated business. Indeed, the core innovation of Bitcoin is the ability to conduct borderless, peer-to-peer electronic payments without the involvement of regulated institutions. This meant that there would always be some payments between counterparties in the cryptocurrency ecosystem that did not involve a regulated VASP on one or both sides of a transaction, and where the Travel Rule therefore could not apply.

This presented the FATF with a conundrum: its standards were developed beginning in the 1980s based on the premise of regulating centralized intermediaries in the banking world. This was also the premise that the FATF and regulators such as FinCEN had relied upon in setting out the initial rules for cryptocurrencies, namely, that regulations should focus on imposing obligations on intermediaries such as cryptocurrency exchanges and other VASPs, rather than imposing restrictions on individual users of the technology. The Travel Rule, however, had exposed that cryptocurrencies by their design clashed with long-standing regulatory frameworks. The FATF therefore had to consider a fundamental problem: how to deal with decentralized, peer-to-peer cryptocurrency activity within the context of AML/CFT requirements that are normally designed for centralized intermediaries.

This debate was highly relevant to the response to ransomware. After all, one common feature of ransomware attacks was that they relied upon the peer-to-peer nature of cryptocurrencies to extract profits from victims. When demanding payment from

victims, ransomware attackers demanded that victims send funds
to the attackers' private wallets, or "unhosted wallets" in the FATF's
parlance – a term used to denote any wallet where the user retains
full control over her private keys, without the involvement of a regulated VASP in securing custody of the funds.

The FATF's approach to the matter was an imperfect resolution
to one of the thorniest regulatory problems involving the cryptocurrency space. Ultimately, the FATF concluded that it would continue
with its historical approach; that is, it would not attempt to extend
AML/CFT obligations to individual users of private unhosted wallets. Rather, it stated that regulators should oblige VASPs, such as
cryptocurrency exchanges, to gather information about the identities of those individuals behind the unhosted wallets with whom
their customers transact. For example, if a customer of a cryptocurrency exchange wished to send a payment from her account at the
exchange to a pseudonymous, unhosted wallet, then according to
the FATF Standards, the exchange needed to ask its customer to
provide the name of the person holding the unhosted wallet before
effecting the transfer.

The aim of this approach, naturally, is to ensure that the coun-
terparty to the payment behind the unhosted wallet cannot hide
behind their pseudonymous cryptocurrency address – in essence,
so the unhosted cryptocurrency wallet cannot act as the equivalent
of a numbered Swiss bank account. In the context of ransomware
payments, this would, in theory, help to unmask the identity of ransomware attackers and their networks, since VASPs would need to
obtain information about the individuals behind the unhosted wallets where attackers receive ransoms. But to cryptocurrency enthusiasts, the possibility of regulatory intrusion into the use of private,
unhosted wallets was practically sacrilegious. After all, cryptocurrencies were established to uphold a right to transactional privacy. In
the eyes of cryptocurrency advocates, it was unreasonable for governments to seek to unmask the users of private cryptocurrency wallets.

Then–US Treasury Secretary Steve Mnuchin, however, had different ideas. Mnuchin, who had once stated, "We're going to make
sure that bitcoin doesn't become the equivalent of Swiss-numbered

bank accounts,"[35] was unpersuaded by the crypto industry's concerns, and in late 2020 he acted to tackle the perceived risks of unhosted wallets.

On December 18, 2020, at Secretary Mnuchin's insistence, FinCEN issued a draft rule entitled *Requirements for Certain Transactions Involving Convertible Virtual Currency or Digital Assets*. The draft rule proposed that when a FinCEN-regulated cryptocurrency exchange processed a transaction greater than $3,000 with an unhosted wallet, it should have to verify the identity of the user of the unhosted wallet. Where transactions of $10,000 or greater involved an unhosted wallet, exchanges would be required to file a disclosure form known as a currency transaction report (CTR) – a type of report that banks already file for high-value cash transactions. The draft rule argued that these measures were needed to combat financial crime, noting that "ransomware attacks and associated demands for payment. . . are increasing in severity," and claiming that "The proposal seeks to establish appropriate controls to protect United States national security from a variety of threats from foreign nations and foreign actors, including state-sponsored ransomware and cybersecurity attacks, sanctions evasion, and financing of global terrorism, among others."[36]

The reaction of the cryptocurrency industry was instant and vigorous opposition. In response to the public notice about the proposed rule, FinCEN received thousands of responses from the industry arguing that the requirements threatened the privacy rights of legitimate crypto users. CoinCenter, a cryptocurrency industry lobbying non-profit organization, argued that the proposed measures were unconstitutional, claiming that the rule "is by its nature an undemocratic and potentially unaccountable activity through which an unelected bureaucracy, exercising broad delegated powers, enacts law that is binding on individuals with few if any checks. . . it would mandate the unconstitutional, warrantless search and seizure of private information, and would obligate financial institutions to keep and report to government lists of persons engaged in the exercise of their First Amendment rights to assemble anonymously."[37] What's more, industry representatives pointed out that likening unhosted wallets to numbered Swiss bank accounts was flawed. After all, the ability of investigators to trace the flow of funds through unhosted wallets by monitoring the blockchain enabled a degree of transparency in crypto transactions that had never been possible with secret bank transactions.

Ultimately, the industry's pushback helped ensure that the rule was never finalized before the end of the Trump administration. This led the incoming Biden administration to pause work on it, though the draft was never formally withdrawn from the rulemaking processes, leaving open the potential for it (or a version of it) to be revived someday. Unhosted wallets would remain one of the most hotly contested policy issues in the cryptocurrency space, with similar proposals from the European Union and elsewhere sparking intensive debate.

Alongside the controversy around unhosted wallets, another debate in global policymaking circles involved an even more fundamental question: Should ransomware payments be banned? Because ransomware had become such a lucrative business and was seemingly motivated overwhelmingly by profit, some observers argued that the most appropriate policy response would be to cut off attackers' financial lifeline by criminalizing ransom payments. The primary argument made in favor of banning ransoms was that victims of attacks had an enormous incentive to pay ransoms – as payment often offered the quickest route to restoring access to critical IT systems – and that this guaranteed attackers an almost constant stream of revenue that incentivized further attacks. At state level in the United States, some legislatures instituted local bans on ransomware payments. Both North Carolina and Florida passed laws prohibiting state government agencies and departments from paying ransoms, with the hope that this would dissuade attackers from targeting their infrastructure.[38]

For several months in the summer of 2021, when the ransomware epidemic was at its height, speculation mounted around whether the Biden administration would implement a federal ban on ransomware payments. But many officials were skeptical of the merits of a ban, and the US government ultimately decided not to pursue one.

The argument against banning ransomware payments rested on several points: firstly, that a ban would merely punish victims of attacks who had already suffered greatly, and who sometimes faced little option but to pay; secondly, that determined attackers would always find victims willing to pay, undermining any ban; and lastly, that a ban threatened to undercut one of the key sources of intelligence about ransomware networks, namely, the payments trail they left on the blockchain when moving their ill-gotten gains.

Unpersuaded that a ban on paying ransoms would prove implementable or effective, the Biden administration decided instead to pursue other approaches.

Wielding the Sanctions Hammer

As global policymakers continued to debate the best response to the ransomware threat, OFAC once again took center stage as part of the US effort to hit back. As US authorities considered how to undermine the ransomware ecosystem, they began to focus on a key set of enablers: unregulated and non-compliant cryptocurrency exchange platforms that attackers used to swap their Bitcoin profits into fiat currencies.

The first target in this effort was a small cryptocurrency exchange registered in the Czech Republic but operating out of a skyscraper in Moscow. SUEX OTC, S.R.O., marketed itself online as a small, boutique cryptocurrency exchange that allowed users to swap bitcoins for euros and other fiat currencies. This ostensibly small and unassuming Czech cryptocurrency exchange was in fact a key facilitator of the Russian cybercrime ecosystem. Elliptic's analysis of SUEX's Bitcoin transactions undertaken on the blockchain indicated that the exchange had processed approximately $370 million in illicit payments between 2018 and 2021 alone.[39] In September 2021, OFAC announced that it had sanctioned SUEX, which it claimed "facilitated transactions involving illicit proceeds from at least eight ransomware variants"[40] – suggesting that in SUEX, criminals had identified a reliable and even complicit party to help them launder their funds. Reports also indicated that SUEX operated a cash-for-crypto swapping service by meeting clients at locations around Moscow and St. Petersburg.[41]

The action against SUEX was just the first in a series of sanctions targeting the Russia-based ransomware ecosystem. In November 2021, OFAC targeted Chatex, a cryptocurrency exchange with a corporate presence in Latvia and St. Vincent and the Grenadines, but which OFAC alleged primarily served a clientele of Russia-based ransomware attackers and had direct ties to the owners of SUEX, operating out of the same Russian skyscraper.[42] In April 2022, OFAC sanctioned another exchange, this time an Estonian-registered exchange known as Garantex, which OFAC claimed handled millions of dollars in funds from the Conti RaaS gang that had attacked Costa Rica.[43]

When it targeted Garantex, OFAC also sanctioned the Russia-based dark web market Hydra, the site where money launderers had advertised the "buried treasure" Bitcoin-for-ruble cash-out schemes. The OFAC sanctions were coordinated with a successful German-led law enforcement action to dismantle Hydra, which had, in only the space of a few years, grown to become by far the largest dark web marketplace ever – dwarfing even AlphaBay by a considerable margin. In 2020 alone, Hydra generated an estimated $1.3 billion in crypto-denominated revenues. In addition to facilitating the trade in drugs, stolen IDs, and other prohibited items, a core part of Hydra's business model was serving as a marketplace for Russia's ransomware ecosystem: RaaS operators sold malware and related distribution kits on Hydra to their affiliates. Just as importantly, Hydra offered attackers a venue for accessing money laundering services such as the buried treasure scheme that they could use to launder bitcoins obtained in ransomware campaigns, as well as a built-in mixing service that enabled users of the site to launder their funds. In addition to the funds that the DarkSide ransomware attackers sent to Hydra, OFAC identified that as much as $8 million worth of bitcoins from perpetrators of the Ryuk, Conti, and other ransomware attacks had been sent to Hydra,[44] potentially to make use of these dark web crypto laundering services.

Set against the backdrop of Russia's invasion of Ukraine in February 2022, this ramping up of sanctions targeting the Russian ransomware ecosystem was also meant to send a message that the United States was intent on stamping out money laundering and other illicit activity in Russia, and formed part of a larger campaign of sweeping economic sanctions the United States and other countries imposed on Russia to isolate it.

In January 2023, FinCEN joined OFAC in taking aim at illicit crypto activity in Russia. Acting under a provision in section 9714 of the Combating Russian Money Laundering Act, FinCEN issued an order preventing US crypto exchanges and financial institutions from engaging in transactions with Bitzlato, a Hong Kong–domiciled crypto exchange owned by Russian nationals. According to FinCEN – which identified Bitzlato as a "primary money laundering concern," the same designation applied to the Liberty Reserve digital currency service nearly a decade earlier – Bitzlato had facilitated hundreds of millions of dollars in illicit payments, including transactions with Hydra and with the Conti ransomware gang.[45]

The US government's ongoing efforts to disrupt ransomware networks with sanctions did not stop with Russia. In September 2022, OFAC had turned its sights back on Iran by sanctioning a ransomware network associated with the Islamic Revolutionary Guard Corp (IRGC), an Iranian paramilitary group and branch of Iran's armed forces. That month, OFAC imposed an asset freeze on numerous individuals and companies that it alleges the IRGC deployed to conduct ransomware attacks. According to the US Treasury, the IRGC-affiliated ransomware network "has launched extensive campaigns against organizations and officials across the globe, particularly targeting U.S. and Middle Eastern defense, diplomatic, and government personnel, as well as private industries including media, energy, business services, and telecommunications. . . In June 2021, the group gained unauthorized access to supervisory control and data acquisition systems associated with a U.S.-based children's hospital."[46]

***

The rise of ransomware reshaped the policy debate around cryptocurrencies, shifting the focus from a primarily law enforcement concern to an issue of pressing international security. Consequently, policymakers looked increasingly to an additional set of tools – particularly the use of sanctions – to respond to emerging risks in the cryptocurrency space.

Despite the tsunami of ransomware attacks that reached their height in the summer of 2021, there were subsequently some signs that the situation might be gradually improving. Across 2022, the total amount of payments made to ransomware attackers decreased by over a third from the previous year. This is likely attributable to improved cybersecurity practices among enterprises, as well as a growing refusal by targets of attacks to pay ransoms – though some analysts suggested that ransomware attackers were simply recalibrating their approach and evolving their techniques before the next wave of aggressive attacks. Even with the best efforts of US and other governments, ransomware simply would not go away. As of mid-2023, ransomware remained a lucrative form of cybercrime, continuing to generate hundreds of millions of dollars for attackers annually, and placing significant demands on already stretched enforcement agencies. Indeed, in the first half of 2023 alone, ransomware attacks generated nearly $450 million in crypto payments from victims, putting 2023 on pace to be the most profitable year ever for ransomware gangs – a testament to the effectiveness of Big Game Hunting techniques that attackers continued to launch relentlessly against vulnerable targets.[47]

Compounding the challenge was the fact that ransomware was only one form of cybercrime leveraging cryptocurrencies. If ransomware formed one front in a battle with cybercriminals that governments found themselves fighting, there was a second front that kept them just as busy. Another form of crypto-enabled cybercrime had proved even more lucrative than ransomware, attracting some familiar protagonists back onto the scene in pursuit of easy digital money.

Chapter 7

Hacked: Crypto Exchange Heists

W hich brings us back to the start of our story, back to August 2016, when the Bitfinex exchange was the target of a major cybercriminal attack resulting in the loss of more than $72 million in customer funds – a sum that swelled to more than $7 billion as most of the stolen bitcoins sat in a private wallet for more than five years, and while blockchain watchers waited anxiously to see where the funds would go. Among cybercriminal attacks on cryptocurrency exchanges, the Bitfinex hack at that point was second in size only to the Mt. Gox hack, and was part of a rapidly mounting wave of exchange heists that would soon become a multibillion-dollar business.

Exchanges: Low-Hanging Fruit for Hackers

Cyber thieves began attacking cryptocurrency exchanges early in Bitcoin's history. It didn't take long after the launch of the first exchanges for hackers to realize that exchanges were attractive honeypots awash with billions of dollars' worth of bitcoins and other cryptocurrencies that they could steal. In October 2011, an early exchange known as Bitcoin7 was hit by a cybercriminal hack that resulted in the theft of 5,000 bitcoins. In September 2012, a US cryptocurrency exchange known as Bitfloor, then one of the largest exchanges, lost 24,000 bitcoins in a hack that ultimately led it to go out of business.[1] As cryptocurrency markets grew, and as the price of Bitcoin increased, the quantity and value of cryptocurrencies traded at exchanges made them increasingly lucrative sources of funding for hackers – with the Mt. Gox and Bitfinex hacks illustrating the potentially enormous scale of these hauls.

The successful hack of a cryptocurrency exchange ultimately rests on one critical step: the hacker must gain access to the private keys that control the exchange's wallets where it holds its customers' funds. Once in possession of the exchange's private keys, the hacker can transfer the funds to a separate wallet that they or their associates control, and from there, attempt to launder the funds. The initial challenge for the hacker is in getting access to the exchange's private keys. No exchange service, after all, would willingly reveal the private keys to its wallets. A hacker therefore must infiltrate the exchange to access the keys. And that requires knowing a thing or two about cryptocurrency storage and custody.

There are two primary methods for storing cryptocurrencies: cold storage and hot storage. Cold storage, as we've already seen, involves retaining the private keys to a wallet offline – a method of storage that makes the funds within the wallet safer from hackers. Providers of cold storage custody services assist exchanges with ensuring the safe custody of their customers' funds, which can involve keeping the private keys to any cold storage wallets in sealed vaults and requiring numerous steps for generating the keys needed to sign a transaction. For example, Xapo, a cryptocurrency custodian registered in Gibraltar that offers cold storage facilities, describes its security arrangements as involving "state of the art Multi-Party Computing (MPC) 'keyless' wallets, whose signing shares are managed by Xapo as well as a trusted SOC2 Type II compliant third party. They are secured using Hardware Security Modules (HSM) devices and we employ strict controls and access rights to both the assets and supporting infrastructure. Cold storage of key material is supported by bank-grade Class III vaults in geographically dispersed locations."[2]

It is good cybersecurity practice for exchanges to maintain a large proportion of their customers' funds in cold storage. But to satisfy customer demand for rapid trading, and to facilitate ease of use, exchanges inevitably retain some funds in hot storage, or in wallets where private keys are retained online. Hot wallets that are single-signature, or that only require authorization from one private key to transact, are particularly vulnerable to theft because a hacker need only obtain access to one set of credentials to gain control of the funds in the wallet. Where hot wallets are multi-signature ("multi-sig"), they are generally more robust from a cybersecurity perspective because more than one set of private keys is required to undertake a transaction. To steal funds from a multi-sig hot wallet, a hacker must either identify a flaw in the wallet's design that allows them to drain funds from it, or they must manage to coerce the holders of the wallet's keys into surrendering a sufficient set of credentials to withdraw funds from the wallet. In either case, the hacker must gain control of the exchange's hot wallet infrastructure, and that requires finding a way into the exchange's IT systems where private keys are retained.

To infiltrate an exchange, hackers engage in phishing attacks – sending malicious emails to the exchange's staff. Posing as job applicants, prospective clients or business partners, or under some other guise, the hackers send emails with file attachments infected with malware that, if downloaded by an employee of the exchange, allows the hackers to gain access to its systems. Once inside, the hacker can search around for the exchange's wallet credentials – and, if successful, can drain funds sitting in any associated hot wallets. Hackers also infiltrate exchanges through "social engineering" campaigns – or by forming direct relationships with employees of an exchange under an assumed guise, using the trust they build with staff to convince them to turn over the exchange's private keys, or to execute a transaction on the hacker's behalf.[3]

Many cryptocurrency exchanges, particularly in the first decade after Bitcoin's launch, had insufficient cybersecurity defenses to

prevent theft. Exchanges sometimes left too large a portion of customers' funds vulnerable in hot storage wallets, and many exchanges
also did not educate their staff on the risks of cyber intrusion, which
left them prone to phishing attacks and social engineering. The
result was an ecosystem of exchanges that were often incredibly easy
prey for hackers, with hacks growing in value and frequency over
the years. One analysis in 2018 found that as many as 54% of cryptocurrency exchanges had security gaps that made them easy targets.[4]

Like ransomware attackers, exchange hackers also benefited
from ready access to an increasingly complex money laundering
ecosystem that enabled them to move the large stashes of cryptocurrencies they acquired. In addition to the familiar techniques
of cashing out through non-compliant exchanges, washing funds
through mixers and coinswap services, or laundering funds through
the dark web, hackers could look to other methods to dispose of
their large stashes of crypto. Stolen credit cards, debit cards, and
pre-paid cards are widely available on both the dark web and the
surface web – with some sites doing a massive business in selling stolen card details for bitcoins. Hackers used these sites to buy
stolen card details with the cryptocurrencies they acquired from
thefts, and could then use the stolen cards for purchasing goods
and services. Hackers could also purchase stolen personal identifying information on the dark web that enabled them to circumvent
AML/CFT controls at regulated exchanges, where they could cash
out the funds they had stolen from other exchanges. Some dark
web sites feature packages of stolen or forged identity information
that include photo IDs, such as driving licenses or passports, that
a money launderer can use to create an account at a cryptocurrency exchange.[5] These kits can even include selfies or short videos
of the individual whose identity has been exploited, allowing the
criminal to circumvent compliance controls at exchanges if asked
to provide more information than a simple image of a photo ID.
With these kits, hackers could deploy teams of money mules, or
surrogates recruited to open accounts and launder funds on their
behalf – equipping hackers with the support networks required to
launder billions of dollars from heists.

North Korea's Crypto Billions

As exchange hacks intensified, so did efforts to unmask their perpe-trators. Russian cybercriminals were identified as behind some early hacks, including the Bitcoin7 hack in 2011. In September 2020, the US Treasury's Office of Foreign Assets Control (OFAC) imposed an asset freeze on Danil Potekhin and Dimitrii Karasavidi, two Russian nationals it accused of launching phishing attacks on customers of cryptocurrency exchanges in 2017 and 2018 that resulted in the theft of at least $16.5 million in customer funds.[6] As investigators dug into other major thefts, they found evidence that some pointed back to a familiar foe: North Korea's Lazarus Group.

It turned out that after the WannaCry attack, the Lazarus Group had been busy finding other sources of crypto income to circumvent sanctions, and to fund the activities of the North Korean regime, including, presumably, sustaining its nuclear weapons program. Shortly after the WannaCry attack, South Korean security analysts identified a campaign of crypto-jacking in which North Korean hackers targeted a South Korean company's servers to mine Mon-ero totaling $25,000.[7] Revelations about North Korea's efforts to hack exchanges were therefore hardly surprising – its motivations for obtaining crypto in order to evade banking restrictions were evi-dent, it possessed the sophisticated cybercrime apparatus needed to pull off large thefts, and it was familiar with the intricacies of the cryptocurrency ecosystem. Given the challenges of attribution in some cases, cybersecurity analysts did not always agree on the exact number of crypto thefts the Lazarus Group had perpetrated. But overwhelming consensus emerged that North Korea was behind some of the most significant hacks targeting exchanges in neigh-boring Asian countries, and particularly in South Korea.

North Korea's exchange hacking activity appears to have started in earnest in the spring of 2017. South Korean intelligence services later confirmed that the Lazarus Group was behind the suspected hack of bitcoins totaling approximately $5 million from the YouBit exchange on April 22 of that year. Before the end of 2017, North Korea managed to undertake at least three more successful hacks of

South Korean cryptocurrency exchanges, including stealing a further undisclosed amount from YouBit in December. South Korea's national police agency also revealed that between May and August 2017, North Korean cybercriminals sent phishing emails to 25 employees at four different crypto exchanges, in what fortunately turned out to be unsuccessful attempts at further hacks.[8]

These cases indicated that South Korea's cryptocurrency exchange industry was under full-scale attack from the Lazarus Group. As more information about North Korea's exchange hacking came to light, it also became apparent that North Korea had developed highly sophisticated techniques for laundering the cryptocurrencies it stole. Desperate for hard cash, North Korea needed a way to convert the cryptocurrencies it obtained into fiat currencies that it could in turn launder through the banking system, from which sanctions largely excluded it. This required the Lazarus Group to come up with intricate methods of crypto laundering. One case that illustrated North Korea's crypto laundering capabilities occurred in the summer of 2018, after the first wave of attacks on South Korean exchanges, this time involving a South Korean exchange called Bithumb.

On June 20 of that year, Bithumb announced on Twitter that its hot wallet had been compromised, resulting in the theft of approximately $30 million worth of cryptocurrencies, and leading the exchange to temporarily halt deposits and withdrawals.[9] Several days later, Bithumb indicated that the hack had included the theft of at least 11 different cryptocurrencies, though most of the funds stolen were bitcoins. An investigation conducted by Elliptic illuminated the flow of these bitcoins after the theft. Across June 19 (when the original breach appears to have occurred) and June 20, the hackers undertook 400 separate transactions to move more than 1,900 bitcoins valued at approximately $13 million from Bithumb's hot wallet to an external wallet the hackers controlled. The funds remained in this wallet for approximately one month, when they began to move again. The hackers then conducted a series of 68 separate transfers, sending the funds through numerous Bitcoin addresses in a money laundering technique known as a "peeling chain."[10]

To understand peeling chains, recall Satoshi Nakamoto's advice that users could protect their privacy by sending funds to unused Bitcoin addresses for each new transaction. A peeling chain involves transferring funds through multiple, previously unused Bitcoin addresses to create the impression that the funds sent through each unused address are unconnected to the original wallet that received the illicit funds (see Figure 7.1). The "peeling" component of this technique refers to the method of taking a portion of the funds from the original wallet, depositing a smaller amount in a new address, using the remaining balance in the original wallet to make a transfer to yet another address, and repeating this cycle continuously until all the funds have been drawn down through different, previously unused addresses. A peeling chain offers a method of "layering" funds in the money laundering process, similar to the method of depositing cash into dozens of seemingly unrelated bank accounts. Cybercriminals often rely on peeling chain techniques to send funds through dozens or even hundreds of separate addresses prior to cashing them out at a cryptocurrency exchange, where the funds can be converted into fiat currencies. The technique is aimed at undermining the ability to identify linked addresses, though sophisticated blockchain analysis can ultimately trace the funds back to their original common source.

In the case of the Bithumb hack, after undertaking this peeling chain process, the hackers then transferred the bitcoins to a

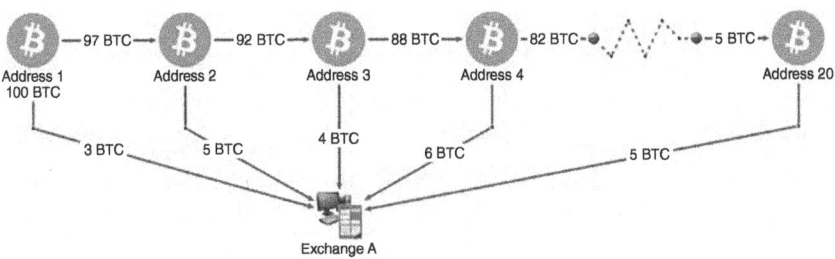

Figure 7.1 Example of a peeling chain process, as illustrated in the criminal complaint against Tian Yinyin and Li Jaidong.
SOURCE: US Department of Justice / Public Domain.

cryptocurrency exchange service called YoBit – a Russia-based cryptocurrency exchange that, unsurprisingly, allowed users to create anonymous accounts. While the use of a Russian exchange to launder the funds might have created the impression that Russian cybercriminals were behind the attack, within days of the attack cybersecurity researchers had linked the malware used in the hack to the Lazarus Group.[11] With a substantial portion of the funds sent to an unregulated exchange service outside South Korea, most of the bitcoins stolen from Bithumb were as good as gone.

Another case that demonstrated North Korea's ability to leverage sophisticated crypto laundering techniques came to light in March 2020. That month, the US Department of Justice (DOJ) unsealed a criminal indictment against Tian Yinyin and Li Jaidong, two Chinese nationals the US government alleges were hired by the Lazarus Group to launder funds from at least three exchange hacks. According to the US government's indictment against the pair, in the summer of 2018 the Lazarus Group managed to steal cryptocurrencies worth $234 million from an exchange in Asia by targeting an employee of the exchange with an email designed to appear as though it came from a potential client, but which in fact contained malware.[12] Once in control of the exchange's private keys, the Lazarus Group began withdrawing more than 10,000 bitcoins they had stolen.

From there, the attackers deposited the funds at four different cryptocurrency exchanges, at least one of which was based in South Korea. Tian Yinyin and Li Jaidong had registered accounts at the exchanges using fake IDs, and with an email address of a South Korean engineering company whose email account the Lazarus Group had hacked.[13] Information the US government obtained from the exchanges indicates that to open the accounts, the pair submitted fake ID documents that included heads that had clearly been photo-shopped onto the body of another individual, and used those images to create fraudulent accounts to convert the funds from the hack into fiat currencies. Consistent with the peeling chain technique, the Lazarus Group transferred the stolen funds through dozens of intermediary Bitcoin addresses before depositing the funds at the four exchanges where Tian Yinyin and Li Jaidong held accounts.

For example, between May and July 2018, approximately half of the stolen bitcoins were sent through 146 separate transactions in a peeling chain before being deposited at one of the exchanges.[14] After receiving the stolen bitcoins into the accounts at the four exchanges, Tian Yinyin and Li Jaidong then sent the funds onwards to additional exchanges, undertaking more peeling chains in a further attempt to obfuscate their origin. The US government's allegations suggest that the laundering process undertaken was highly sophisticated, noting that "the transactions that occurred in the peel chain were automated. That is, the North Korean co-conspirators had a computer script that rapidly laundered the [bitcoins] to and from addresses and exchanges. In fact, many of the transactions occurred during the same minute."[15]

The US government alleges that Tian Yinyin and Li Jaidong, who advertised cryptocurrency swapping services online under the usernames "snowjohn" and "khaleesi," respectively, converted approximately $100 million worth of the stolen funds for the Lazarus Group into fiat currencies, which they then laundered through the banking system – presumably to other accounts the Lazarus Group controlled, though the ultimate destination of the funds after they reached the banking system is unclear. After swapping the bitcoins for Chinese yuan at an exchange where he held an account, Tian Yinyin sent approximately $34 million worth of yuan to an account at China Guangfa Bank, while Li Jaidong sent approximately $32 million worth of yuan he had converted from stolen bitcoins through nine separate Chinese bank accounts. Tian Yinyin also used funds from one of his crypto exchange accounts to purchase approximately $1.4 million worth of Apple iTunes gift cards (which can be used to buy goods and services) with the proceeds of the crime, thereby breaking the funds' trail back to the original source. In addition to the hack that occurred in 2018, the US government alleges that Tian Yinyin and Li Jaidong assisted the Lazarus Group in laundering funds from at least two other hacks, which occurred in 2017 and 2019. At the same time that the DOJ announced its indictment of the pair, OFAC imposed sanctions on Tian Yinyin and Li Jaidong, freezing their assets. US Treasury Secretary Steve Mnuchin declared that the action demonstrated that the "United States will continue to protect the global financial system by holding accountable those who help North Korea engage in cyber-crime."[16]

With concerns mounting about the scale of the Lazarus Group's crypto heists, US agencies also drew attention to the increasing sophistication of North Korea's attempts to infiltrate exchanges. In a jointly issued guidance document in May 2022, the US Treasury, Department of State, and DOJ warned that IT workers from North Korea were increasingly attempting to gain employment at cryptocurrency exchanges in the United States and elsewhere by posing as IT workers from third countries. According to the agencies, North Korean IT workers were attempting to obtain jobs assisting with the development of cryptocurrency exchanges' websites, or other seemingly harmless activities. Once ensconced, the IT workers provided proxy access to North Korean hackers, such as those from the Lazarus Group, and would gain "access to virtual infrastructure, facilitate sales of data. . . or assist with [North Korea's] moneylaundering [sic] and virtual currency transfers."[17]

The growing evidence of North Korea's involvement in these lucrative exchange hacks grabbed the attention of another set of watchdogs at the United Nations Security Council (UNSC). Since the 1990s, the UNSC had imposed multiple rounds of sanctions on North Korea for its nuclear proliferation activities. To oversee the implementation of these sanctions, in 2006 the UNSC created a panel of experts known as the 1718 Sanctions Committee (named after the UNSC resolution number that established it), charged with monitoring whether countries are enforcing the sanctions on North Korea, and to investigate cases of sanctions evasion. In a report it issued in March 2022, the 1718 Committee acknowledged cyberattacks on crypto exchanges as "an important revenue source" for the North Korean government,[18] and in another report that September warned that these attacks were "becoming more sophisticated. . . The absence of global regulatory mechanisms governing cryptocurrencies exacerbates the issue."[19]

While the total value of funds derived from North Korea's hacking activity is difficult to pinpoint, based on known hacks that cybersecurity firms have attributed to the Lazarus Group with a high level of confidence, Elliptic estimates that North Korea has obtained cryptocurrencies totaling approximately $2 billion from cryptocurrency exchange hacks.[20] It remains unclear exactly how much of this money has been successfully laundered for the benefit of North Korea's regime through the banking system after being converted from cryptocurrencies. But even a relatively small success rate in laundering these funds back to North Korea could provide the heavily sanctioned country with tens or hundreds of millions of dollars' worth of much-needed cash, goods, and services. In April 2023, OFAC and the DOJ unveiled another case that revealed a network of crypto brokers based in mainland China and Hong Kong who helped North Korea to convert stolen crypto into US dollars, which they then used to buy tobacco products, electronic goods, and other items that North Korea struggles to access due to sanctions.[21]

The Blockchain Leads to Dutch and Razzlekhan

All the while, the 94,643.29 bitcoins from the Bitfinex theft continued to sit in the wallet where they'd been transferred in August 2016, their value rising massively as the price of Bitcoin spiked over the years, until that day in early February 2022 when the funds all moved.

Articles in the press speculated about the potential destination of the funds: Were the hackers finally attempting to launder their stash? And how would they do so? Would they attempt to move the billions' worth of bitcoins through mixers, exchanges, or other services? It turned out, however, that it wasn't the Bitfinex hackers behind the February 1 transfer of the massive Bitcoin stash after all. It was the US government.

On February 8, one week after the 94,643.29 bitcoins were transferred, the DOJ announced that it had arrested two individuals it accused of possessing the funds from the Bitfinex hack. US law enforcement agencies had arrested Ilya Lichtenstein and his wife Heather Morgan on charges of conspiracy to engage in money laundering and fraud, alleging that they "employed numerous sophisticated laundering techniques" in an attempt to hide the 25,000 bitcoins from the hack that they had withdrawn from the infamous wallet between 2017 and 2021.[22] By all accounts, Lichtenstein and Morgan were a flamboyant and eccentric pair – certainly among the oddest characters in the long list of those accused of crypto laundering. Lichtenstein, who also went by the nickname Dutch, was originally from Russia but had emigrated to the United States, where – in addition to working as an investor – he worked as a mentalist magician. Morgan, an American citizen who went by the nicknames Razzlekhan, Turkish Martha Stewart, and the Crocodile of Wall Street on her numerous social media accounts, was an aspiring rapper. A Bitcoin enthusiast, Morgan also worked as a freelance writer covering cryptocurrency topics for business and finance publications, at one point even penning a column for *Forbes* entitled "Experts Share Tips To Protect Your Business from Cybercriminals."[23] The couple had an extensive social media presence – including maintaining an Instagram account for their pet Bengal cat, Clarissa. In one post, Morgan filmed Lichtenstein as he ate Clarissa's cat food. Their social media profiles featured the couple flaunting a jet-setting and luxurious lifestyle that US prosecutors allege was the result, at least in part, of their crypto laundering activity.[24]

According to the federal criminal complaint lodged against them, the wallet that received the original 119,756 bitcoins directly from the Bitfinex hack was a private, unhosted wallet controlled by Lichtenstein, the keys to which he maintained in a cloud storage account, and where most of the stolen funds had sat until his arrest in February 2022. The United States alleges that beginning in January 2017 Lichtenstein, along with Morgan, managed to launder 25,000 bitcoins from the wallet, and in doing so employed a range of sophisticated – and familiar – techniques.

In early 2017, Lichtenstein undertook a series of peeling chain transactions using automated scripts – much like the Lazarus Group's methods – before sending the bitcoins to accounts he had established at the AlphaBay dark web marketplace. The law enforcement takedown of AlphaBay in 2017 would have enabled agents to obtain the market's account and user logs, allowing them to identify payments from the Bitfinex hack that flowed into accounts there, and subsequently to trace those same funds as they left the marketplace. According to the US government, "The AlphaBay accounts were used as a pass-through for the stolen [bitcoins]," before the funds were transferred onwards to various cryptocurrency exchanges with the aim of cashing them out.[25]

Lichtenstein and Morgan operated dozens of accounts at 10 crypto exchanges that US investigators had identified. Many of these accounts were opened using false IDs and under fictitious names, but investigators managed to link them to Lichtenstein and Morgan through analysis of IP and email addresses the couple used, and based on records Lichtenstein maintained on his computer that US investigators had seized during his arrest. At two of the exchanges, the couple maintained not only Bitcoin but also accounts in the privacy coin Monero, which federal prosecutors claim was part of an attempt to launder the funds from the hack using "chain-hopping" techniques by swapping the stolen Bitcoin for Monero. At another exchange, the couple converted bitcoins into Dash, another apparent attempt to engage in chain-hopping through a privacy coin.[26] The couple also cashed out a portion of the bitcoins from the Bitfinex hack at a Bitcoin ATM. Research by Elliptic indicated that other familiar crypto laundering techniques were used to hide the Bitfinex bitcoins, including sending some of the funds through Wasabi Wallet and other privacy-enhancing services after engaging in peeling chains.[27] A portion of the stolen bitcoins was also sent to the Hydra dark web market in January 2021, potentially an attempt to make use of money laundering services there, such as the "hidden treasure" scheme, after AlphaBay was shut down.[28]

The Bitfinex hack case featured nearly every scheme in the crypto laundering playbook – and ultimately, it was this extensive trail on the blockchain that investigators followed. As so often happens, it was a series of careless mistakes that created the final clues law enforcement needed to make an arrest. According to the US government's criminal complaint, Lichtenstein sent funds between his various exchange accounts, engaging in peeling chains as he swapped funds from one exchange to the next. At one of the exchanges he used for undertaking the transfers, he had made an error: he used his personal California driver's license to register the account, offering up his own identity. He then used the funds in that exchange account to purchase gold bars, which he had shipped to his home in New York City where he lived with Morgan. The couple also erred when they purchased more than a dozen Walmart gift cards using the funds in another of their crypto exchange accounts and registered the cards in Morgan's name and to their home address. This series of transactions led law enforcement agents to the couple's Manhattan apartment.[29] At the time of their arrest, Lichtenstein and Morgan possessed $40,000 in cash, as well as fake IDs and SIM cards that had been purchased from the dark web.[30]

Because Lichtenstein had left most of the funds stolen from the Bitfinex hack sitting in the original wallet whose keys were accessible online, at the time of the couple's arrest federal agents managed to seize the remaining 94,643.29 bitcoins in the wallet, totaling more than $3.5 billion – providing the US government with its largest ever financial seizure. It was the transfer of those funds to the US government's own wallet on February 1 that the whole world had seen on the blockchain.

The case was a triumph for US law enforcement agents, who had succeeded in using blockchain analytics to trace the complex flow of funds from the hack, and who also relied on information from regulated cryptocurrency exchanges to assist in identifying the perpetrators. At the time of their arrest, US Deputy Attorney General Lisa Monaco said: "In a futile effort to maintain digital anonymity, the defendants laundered stolen funds through a labyrinth of cryptocurrency transactions. Thanks to the meticulous work of law enforcement, the department once again showed how it can and will follow the money, no matter what form it takes."[31]

But for more than a year after Lichtenstein and Morgan were arrested, one mystery remained: Who hacked Bitfinex? Lichtenstein and Morgan were only charged with laundering the funds from the hack – not with the cyber theft itself. Speculation abounded that the couple may have been acting on behalf of more sophisticated Russian cybercriminals who carried out the attack and hired Lichtenstein and Morgan to launder the funds, while others speculated that the couple were likely acting on their own. Although the US government had apprehended those it accused of one of the most intricate cases of cryptocurrency laundering yet, it remained unclear whether others who may have undertaken the Bitfinex hack were still free.

On August 3, 2023, the answer to this mystery was revealed. In a plea hearing held at a federal court in Washington, DC, Lichtenstein admitted that he was the hacker who stole the funds from Bitfinex. According to the DOJ, Lichtenstein "used a number of advanced hacking tools and techniques to gain access to Bitfinex's network," enabling him to undertake more than 2,000 separate withdrawals of bitcoins from the exchange.[32] He then covered up his tracks by deleting access logs and user credentials in Bitfinex's systems that might have revealed his identity.

According to Morgan, who entered a guilty plea to money laundering and fraud charges on the same day, it was only in 2020, more than three years after the hack, that Lichtenstein told her he had hacked Bitfinex and needed her help to launder the stolen bitcoins. The couple admitted that Morgan joined Lichtenstein in trips to Ukraine and Kazakhstan, where he met with money mules who converted a portion of the stolen bitcoins into cash that Lichtenstein and Morgan deposited into their US bank accounts. Morgan also admitted to burying in the ground in California some of the gold coins Lichtenstein had purchased with the stolen funds.[33] Before their arrest, Lichtenstein and Morgan had devised a plan to relocate eventually to Russia, but the blockchain led US law enforcement to the couple before they could manage to get away.

As this book went to production, Lichtenstein and Morgan were still awaiting sentencing.

* * *

The wave of major cryptocurrency exchange hacks combined highly lucrative cybercrime with sophisticated crypto laundering.

Ultimately, funds from hacks – like those from other forms of crypto-enabled crime – could be traced and seized, as the Bitfinex case showed, ensuring that criminals could not benefit from the full spoils of cyber heists.

But the overall scale of thefts suggested that even with successful law enforcement actions taking place, hackers such as the Lazarus Group had still reaped substantial profits. Exact figures vary, but analysis of blockchain data suggests that the total value of cryptocurrencies stolen from all exchange thefts to date could be as high as $13 to $15 billion.[34] Even though law enforcement agencies scored major victories along the way and retrieved several billion dollars in funds, that still left billions more unaccounted for.

With time, centralized cryptocurrency exchanges would become less vulnerable to hacks. Between 2019 and 2020, the total number of hacks targeting crypto exchanges decreased for the first time, the result of improved cybersecurity measures at exchanges, which began heeding the lessons of earlier attacks.

Inevitably, as the public and private sectors established defenses against exchange hacking, criminals looked to new frontiers to boost their profits. The next frontier of crypto crime was one that illustrated more vividly than ever before how new and rapidly evolving iterations of cryptocurrencies could force governments to adapt continuously. And the first hints of that new frontier were gleaned in a case involving, perhaps unsurprisingly, North Korea.

Chapter 8
DeFi: Tornadoes, Bridges, and the Frontiers of Regulation

In September 2020, the Lazarus Group hacked yet another exchange – the KuCoin exchange in Singapore. On September 25, KuCoin announced that the theft had resulted in the loss of approximately $280 million worth of cryptocurrencies – and the UN Security Council later acknowledged that North Korea was the suspected culprit.[1]

A small portion of the stolen funds, approximately $8 million worth, was in bitcoins. The North Korean hackers laundered these stolen bitcoins using a popular mixing service known as ChipMixer, which had emerged as the preferred service for illicit users after the demise of the Helix and Bitcoin Fog services, as well as with Wasabi Wallet – by then - familiar obfuscation techniques to blockchain investigators.

But most of the funds stolen in the KuCoin hack, approximately $152 million worth, were not in bitcoins, but tokens based on the Ethereum blockchain. The Lazarus Group had stolen ether – the native token of the Ethereum network – as well as Tether, Chainlink,

Ocean Protocol, and other Ethereum-based tokens. And the trail of transactions on the blockchain showed that the funds did not follow the same path as in cases of Bitcoin laundering. Most of the funds from the KuCoin hack that the Lazarus Group laundered were instead sent through the ecosystem of decentralized finance (DeFi), an evolution of crypto and blockchain technology that threatened to up-end the regulatory approach to cryptocurrencies that had been crafted until then, and that demonstrated the ability of illicit actors to evolve sophisticated new approaches to crypto laundering.

The Birth of Ethereum

Next to the creation of Bitcoin, arguably the most important development in the history of cryptocurrencies was the launch of Ethereum. The idea for Ethereum was conceived across 2013 and formally set out in a White Paper the following year by Vladimir Buterin, who was born in Russia in 1994 but emigrated to Canada with his parents when he was six years old. A math and computer science whiz-kid, Buterin learned of Bitcoin as a teenager and quickly became obsessed with cryptocurrencies, co-founding and writing for *Bitcoin Magazine*, which became a popular trade publication. In his spare time, Buterin was dreaming up a complete reimagining of the cryptocurrency ecosystem, ultimately resulting in the birth of Ethereum, which he described as a "Next-Generation Smart Contract and Decentralized Application Platform" when he formally articulated his ideas in the Ethereum White Paper.[2]

With Ethereum, Buterin sought not to overtake Bitcoin or make it irrelevant; rather, he sought to advance what he saw as the next natural step in the evolution of cryptocurrencies. Bitcoin, Buterin acknowledged, offered the first successful, fully decentralized, peer-to-peer form of digital cash. This was revolutionary, but it was also of limited utility: Bitcoin demonstrated that decentralized digital cash was possible, but its blockchain did not provide ready support for a wide range of practical applications, with the result that its primary, and nearly only, use was in speculative trading. This was the result, in part, of the programming script that Nakamoto had devised, which meant that Bitcoin could not support a wide range of "blockchain-native" applications – or automated services directly coded into the blockchain – and instead required third-party services sitting apart from its blockchain to enable any practical usability. Consequently, despite Nakamoto's stated aim to reduce intermediation in finance, the Bitcoin ecosystem remained heavily populated with centralized intermediaries – particularly cryptocurrency exchanges, which functioned like traditional financial institutions by taking custody of customer funds and actively managing user accounts.

In the Ethereum White Paper, Buterin envisioned an entirely new type of ecosystem that leveraged the core innovation of Bitcoin – decentralized, peer-to-peer payments – but that would enable a wide variety of decentralized applications (Dapps) where traditional intermediaries were absent. As Buterin described it in the Ethereum White Paper, he sought to explore how "the blockchain concept can be used for more than just money."[3] For Buterin, this meant a world where users could participate in a wide range of commercial, economic, and social activities beyond just payments – from asset exchange to lending to trading derivatives to managing ownership of real-world assets to purchasing insurance to online gaming to running entire organizations, and even to cultivating one's digital identity – in ways that were truly decentralized, and, therefore, genuinely free.

Buterin's solution was to create a new blockchain – Ethereum – that was "Turing-complete," that is, which used a programming language that allowed it to implement, theoretically, any conceivable function. By weaving a Turing-complete script into the design of the Ethereum blockchain, Buterin intended for it to be more dynamic than Bitcoin. Automated apps and services could be coded directly into the Ethereum blockchain, a feat achieved by deploying protocols known as "smart contracts." Smart contracts are automated scripts that set out conditions of interaction, which, as Buterin described them, allow anyone to "create their own arbitrary rules for ownership, transaction formats and state transition functions."[4] In short, Buterin's blockchain would allow anyone to create a Dapp and define parameters governing nearly any form of financial or social interaction, executed in a decentralized fashion, eliminating the need for middlemen, with cryptocurrencies functioning as the medium of exchange. What ultimately emerged was a complex ecosystem of Dapps that enabled users to access a broad array of financial services – an ecosystem that took on the name DeFi.

To understand this more clearly, it helps to consider a concept Buterin explored in the White Paper, that of decentralized autonomous organizations (DAOs). Before Ethereum, if you wanted to establish a corporate entity or other organization – such as a charity or association – you needed to formally organize it under the corporate registration laws of a particular jurisdiction, register it at a physical address, and (to capitalize it) establish accounts at a bank, where the entity's money could be managed. Shareholding details had to be recorded in corporate filings, and any purchases and sales of shares were typically executed through a broker – yet another intermediary. With DAOs, Buterin imagined a world where diffuse sets of individuals around the world could engage and collaborate in common enterprises, but without the involvement of all those middlemen.

Much like a traditional corporation, a DAO would enable participants to vote on activities and have a stake in the future of an underlying enterprise, but its method of delivery and execution would be entirely different. The rules and activities of a DAO would be encoded in a smart contract – automating the activities of the enterprise, whatever its underlying economic or social function. Ownership in a DAO would be allocated in cryptocurrencies – with holders obtaining a voting share equal to the size of their token holdings, and able to vote on changes to the underlying code governing a DAO's smart contract. Brokers, banks, stock exchanges – none of these intermediaries would be required. A DAO could simply function as a self-executing enterprise, with the ownership stake held by individuals trading peer-to-peer cryptocurrencies, participating in the governance of the DAO from anywhere in the world, so long as they had access to an Internet connection. A DAO could underpin, theoretically, any type of enterprise, cause, or activity that a group of individuals sought to undertake in the real world, but with democratized and fully open ownership.

Having articulated these ideas, on July 30, 2015, Buterin and his partners with whom he formed the non-profit Ethereum Foundation launched the Ethereum blockchain.

The Rise of DeFi Laundering

Soon, Ethereum began hosting decentralized applications using smart contracts that would reshape the entire cryptocurrency space. As these innovations emerged, several had particularly significant impacts on the future of crypto laundering. First among these were decentralized exchanges (DEXs).

As their name suggests, DEXs contrast with the centralized exchange model that predominated for much of the early history of cryptocurrencies by allowing users to swap cryptocurrencies in a fully disintermediated, peer-to-peer fashion. Unlike centralized exchanges, DEXs do not actively match users' trades or take custody of funds; rather, DEX smart contracts enable automated market making (AMM), which involves users depositing funds into "liquidity pools" – or collections of token pairs that counterparties can trade peer-to-peer, with prices set based on the ratio of tokens in the pool. Because the smart contract protocols powering DEXs are open source, anyone can access a DEX and trade tokens in a liquidity pool by transacting on the blockchain, obviating the need for large, centralized exchanges in the ecosystem – though for convenience many users tend to interact with DEXs through dedicated, front-end interfaces that are typically managed by the developer teams and sponsoring foundations who launch DEXs.

Changes to the code of a DEX's smart contracts require consent from members of a DAO associated with the DEX, who have their say in the governance around the ongoing development of the underlying protocol and related activities of its community of users.

Fiat currencies cannot be traded on DEXs, and Bitcoin also cannot be traded directly on Ethereum-based DEXs – but DEXs nonetheless function as a critical way for users of the DeFi space to swap thousands of cryptocurrencies directly for one another. Additionally, because DEXs run using self-executing smart contracts that automate swaps, users can access DEXs without having to undergo due diligence checks, such as providing their names or identifying documents, as a regulated centralized exchange service would require. This has obvious benefits from the vantage point of a money launderer, since traders in liquidity pools remain pseudonymous to their counterparties, and to members of any associated DAO.

The largest DEX on Ethereum by a substantial margin for much of the relatively young history of DEXs was Uniswap, established in 2018 by an engineer in the United States named Hayden Adams. Uniswap allows users to access more than 1,500 trading pairs across different cryptocurrencies. Changes to its protocol are voted on by participants from its community of governance token holders and implemented by developers from the community. Uniswap Labs, a corporate entity registered in Delaware, promotes the activities and growth of the ecosystem and manages the operation of a web domain through which users can access the underlying protocol. Other popular DEXs that have emerged alongside Uniswap include Curve, dYdX, Balancer, Pancake Swap, DODO, and Sushiswap.

A second and closely related innovation that influenced money laundering in DeFi relates to Ethereum's ability to facilitate the creation of new tokens. When Buterin launched Ethereum, he included in its design a native cryptocurrency known as ether, so that when developers launched new Dapps on Ethereum they would have a ready-made coin they could integrate into their projects. Shortly after Ethereum's launch, however, a member of the Ethereum community put forward a proposal for a standard that could be integrated into the network, known as the ERC-20 standard. ERC-20 is a protocol that defines a common approach for creating a new token and implementing it within an Ethereum smart contract. This ensures that as new tokens are created, they can operate in the Ethereum ecosystem and that transactions in the new tokens are recorded correctly on the

Ethereum blockchain. The introduction of this standard drastically reduced the time and effort needed to create and launch new tokens: if a developer had an idea for a new cryptocurrency they wished to create, rather than developing an entirely new blockchain, they could simply launch a new token on Ethereum.

Using the ERC-20 standard, when a developer creates a new app, such as a DEX, they can issue a dedicated token for use within that app. In the case of the Uniswap DEX, for example, there is a token (UNI) that is issued to participants in the community DAO representing their governance stake for voting on new initiatives and changes to the protocol. The UNI token can then be swapped on DEXs for ether or other tokens, which the holder can then use within different apps across the Ethereum ecosystem.

This innovation revolutionized the cryptocurrency space, resulting in the launch of thousands of new tokens from 2016 onwards – one consequence of which was the ICO boom and bust of 2017. The ERC-20 standard was also pivotal to the growth of a class of cryptocurrencies known as stablecoins – or cryptocurrencies that seek to eliminate price volatility by maintaining a peg to a fiat currency such as the US dollar, or to other assets. The wild speculative price swings that had predominated in cryptocurrency markets had always been an impediment to their use in broader financial applications: it was simply impractical to use a cryptocurrency like Bitcoin in day-to-day payments with its price constantly, and often dramatically, fluctuating. Stablecoins offered a potential solution and raised the prospect that cryptocurrencies could feature in more practical applications. Among popular stablecoins, USDC – a stablecoin created by Circle, an American cryptocurrency payments business – was originally issued as an ERC-20 token. By early 2022, stablecoin markets had a total value of approximately $185 billion, and roughly three-quarters of all stablecoins created globally were issued on the Ethereum network, including an ERC-20 version of Tether, the largest of the stablecoins, which was originally issued on its own separate blockchain.[5]

The rise in the number of tokens traded across the Ethereum ecosystem helped to facilitate the rapid increase in volumes of

trading on DEXs. The creation of stablecoins in particular enabled users to move funds in and out of DEXs more swiftly, greatly
bolstering DEXs' liquidity. Trading on DEXs was relatively small
across the period from 2017 to 2019, but grew substantially during
2020. By mid-2021, DEXs were facilitating more than $160 billion
in trades monthly. At their height, the Uniswap and Curve DEXs
accounted for as much as $2 billion in daily trading volume, and in
May 2022, Uniswap reached the milestone of having facilitated $1
trillion in total trades in less than four years – rivaling major centralized exchanges such as Coinbase and Bitfinex. This rapid growth in
turn had a significant impact from a money laundering perspective: an ecosystem of highly liquid DEXs that require no identifying information of users, where trades are fully automated with no
intermediary brokers, and where thousands of tokens can be traded
seamlessly and rapidly, created new opportunities for criminals to
engage in chain-hopping typologies of money laundering, swapping tokens to try and obfuscate their activity.

A third feature of the Ethereum ecosystem impacting money
laundering relates to transparency. Like Bitcoin, transactions on
the Ethereum blockchain are highly traceable, and feature limited
privacy – users are pseudonymous, rather than anonymous, and
similar techniques that blockchain analytics companies employ to
identify the users of Bitcoin addresses can be used for unmasking
Ethereum users. Indeed, transactions in Ethereum are often even
more transparent than in Bitcoin, owing to the open nature of smart
contracts. Because all trades executed via DEXs and other Dapps
are recorded on the Ethereum blockchain, every individual token
swap made through a smart contract is broadcast for all to see. This
extreme traceability created a demand for privacy-enhancing services like mixers on the Ethereum blockchain. But unlike in Bitcoin,
where numerous mixing services had co-existed, in the Ethereum
network one mixer dominated the landscape.

On December 17, 2019, a trio of Russian-born developers –
Roman Semenov, Alexey Pertsev, and Roman Storm – launched
Tornado Cash, a mixing service created, in their words, to enable
"non-custodial private transactions on Ethereum."[6] Like other

applications on Ethereum, Tornado Cash uses smart contracts, with changes to its protocol requiring approval from members of a DAO, the Tornado DAO, whose members own a stake in the project through their holdings of an ERC-20 token known as TORN. Tornado Cash employs anonymizing techniques such as zero-knowledge proofs, and it achieves the same outcome as Bitcoin mixers, enabling the obfuscation of a user's source of funds. But because it operates on Ethereum, Tornado Cash is decentralized. It does not take custody of user funds, as in the manner of Bitcoin mixers such as Helix, but rather allows users to send their ether into Tornado Cash pools via smart contracts, where the funds are broken into smaller denominations and co-mingled with those of other users, with the user retaining ownership of their tokens throughout the entire mixing process. Additionally, because Tornado Cash is essentially just the smart contracts that define it encoded on the Ethereum blockchain, it can continue operating indefinitely – described by the members of its community as an "unstoppable privacy protocol."[7] As long as the Ethereum blockchain continues to function, Tornado Cash can mix users' tokens, offering a perpetual, permanent mixing option for anyone seeking private transactions on Ethereum.

In the case of the September 2020 KuCoin hack perpetrated by North Korea, all three of these innovations of the Ethereum ecosystem – DEXs, ERC-20 tokens, and Tornado Cash – factored into the money laundering process.

After obtaining approximately $152 million in Ether and ERC-20 tokens from the hack, the Lazarus Group needed a way to convert the funds. They sent a portion of the stolen ether into the Tornado Cash mixer, after which the trail went dark. Tornado Cash, however, counted for only a small portion of the funds laundered from the KuCoin hack. Rather, the Lazarus Group sent most of the ERC-20 tokens stolen in the hack to DEXs.

In addition to offering the ability to swap funds free of identity checks, DEXs were useful for the Lazarus Group for another reason. One feature of many ERC-20 tokens is that their creators can design them to be freezable; that is, creators of those tokens can freeze the Ethereum accounts that hold ERC-20 tokens suspected of being used in illicit activity if required by law enforcement agencies, or if they have another compelling reason to do so. Other cryptocurrencies, such as Bitcoin and ether, are censorship-resistant, and their protocols do not allow transactions to be forcibly changed or for funds to be frozen in specific wallets. This meant the Lazarus Group, once in possession of freezable ERC-20 tokens from the hack, needed to swap them for other non-freezable coins, such as ether, to avoid having the funds seized. And that is precisely what they did. The Lazarus Group hackers sent ERC-20 tokens to several DEXs – including Uniswap and Curve – where they swapped the stolen funds for ether, which they could in turn transfer onward to centralized exchanges for conversion into fiat currencies. This required a relatively sophisticated understanding of the DeFi ecosystem on the part of the Lazarus Group.

This may have seemed a foolproof way to launder funds, but as usual in the world of crypto, the truth proved more complex. After the hack, KuCoin announced that it had managed to recover a substantial portion of the ERC-20 tokens before the hackers managed to launder them all.[8] Additionally, because the smart contracts underpinning the DEXs that the hackers used recorded every single swap on the blockchain, analytics firms were able to follow the funds trail *through* the DEXs where the Lazarus Group swapped their stolen coins, and onwards in their journey through the blockchain, allowing for a complete end-to-end view through the chain-hopping process. For example, when the hackers swapped an ERC-20 token, such as Chainlink, at a DEX for ether, blockchain analytics firms could establish a clear link between the wallets used to hold both the Chainlink tokens and ether, ensuring that the funds trail leading back to the hack was never fully broken. DeFi, it turned out, offered money launderers new avenues for swapping coins, but also afforded an enhanced level of traceability that law enforcement could leverage. In future cases, the Lazarus Group heeded this lesson, and leaned increasingly on Tornado Cash to mix its funds.

Nonetheless, DEXs featured increasingly in cases of money laundering – with a growing number of hackers, ransomware attackers, and other criminals using them to swap illicit-origin tokens. Between 2020 and 2022, according to research from Elliptic, more than $1.2 billion in criminal funds was laundered through DEXs, with approximately half of that figure through the Uniswap and Curve DEXs alone.[9]

Hacking DeFi

As criminals experimented with laundering funds through the DeFi ecosystem, they also began to exploit it for other purposes – particularly by hacking DeFi protocols to steal crypto. DeFi protocols are often described as containing a certain amount of "total value locked" (TVL) within them. That is, a certain amount of funds on the blockchain are allocated to the smart contracts associated with Dapps as users engage with them, whether depositing funds into a DEX liquidity pool, providing collateral for a DeFi lending protocol, or interacting with another Dapp. If flaws exist in the code of a smart contract, an attacker can exploit it, draining funds from the Ethereum accounts associated with the smart contracts. As usage of DEXs and other apps grew during the period from 2017 to 2022, the TVL in DeFi protocols grew substantially, reaching nearly $250 billion at one stage in late 2021.[10] It didn't take long for cybercriminals to recognize that they could rake in significant sums of cryptocurrencies by attacking DeFi protocols.

The first major DeFi hack occurred in June 2016 from the exploit of a DAO known simply as "The DAO," which acted as a pooled, democratized investment fund. An attacker – who has never been formally identified, but whom the journalist Laura Shin alleges is likely an Austrian programmer named Toby Hoenisch[11] – managed to exploit flaws in The DAO's smart contracts, resulting in the theft of $55 million worth of ether. In response, the Ethereum community decided to "fork" the Ethereum blockchain to reverse the hacker's transaction and return the funds to The DAO community. The result was a split into two blockchains – a new Ethereum blockchain, where the hacker's profits had been reversed, and the original blockchain, now known as Ethereum Classic, where the original tainted transactions remain.

As the number of Dapps on Ethereum grew, so did the number of attacks aiming to exploit them, with many of the most significant hacks targeting DeFi lending protocols. Lending Dapps allow cryptocurrency users to deposit funds into lending pools maintained via smart contracts. Other users can borrow those funds from the pool, putting up other cryptocurrencies as collateral, and with interest rates determined by the underlying smart contract based on the amount of funds within the pool. The promise of high yields and rapid settlement times ensured that DeFi loans became one of the most popular DeFi use cases. Consequently, the large TVL in lending protocols made them an attractive target for hackers. One such hack occurred in October 2021, when hackers stole $130 million from Cream Finance, a DeFi lending protocol, by exploiting a bug in its smart contracts.[12] Elliptic estimates that between 2020 and 2022, the total value of funds stolen from DeFi protocols was $5.1 billion, with more than $2.7 billion occurring during 2022 alone – amounting to an average of $7.6 million stolen from DeFi protocols every day that year.[13]

With lucrative attacks on DeFi protocols accelerating, it was only a matter of time before North Korea got in on the spoils. On March 29, 2022, staff at Sky Mavis, a Vietnamese company that created a video game app in 2018 called Axie Infinity, received emails from a job recruiter offering them new roles. One staff member at Sky Mavis responded to the inquiry from the supposed recruiter, and engaged in ongoing correspondence with them – eventually clicking on a PDF file that supposedly contained information about the proposed role. The file, it turned out, was infected with malware, and the job recruiters were in fact members of the Lazarus Group, who were now embedded in Sky Mavis's IT systems.[14]

Axie Infinity is a video game where users purchase and breed digital pets for battle against one another, with purchases made using cryptocurrencies. This gaming ecosystem was built atop the Ronin Network, a parallel blockchain to Ethereum known as a "sidechain." To enable users to bring tokens into this video game ecosystem, the developers at Sky Mavis had created a Dapp known as the Ronin Bridge. In the DeFi space, bridges are smart contract–based mechanisms that allow users to move funds seamlessly from one blockchain to the next. While the advent of DEXs enabled users to swap tokens within the Ethereum ecosystem, users of Dapps still had to go to centralized exchanges if they wished to swap ether or ERC-20 tokens for other cryptocurrencies, such as Bitcoin, that reside on entirely different blockchains. DeFi bridges surmounted the need to swap coins at centralized exchanges, allowing users instead to move funds directly from one blockchain to the next. The Ronin Bridge allowed users of ether and ERC-20 tokens to transfer their funds directly into the Axie Infinity gaming ecosystem from the main Ethereum blockchain. Because Axie Infinity players were constantly moving funds across the Ronin Bridge, substantial values of tokens were locked into the bridge's smart contracts – and that is precisely what the Lazarus Group was after. By obtaining access to Sky Mavis's IT systems, the Lazarus Group got hold of the keys controlling a majority of the validator nodes for the Ronin Bridge – effectively, the credentials for controlling the bridge's smart contracts – and drained funds from it.[15]

The haul for the Lazarus Group was massive: they managed to steal cryptocurrencies worth approximately $625 million from the Ronin Bridge, with most of the stolen funds comprised of ether and the USDC stablecoin. Of course, once in possession of this huge haul, they needed a way to launder the stolen funds, and they turned to some familiar tricks to do so.

As in the case of the KuCoin hack, the Lazarus Group needed to convert the stolen USDC stablecoins so that transactions could not be reversed. They did this by swapping the USDC for ether at DEXs, including through Uniswap. The hackers then sent more than $450 million worth of the stolen funds through the Tornado Cash mixer to obfuscate the funds trail. But moving a massive stash of funds through Tornado Cash created a problem. Mixing, recall, is most effective where moderate amounts of funds are sent into large pools of other coins, enabling the owner of any tainted funds to hide their coins among those of other users. But where tainted coins make up most of the funds sent into a mixer, they can no longer be hidden effectively, and it becomes much easier to establish the identity of the party who contributed the large set of coins to the pool. Because the Lazarus Group had sent such a large volume of funds into Tornado Cash all at once, observers using blockchain analytics managed to identify where the funds came out on the other end – essentially "de-mixing" the transactions.

Consequently, when the Lazarus Group sent some of the stolen funds to cryptocurrency exchanges after passing them through Tornado Cash, US law enforcement agencies managed to work with compliance staff at those exchanges to seize approximately $30 million worth of the stolen ether.[16]

DeFi offered yet another attack vector for cybercriminals, but the transparency of the blockchain remained one of governments' best assets for preventing hackers from realizing the full benefit of their crimes.

The Regulators Come for DeFi

The rise in cyberattacks and money laundering in the DeFi space led the usual suspects among watchdogs and regulators to respond. With the ink barely dry on its 2019 guidance, the FATF took up the question of how to apply its global AML/CFT standards to the DeFi space. Like the debate at the FATF over unhosted wallets, the debate over DeFi raised fundamental questions about the applicability of regulation to crypto-related technology. The FATF's Standards, recall, were designed for a world of centralized intermediaries – banks, securities brokers, money transfer businesses, and even centralized crypto exchanges – but were not created with a world of decentralized virtual transactions in mind when set out in 1990. The FATF's previous guidance – as well as guidance in May 2019 from FinCEN – had also stressed that a key benchmark for whether a cryptocurrency service should be subject to regulation was whether it took custody of user funds. Because DeFi protocols do not take custody of user funds and instead enable users to retain control of their own funds throughout the entire trading process, some observers assumed that innovations such as DEXs and DeFi lending protocols might sit entirely outside the regulatory framework. An important question therefore emerged: Was it possible to apply AML/CFT regulation to the DeFi ecosystem at all? Could developers create DEXs, DeFi lending protocols, and other Dapps, with no requirements to identify users, or comply with other AML/CFT measures? Would this new ecosystem be one where North Korean hackers would have unfettered access with no barriers to entry?

From the perspective of AML/CFT watchdogs, the prospect of a DeFi ecosystem completely impervious to regulation was simply unacceptable. A parallel universe could not be allowed to emerge where North Korean cybercriminals engaged in theft and money laundering unhindered. The question, from the FATF's perspective, was not "should DeFi be regulated?," but how to regulate it.

After a period of considerable debate, in October 2021 the FATF updated its guidance on virtual assets to provide an answer. According to the FATF, the term "DeFi" was really a misnomer. While some projects in the DeFi space could claim to be truly decentralized, many, according to the FATF, "often still have a central party with some measure of involvement or control."[17] While the protocols underlying Dapps enable peer-to-peer transactions, and their smart contracts are fully automated, the FATF pointed out that people were inevitably involved in the creation and ongoing maintenance of a Dapp – from those designing the protocol and creating and issuing any tokens used in it, to those running associated web interfaces that enable users to access the protocol. From the FATF's perspective, merely because something claimed to be "decentralized" did not exempt it from AML/CFT regulation if it allowed people to access a financial service. According to the FATF, regulators should identify the individuals who exercise control and influence over a Dapp – for example, members of a DAO who also help to maintain an associated user interface and benefit from its operations – and subject them to AML/CFT regulation. In short, the FATF's message was that someone, somewhere, must be held accountable for the activities being undertaken in DeFi.

If that sounds oversimplified, that's because, in many respects, it was. One major problem for regulators that would persist is that in many cases it could be difficult, if not entirely impractical, to identify where people associated with a DeFi project or DAO resided – which made establishing regulatory jurisdiction over a Dapp problematic. Another challenge related to how to establish liability. Could token holders involved in the governance arrangements of a DAO really be said to have a meaningful influence over its activities in a way that would convince a court that they should be responsible for open-source smart contracts being abused by the likes of North Korea? DeFi would remain a gray area of significant regulatory uncertainty, often raising more questions than it offered answers.

As these policy debates unfolded, US authorities grew increasingly concerned about North Korea's ability to exploit an ecosystem where there was still so much regulatory flux. The US Treasury decided to wield one of the bluntest instruments available to it: the Office of Foreign Assets Control (OFAC)'s sanctions powers.

On April 14, 2022, OFAC added to its SDN List an Ethereum address that the Lazarus Group had used to launder a portion of the funds from the Axie Infinity hack. On April 22, OFAC added three more of the Lazarus Group's Ethereum addresses to the SDN List (see Figure 8.1). In doing so, the US Treasury not only prohibited cryptocurrency exchanges and others from handling funds from those addresses – but by blacklisting them within weeks of the Ronin Bridge hack, the Treasury sent a message that it was actively watching North Korea's crypto laundering activity, and was determined to curtail it.

A few months later, OFAC took another action with far-reaching repercussions, one that revived the heated debate over privacy. On August 8, 2022, OFAC announced that it had sanctioned the Tornado Cash mixer, which OFAC declared had been "used to launder more than $7 billion worth of virtual currency since its creation in 2019," including at least $455 million worth of funds that had been stolen by the Lazarus Group – a finding that OFAC claimed allowed it to target Tornado Cash using its authorities for countering cybercrime.[18] The sanctions meant that US citizens and companies – including cryptocurrency exchanges – could not

LAZARUS GROUP (a.k.a. "APPLEWORM"; a.k.a. "APT-C-26"; a.k.a. "GROUP 77"; a.k.a. "GUARDIANS OF PEACE"; a.k.a. "HIDDEN COBRA"; a.k.a. "OFFICE 91"; a.k.a. "RED DOT"; a.k.a. "TEMP.HERMIT"; a.k.a. "THE NEW ROMANTIC CYBER ARMY TEAM"; a.k.a. "WHOIS HACKING TEAM"; a.k.a. "ZINC"), Potonggang District, Pyongyang, Korea, North; Digital Currency Address - ETH 0x098B716B8Aaf21512996dC57EB0615e2383E2f96; Secondary sanctions risk: North Korea Sanctions Regulations, sections 510.201 and 510.210; Transactions Prohibited For Persons Owned or Controlled By U.S. Financial Institutions: North Korea Sanctions Regulations section 510.214 [DPRK3]. -to- LAZARUS GROUP (a.k.a. "APPLEWORM"; a.k.a. "APT-C-26"; a.k.a. "GROUP 77"; a.k.a. "GUARDIANS OF PEACE"; a.k.a. "HIDDEN COBRA"; a.k.a. "OFFICE 91"; a.k.a. "RED DOT"; a.k.a. "TEMP.HERMIT"; a.k.a. "THE NEW ROMANTIC CYBER ARMY TEAM"; a.k.a. "WHOIS HACKING TEAM"; a.k.a. "ZINC"), Potonggang District, Pyongyang, Korea, North; Digital Currency Address - ETH 0x098B716B8Aaf21512996dC57EB0615e2383E2f96; alt. Digital Currency Address - ETH 0xa0e1c89Ef1a489c9C7dE96311eD5Ce5D32c20E4B; alt. Digital Currency Address - ETH 0x3Cffd56B47B7b41c56258D9C7731ABaDc360E073; alt. Digital Currency Address - ETH 0x53b6936513e738f44FB50d2b9476730C0Ab3Bfc1; Secondary sanctions risk: North Korea Sanctions Regulations, sections 510.201 and 510.210; Transactions Prohibited For Persons Owned or Controlled By U.S. Financial Institutions: North Korea Sanctions Regulations section 510.214 [DPRK3].

Figure 8.1 The Lazarus Group's entry on the OFAC SDN List, showing the group's Ethereum addresses.
SOURCE: US Department of the Treasury / Public Domain.

process transactions with Tornado Cash, criminalizing use of the mixer. At the time of the action, Brian Nelson, the Treasury's Under Secretary for Terrorism and Financial Intelligence, stated: "Treasury will continue to aggressively pursue actions against mixers that launder virtual currency for criminals and those who assist them."[19]

The evidence indicating that the Lazarus Group and other criminals had used Tornado Cash was overwhelming, and the US government seemed to have struck a major blow to the prolific mixer. Within weeks of the OFAC sanctions, the volume of transactions being sent through Tornado Cash declined substantially, falling by more than 50%.[20] While the US Treasury couldn't shut Tornado Cash down – its smart contracts would always exist on the blockchain – by preventing US exchanges from processing transactions involving Tornado Cash, the mixer's liquidity plummeted, undermining its ability to obfuscate transactions.

The cryptocurrency community, however, saw the Tornado Cash sanctions as an all-out threat to privacy. Immediately after OFAC's designation of Tornado Cash, the industry advocacy group CoinCenter, which had led the charge against the Treasury's efforts to require exchanges to identify users of unhosted wallets, declared that "this action potentially violates constitutional rights to due process and free speech and that OFAC has not adequately acted to mitigate the foreseeable impact its action would have on innocent Americans."[21] One writer in *CoinDesk*, a crypto industry news source, called the Tornado Cash sanctions "a terrifying precedent."[22]

At the heart of these concerns was a fear that if the US government could sanction a DeFi protocol that was ultimately just a piece of code on the blockchain designed to ensure private transactions, then there might be no end to surveillance of transactions that eroded legitimate crypto users' privacy rights. While opponents of the OFAC sanctions did not dispute that Tornado Cash had enabled the mixing of illicit transactions, they pointed out that ordinary, legitimate users of cryptocurrencies also used Tornado Cash to ensure their own privacy. Vitalik Buterin, for example, acknowledged that before the sanctions were put in place he had sent ether through Tornado Cash to donate funds to the Ukraine in the aftermath of the Russian invasion in February 2022 – part of a tremendous fundraising effort that saw the Ukrainian government and non-governmental organizations raise more than $210 million in crypto-denominated donations from supporters around the world while the Ukrainian banking sector was crippled during the conflict.[23] Crypto advocates argued that ensuring privacy in transactions for these types of legitimate charitable fundraising efforts was essential to protect the identities of donors and recipients from having their transactional details revealed to the Russian government – and that the sanctions on Tornado Cash threatened to undermine the potential for cryptocurrencies to act as an alternative financial lifeline for a country in dire straits, like Ukraine.

What's more, opponents of the OFAC sanctions argued that blacklisting Tornado Cash for facilitating illicit transactions was misguided and disproportionate. Brian Armstrong, CEO of the cryptocurrency exchange Coinbase, argued that "Sanctioning open source software is like permanently shutting down a highway because robbers used it to flee a crime scene. It's not the best way to solve a problem. It ends up punishing people who did nothing wrong and results in people having less privacy and security."[24] The OFAC action was not just a matter of mistaken policy, the crypto industry argued, but a direct assault on the right of law-abiding Americans to use open-source technology for legitimate and beneficial ends.

In September 2022, within a month of the Tornado Cash action, the stakes were raised when Coinbase funded a lawsuit brought by a group of Ethereum users challenging OFAC's sanctions on the mixer, and requesting the sanctions be lifted. In October, CoinCenter filed an additional lawsuit seeking to reverse the sanctions. The lawsuits argued that OFAC had overstepped its authority by prohibiting US citizens from transacting through open-source code, and in doing so had violated the constitutional rights of US citizens to free speech and due process. In August 2023, however, a US federal judge rejected the arguments put forward in the Coinbase-backed lawsuit, and held that OFAC had acted reasonably and legally in sanctioning Tornado Cash. (As this book went to production in mid-2023, no judgement had been issued in the separate court filing brought by CoinCenter.)

The stakes were also high because of another development: police in the Netherlands had arrested one of Tornado Cash's developers. On August 11, just two days after the OFAC action, Alexey Pertsev was taken into police custody in Amsterdam, where the 29-year-old developer had been residing at the time of his arrest. The FIOD, the Dutch anti–money laundering agency, issued a press statement indicating that Pertsev had been arrested for "involvement in concealing criminal financial flows and facilitating money laundering through the mixing of cryptocurrencies," following an investigation that had commenced in June 2022.[25] To privacy advocates in the crypto industry, this represented another terrifying step toward the destruction of freedom – and Pertsev's supporters gathered for public protests in Amsterdam to demand his release. If authorities could arrest the developers of privacy-enhancing technologies for the mere act of writing open-source code, they worried, then how could privacy rights ever be safe? (As this book went to production, Pertsev was still awaiting trial under house arrest.)

Back in the United States, the Treasury Department remained steadfast in defense of its sanctions on Tornado Cash, despite the opposition. In November 2022, the Treasury's Assistant Secretary for Terrorist Financing, Elizabeth Rosenberg, said in a speech that while policymakers understood the desire "to maintain privacy and shield against arbitrary or unlawful surveillance. . . mixers, as currently operating, provide anonymity, a way for illicit actors to obfuscate the movement and the origin or destination of funds, while reducing law enforcement's visibility into these transfers. . . The Treasury Department cannot allow such egregious activity to occur."[26] Indeed, in August 2023, the US government doubled down in its efforts against Tornado Cash when it announced a criminal indictment against the mixer's two other founders – Roman Storm and Roman Semenov – on allegations related to facilitating money laundering and sanctions evasion.

FTX and the DeFi Maze

As 2022 drew to a close, the crypto industry was shaken by its biggest-ever scandal when news broke of the collapse of the cryptocurrency exchange FTX. Established in 2019 by Sam Bankman-Fried, the son of Stanford law professors and himself a former Wall Street trader, FTX focused primarily on enabling users to buy and sell crypto-based futures products. Bankman-Fried founded the exchange after having earned himself a small fortune arbitraging Bitcoin trades on other exchanges, which he realized offered wildly different prices for Bitcoin. In 2017, Bankman-Fried established a trading fund called Alameda Research, later launching FTX to offer a consumer-facing crypto trading venue.

FTX was part of a sprawling – and it turned out, incredibly opaque – corporate network that featured more than 150 companies globally, and was headquartered in the Bahamas after a move away from its original hub in Hong Kong. FTX's growth was explosive: by mid-2022, less than three years after its founding, FTX had grown to become the third largest cryptocurrency exchange in the world, with over one million users and a daily trading volume that hit $21 billion at its peak. The company obtained funding from some of the largest venture capitalist firms in the world, and in the summer of 2021 announced a $900 million round of investment, earning FTX a valuation of $18 billion – to be followed by a further $400 million investment round just six months later in January 2022, with a near doubling of its valuation to $32 billion.[27] In the process, Bankman-Fried's net worth grew to more than $25 billion, making him one of the hundred richest people in the world at just 29 years old. Along the way, he obtained investment from celebrities such as Tom Brady and Gisele Bundchen, pledged to devote his wealth to philanthropic causes as part of his professed devotion to the Effective Altruism movement, and donated funds to political campaigns to champion issues from regulation of the cryptocurrency industry to climate change to pandemic preparedness. Bankman-Fried, who appeared at FTX-sponsored conferences in shorts and a t-shirt, earned a reputation as a selfless, and self-effacing, boy genius billionaire.

It all turned out to be a mirage, as FTX imploded in a swirl of contagion that spread through crypto markets across 2022. In April of that year, the cryptocurrency industry witnessed the collapse of a stablecoin known as Terra USD, which had failed to maintain its peg to the US dollar and consequently cost holders billions of dollars in losses when they were unable to redeem their tokens. The collapse of Terra USD in turn caused a hedge fund in Singapore – Three Arrows Capital (3AC) – to go bankrupt, owing to its exposure to the coin. The collapse of 3AC led investors across cryptocurrency markets to start calling in some of their bets, which included loans they had extended to Alameda Research. There was a problem, though: Alameda didn't have the money to pay. The trading firm had become horribly overextended and didn't have the cash. Instead, in an attempt to raise funds, Alameda began selling its holdings of an ERC-20 token known as FTT, which FTX had issued to users of the exchange. As markets got wind of the fact that something was wrong, other holders of FTT tokens began dumping the coin, leading to a plummeting in its value. FTX customers then began making panicked withdrawals from the exchange, which, it turned out, FTX couldn't cover.

A full-blown liquidity crisis was underway. Soon, allegations were swirling that FTX had been covertly using customer funds to fill the giant hole at Alameda Research. Bankman-Fried ultimately resigned as CEO, and the company was put in the hands of John J. Ray III, a lawyer who specialized in corporate restructuring and had overseen the bankruptcy case of disgraced energy giant Enron. On November 11, FTX and most of its global affiliated entities filed for Chapter 11 bankruptcy in the United States. The case carried hints of the Mt. Gox collapse nearly a decade earlier, with furious creditors demanding their funds back from Bankman-Fried – though the cost was even more severe, and in this case, the losses couldn't be blamed on a hack. FTX creditors had lost as much as $8 billion, and because the exchange had become so interconnected across the cryptocurrency industry, its collapse sparked cascading failures across other crypto trading venues.

The story was only beginning for Bankman-Fried. On December 12, he was arrested in the Bahamas, where he had been living since relocating the company there. The following day, US prosecutors unsealed an indictment charging him with multiple counts of fraud and money laundering. The US government alleged that Bankman-Fried systematically misled investors and FTX customers about the health of the firm, and illegally used customer funds to repay Alameda's outstanding debts. Prosecutors also accused him of using customer funds to make political donations – in breach of campaign finance laws – as well as with bribing Chinese government officials.[28] The US Securities and Exchange Commission (SEC) and the Commodity Futures Trading Commission (CFTC) also unveiled further charges against Bankman-Fried, FTX, and Alameda for allegedly engaging in securities and commodities trading fraud.[29]

As US agencies built their case against Bankman-Fried, the attention of blockchain watchers around the world was focused on $477 million worth of cryptocurrencies tied to FTX's collapse.

On November 12, the day after FTX filed for bankruptcy, approximately $477 million worth of cryptocurrencies, primarily ERC-20 tokens, left the exchange's wallets and were deposited in a separate private wallet – a transfer large enough that it attracted immediate attention from blockchain analytics companies. Some observers initially wondered if the funds were related to an asset seizure order that regulators in the Bahamas had issued against the exchange, and speculated that the transfer might have represented FTX surrendering funds to Bahamian authorities. But the new leadership of FTX – who had taken over to steer the company through bankruptcy – later confirmed that the transfer was unauthorized. Someone, it seemed, had stolen funds from FTX as it was imploding. And as the $477 million in crypto from FTX moved, the blockchain revealed a pattern of transactions that bore all the hallmarks of DeFi laundering.

Shortly after being moved off FTX, the funds were sent from the private wallet that had received them and onward to DEXs, where the ERC-20 tokens were converted into ether. A week later, on November 20, the funds were converted into a token known as RenBTC and sent through a DeFi bridge known as the RenBridge. The RenBridge allowed users to transfer funds across the Ethereum, Bitcoin, and other blockchains – and in this case, allowed for the funds to move from the Ethereum ecosystem into the Bitcoin ecosystem seamlessly, without having to pass through a regulated exchange. This was not the first time that RenBridge had appeared in cases of suspected money laundering. In fact, even before the FTX case, more than $540 million worth of cryptocurrencies had been laundered through RenBridge over the previous two years. Research by Elliptic revealed that ransomware gangs had laundered more than $153 million through RenBridge, and the Lazarus Group had also used it to launder about $33.8 million from the August 2021 hack of a Japanese cryptocurrency exchange known as Liquid.[30] Whoever was in control of the $477 million in FTX funds seemed to be attempting the same method of money laundering, with the hope that by moving funds from the Ethereum blockchain to the Bitcoin blockchain, they might throw investigators off their trail.

Who was behind the apparent laundering of nearly half-a-billion dollars from FTX? Was it an inside job, or a hack by an external infiltrator? If it was someone on the inside, they would have been familiar with RenBridge's functionality: in early 2021, Alameda Research had acquired a stake in the RenBridge project to provide it with funding for ongoing development.[31] On December 27, 2022, Bloomberg reported that the DOJ was investigating the misappropriated funds.[32]

As of mid-2023, it remained unclear who had possession of the $477 million stolen from FTX. The funds continued to swirl around deep in the plumbing of the crypto laundering ecosystem, leaving behind a trail that might, someday, provide an answer.

* * *

DeFi demonstrated that as the boundaries of the cryptocurrency space expanded to new frontiers, criminals would follow. The frontiers of DeFi again put regulators and law enforcement agencies to the test, but as always, they would continue to pursue the funds trail wherever it led, and use every weapon in their arsenal to hit back – though not without reviving, and upping, the stakes in the already intense debates about financial privacy.

But just as regulators and law enforcement agencies were getting to grips with DeFi, another innovation spawned by Ethereum grabbed their attention, one that provided a further glimpse into the future of crypto-enabled financial crime.

Chapter 9

NFTs: Virtual Art, Virtual Crime

Despite Vitalik Buterin's aim to design a blockchain that could be used for "more than just money," for its first two years in existence the Ethereum blockchain primarily featured Dapps fulfilling use cases related to swapping, lending, or investing with cryptocurrencies – as well as sparking a proliferation in new tokens that helped to inflate crypto market bubbles. As compelling and innovative as decentralized autonomous organizations (DAOs), decentralized exchanges (DEXs), and ERC-20 tokens were, by late 2017 the Ethereum ecosystem remained relatively immature, with Dapps of limited scale. For Ethereum to meet its true promise of offering a complete, expansive, blockchain-native ecosystem, developers needed to be able to launch projects that applied to an even wider range of functions beyond the initial experiments in DeFi – and in particular, more use cases that resembled real-world activities, but in a digital realm.

Enter NFTs

In January 2018, members of the Ethereum community proposed a new standard for the network, known as ERC-721, that expanded the realm of the possible. The ERC-721 standard laid the foundation for a new set of innovations by defining a protocol for the launch of non-fungible tokens (NFTs). The idea was not an entirely new one – like all innovations, the birth of NFTs arose from years of experimentation. In 2013, Buterin had collaborated with Yoni Assia, the CEO of the Israeli investment firm eToro, on a White Paper exploring the potential of "colored coins." Buterin and Assia proposed colored coins as an additional layer to the original Bitcoin protocol, to allow Bitcoin to support a wider range of applications. The idea behind colored coins was that one could label a specific bitcoin to denote its uniqueness from all other coins, and could allow that coin to represent ownership in another item, such as "commodity certificates, smart property, and other financial instruments such as stocks and bonds"[1] – in short, one could theoretically use a specific coin on the blockchain to record ownership in anything. Buterin would ultimately move on from the Bitcoin colored coin concept and focus instead on the potential for a similar functionality on Ethereum.

The notion of non-fungibility on the blockchain was one that the Ethereum community came to see as critical to building a truly successful decentralized ecosystem, and for fully unlocking the value of crypto to transform social and economic interaction. Cryptocurrencies such as ether are fungible: one unit of ether (known as a gwei) will always be worth the same as any other, just as any dollar bill is always worth the same as any other dollar bill. Fungibility is essential for an asset to act as a medium of exchange in financial applications and transactions, but it isn't helpful if you are trading something unique. For example, if you own a rare collectible item such as a historic stamp, you would not expect or want your stamp to carry the same value as every other stamp on earth; indeed, if you decided to sell your historic stamp, you would want to obtain the highest possible price the market would pay for it.

This was the rationale behind the creation of NFTs – to allow users of the blockchain to record, maintain, and track ownership of unique assets.[2] With NFTs, Ethereum could become home to a whole host of new apps on the blockchain. Lottery tickets, customer awards points, subscriptions, and coupons could be issued on the blockchain via DAOs, allowing participants from anywhere in the world to create and participate in a broader variety of online interactions with cryptocurrencies. Ownership in real-world assets, such as real estate, cars, a private jet, or any other item could also be represented as an NFT – a concept known as "tokenization" – enabling globalized, syndicated, and disintermediated ownership over the blockchain. But the first major use case that emerged with NFTs, which put them on the map and etched them into the public consciousness, was the trade in digital collectibles.

Until the advent of NFTs, users of the Internet had no reliable way to ensure the uniqueness of a piece of digital content – whether an image, ebook, song, film, or software. A brand logo or other image broadcast online could simply be copied indefinitely, with no way for the creator of that image to verify the authenticity of the original. Not only did this facilitate counterfeiting and copyright infringement, it also limited creators' ability to maximize the value of their digital content. For example, if a graphic designer created an image and shared it online, anyone could simply copy it and claim it as theirs, which undermined the ability of the creator to monetize her work, since the value of an image is partly a function of its uniqueness. With an NFT, however, a graphic designer could suddenly create a digital image and assign it a unique record on the blockchain (a process known as "minting" an NFT), by specifying its properties in an underlying Ethereum smart contract. No one other than the holder of the Ethereum wallet containing the NFT could claim to own the true image – whose properties and time of creation would be permanently etched and authenticated on the blockchain. Therefore, if the designer created a digital image that others were willing to buy, she could sell the NFT to the highest bidder, transferring ownership over the blockchain to the buyer, who could rightly claim to be the true holder of the unique image. The same process could be used to create not just a single digital representation of art, but an entire collection as well. The same graphic designer could mint 100 NFTs corresponding to the same image and sell each NFT in her collection as part of a limited series. And because the blockchain is open to anyone to access, any content creator anywhere in the world could mint NFTs and begin monetizing content by settling transactions in cryptocurrencies with fans of their work.

NFTs therefore offered the prospect of democratized and decentralized content creation, putting the power back in the hands of the creator to produce, distribute, and monetize her own work. An additional important property of NFTs is that they are compostable, which means they are compatible with an effectively unlimited range of Dapps, allowing users to move them across different blockchain-native Dapps seamlessly. For example, one can buy an NFT in an online gaming Dapp, and then trade it in another Dapp, taking one's digital property from one online environment to the next. NFTs therefore offered the prospect for the blockchain to give birth to increasingly rich digital environments, where value could be unlocked and income generated in new ways, particularly among a younger generation of tech-savvy cryptocurrency users eager to consume content online.

It didn't take long after the launch of the ERC-721 standard before the first full-on NFT collectible craze began, with perhaps the unlikeliest of fads. In late 2017, a Canadian company known as Dapper Labs launched CryptoKitties, an online game that allows users to breed and trade virtual cats, with ownership of the digital felines recorded on the Ethereum blockchain as NFTs, and purchases made in ether. The game became a hit, attracting nearly 15,000 daily users at one stage.[3] By the end of 2019, CryptoKitties had processed more than two million transactions on Ethereum, making it one of the largest Dapps on the network at the time.[4]

Other NFT collectible crazes followed. In April 2021, a blockchain development company known as Yuga Labs launched an NFT collection dubbed the Bored Ape Yacht Club. As the name suggests, the NFTs featured humorous illustrations of weary-eyed apes, minted as a collection of 10,000 images on Ethereum. Holders of Bored Ape NFTs become members of the eponymous "yacht club" – an exclusive organization which features members-only events, preferential access to new NFT mintings, and other perks. When it first launched, individual NFTs from the collection sold for less than $200 each; but the digital apes soon became a viral Internet meme – trading for higher and higher values, with celebrities such as Eminem and Madonna buying Bored Apes, adding to their popularity. After the success of CryptoKitties and the Bored Apes, thousands of other NFT collections launched, attracting buyers eager to explore this new world of digital artwork – and to get in on the skyrocketing sums of money involved.

The major crypto market price surge of 2021 that had sent Bitcoin's price north of $67,000, and ether's above $4,500, also spread to the NFT space, setting off a frenzy of NFT minting, buying, and selling. Across the first quarter of 2021 alone, NFTs generated $1.5 billion in sales, an increase of more than 2,600% on the final quarter of 2020.[5] The number of individual NFT buyers increased by more than 450% over that time frame as well, and by the end of 2021, the global NFT market was worth more than $15 billion.[6]

These exploding NFT sales were conducted through dedicated NFT marketplaces, where users could buy and sell their NFTs, primarily with ether, though NFT-compatible functionality was launched on other blockchains as well, such as Solana and Tron. Amid the craze, the largest NFT marketplace to emerge was the US-based OpenSea, which had originally been established in late 2017 to allow users to buy and sell NFTs peer-to-peer, with the site acting as a venue for NFT auctions.

OpenSea's growth was astounding. In 2018, its first full year of operation, OpenSea processed less than $500,000 in total NFT trades. Between January and August 2021, it processed more than $1 billion in NFT trades, and its user base grew by more than 4,000% during that nine-month period alone.[7] Major cryptocurrency exchanges such as Binance, Coinbase, and Crypto.com saw OpenSea's tremendous success and launched NFT services in a bid to ride the digital art wave, enabling customers to buy and sell NFTs alongside other tokens and cryptocurrencies they could swap. NFT markets were booming, generating growth that resulted in NFT sales of mind-boggling sums. By late 2021, the average Bored Ape NFT was selling for more than $300,000 – with the entire Bored Ape collection valued at more than $1 billion.[8] And the craze was spreading. Traditional art galleries and auction houses, such as Christie's and Sotheby's, soon began auctioning NFTs. These NFT auctions fetched increasingly staggering bids, as epitomized in March 2021 when an NFT created by the American digital artist Beeple (whose real name is Mike Winkelman), entitled *Everydays – The First 5000 Days*, was sold at a Christie's auction for more than $69 million, purchased with more than 42,000 ether by Vignesh Sundaresan, a crypto investor in Singapore.[9]

Major corporations also entered the NFT space, intrigued by the potential market opportunity to monetize digital content in new ways. The sporting industry was especially attracted to the notion of using digital collectibles to sell content to fans. In 2020, the National Basketball Association teamed with Dapper Labs to launch Top Shot, an NFT collection featuring images of professional basketball players such as LeBron James. Top Shot "Moments," as the NFTs were called, resembled physical sports trading cards of old, but in the digital realm – with users able to buy and sell Moments of their favorite players using crypto. During 2021, Top Shot sales boomed alongside other frothy NFT markets, with the site generating $45 million in sales on a single day in February that year. A Moment featuring LeBron James sold for $230,000 that August, making it the most valuable single item in the Top Shot collection. Top Shot's booming sales soon spread to other popular sports-based NFT offerings, including Sorare, a platform allowing users to buy and sell NFTs of soccer stars such as Lionel Messi and Kylian Mbappé.

Other industries followed suit. In March 2021, *TIME* magazine auctioned three NFTs it had minted based on a cover from an old issue, and the following year it launched an entire issue as an NFT, with Vitalik Buterin appearing on the cover.[10] In May 2022, Adidas issued NFTs in the form of "wearables" – digital apparel available for users of online gaming platforms to purchase on OpenSea, and branded with the company's logo.[11] Shopify, eBay, McDonald's, Nike, and Prada were among other brands that launched experiments in advertising and customer loyalty programs with NFTs. The commercialization of NFTs attracted celebrities, who began issuing NFTs to promote their personal brands – from Snoop Dogg to Paris Hilton to former US President Donald Trump, who in December 2022 sold 45,000 NFTs on OpenSea within several hours. The images featured the former president ripping open his suit to reveal a superhero vest beneath.

Frauds and Scams Galore

As had happened many times before, a booming new market in the crypto space attracted those eager to exploit it. Fraudsters soon began targeting NFT markets to take advantage of the rampant FOMO (fear of missing out) among traders eager to profit from the latest fad. NFT markets were rife with rug pulls – a variety of fraud with which the crypto space was all too familiar. In a typical NFT rug-pull scam, a fraudster creates a supposed NFT, which they advertise on OpenSea or other markets. After receiving payment from a buyer, the fraudsters simply disappear, never transferring ownership of the NFT to the purchaser. NFT rug pulls often involved fraudsters mimicking legitimate NFTs and tricking newbie buyers into thinking they were getting the real deal. In January 2022, an NFT collection known as Big Daddy Ape Club – inspired by the Bored Apes – was announced on Twitter, promoting a pending mint on the Solana blockchain. The promoters received $1.3 million in the Solana cryptocurrency from buyers for pre-launch sales of the NFTs; however, the promoters disappeared just hours before the mint was due to take place – and the unfortunate victims never received the NFTs they had been promised.[12]

Another variety of NFT scam involved fraudsters posing as well-known artists and selling NFTs to unsuspecting buyers, who believed they were purchasing digital art from famous creators. In August 2021, a bizarre case was uncovered involving the

British street artist Banksy. On August 31, an image appeared on Banksy's website of an NFT entitled *Great Redistribution of the Climate Change Disaster*, with a link to a posting on OpenSea where users could bid on the work. Within hours, the NFT had sold for $336,000 worth of ether. Nearly as soon as it had been purchased, however, Banksy's press team issued a statement indicating that he had not created the NFT. His website, it transpired, had been hacked, and the link to the OpenSea posting had been placed there to trick his fans into bidding on the NFT.[13] The apparent fraudster who had created and sold the NFT, and who was never identified, returned the funds to the buyer, seemingly in response to the widespread press attention the case received.

NFT markets also became targets for cyber thieves, who found ample opportunity to steal digital art from vulnerable users. NFTs, like cryptocurrencies, can be stolen from users where an attacker accesses the private key of the wallet in which the NFT is held. Hackers devised numerous clever ruses to steal NFTs, which they could then resell to generate profits in ether and other cryptocurrencies. In October 2022, French authorities arrested a group of five alleged NFT thieves who police claim launched phony websites promising to create animated gifs out of Bored Ape NFTs. When Bored Ape NFT owners clicked on malicious links on the websites, they were directed to authorize transactions by disclosing their private keys – allowing the thieves behind the sites to steal the NFTs straight from the victims' wallets. The alleged thieves resold the stolen NFTs for $2.4 million.[14]

These types of thefts became widespread during the NFT market boom. Research by Elliptic indicated that publicly reported NFT thefts between July 2021 and July 2022 totaled more than $100 million.[15] The bonanza in NFT thievery also attracted a familiar guest to the party. In late 2022, cybersecurity analysts indicated that North Korean hackers were likely behind a series of NFT phishing sites targeting users of the Ethereum and Solana blockchains, stealing as many as 1,500 NFTs, as well as ether worth approximately $450,000 from scammed visitors.[16]

Shining a Light on NFT Crime

The US Treasury's anti–money laundering watchdogs were alert to the boom in NFT trading, and the corresponding cases of crime. In a report it published in February 2022 entitled *Study of the Facilitation of Money Laundering and Terror Finance Through the Trade in Works of Art*, the Treasury devoted an entire section to the risks involving NFTs, raising concern that "The ability to transfer some NFTs via the internet without concern for geographic distance and across borders nearly instantaneously makes digital art susceptible to exploitation."[17]

The Financial Action Task Force (FATF), for its part, worried that "[r]egulation and supervision of NFTs is nonexistent in most jurisdictions"[18] – a problem that exacerbated the risks of crime. In asking the question, as it had before, of how to apply its long-standing AML/CFT standards to the world of NFTs, the FATF gave an answer that was unlikely to clarify things: it depends. According to the FATF, an NFT could classify as any number of financial instruments or assets, depending on its characteristics: as artwork (if purely bought and sold in limited numbers); as a virtual asset (if traded widely on secondary markets); or as a security (if sold as an investment offering). The only way to determine whether, and where, an NFT sat within the regulatory perimeter would be to look case-by-case at NFTs to assess their purpose and regulatory classification – a slow and time-consuming approach unlikely to keep pace with a rapidly evolving technology. NFTs, like parallel developments in the DeFi space, sat in a regulatory gray area that often fostered a perception of the NFT space as an uncontrolled Wild West – which, in many respects, it was.

The primary weapon available to those determined to prevent crime in the NFT space was, yet again, the transparency of the blockchain – which enabled insight into the transfer of NFTs and corresponding flows of funds. Because smart contracts record every transfer of an NFT's ownership on the blockchain, investigators discovered that they could trace the transfer of an NFT in cases of fraud or theft, and could identify the wallets where NFTs were held. And because NFT purchases were generally settled in transparent cryptocurrencies such as ether, investigators could trace the corresponding flows of funds related to fraudulent NFT sales or other illicit activity, just as they would with the flows of other illicit funds on the blockchain. NFT fraudsters and hackers, of course, took steps to hide their tracks – using tried and tested methods to disguise ether they obtained, such as laundering their proceeds through DEXs and mixers. Elliptic's analysis of the blockchain found that more than half of the ether generated from NFT hacks and scams was laundered through the Tornado Cash mixer before it was sanctioned by the US Treasury.[19]

Despite the rise in NFT-related crimes, law enforcement agencies ultimately began to arrest perpetrators of NFT frauds and thefts, and to seize their NFTs and cryptocurrency proceeds. In February 2022, UK investigators seized three NFTs during an arrest involving a case of fraud.[20] In June 2022, the US Department of Justice (DOJ) announced fraud and money charges against Le Anh Tuan, who it alleged was involved in a rug pull known as the Baller Ape collection – another scam allegedly inspired by the Bored Apes – which resulted in victims paying Tuan more than $2.6 million in the Solana cryptocurrency for NFTs that they never received[21] (see Figure 9.1). According to a grand jury indictment, Tuan allegedly laundered the proceeds from the rug-pull scam by engaging in chain-hopping, using DEXs to swap the funds from the rug pull for other tokens.[22]

In January 2023, the DOJ announced charges in another rug-pull scheme involving Aurelien Michel, a French national resident in the United Arab Emirates, who the United States alleged stole $2.9 million from NFT buyers in a fraudulent collection entitled Mutant Ape Planet.[23] US investigators identified Michel by following the flow of funds from the sale: after receiving ether from victims, he allegedly transferred the ether from his private wallet to cryptocurrency exchanges, where he had opened accounts using his personal ID.[24]

Figure 9.1 Image from the Baller Ape Yacht Club NFT collection, which the US government alleges was a scam.
SOURCE: US Department of Justice.

In addition to pervasive rug pulls and hacks, the NFT space proved vulnerable to another form of financial crime: market manipulation. Market manipulation involves deceiving investors by engaging in conduct or transactions that interfere with normal market activity, resulting in gains for the perpetrator and losses for other market participants. With NFTs, market manipulation took several forms. One was the use of "pump and dump" schemes – or activity designed to cause a sudden spike in the price of an NFT, allowing the seller to reap a major profit, only for the price to collapse just as abruptly. In pump and dumps, the creator or holder of the NFT takes to social media to hype up the NFT based on false information and misleading claims – such as bogus information about celebrity endorsements – that leads buyers to up their bids. After buyers purchase the NFT at inflated prices, they are left with an NFT of little or no value, which they may struggle to ever sell.

NFT markets also featured instances of wash trading, a form of manipulation in which a user repeatedly buys an NFT from herself, manufacturing numerous transactions to create a rise in the price.

This draws in other buyers, who purchase the NFT at the inflated value and suffer losses when they try to resell it and discover its price was artificial. Some researchers have estimated that wash trading may have accounted for as much as 40% to 60% of total NFT trading volume during the height of the 2021/2022 boom, suggesting that markets were heavily manipulated.[25]

One open question was whether these manipulative practices, which constituted crimes when involving stocks and other asset classes that fall within the regulatory perimeter, necessarily constituted crimes when undertaken with NFTs, given NFTs' uncertain regulatory status. With the regulatory perimeter nebulous, market manipulation in NFTs could prove deeply unfair and injurious, but not necessarily illegal in all cases. But the US government was intent on curtailing abusive conduct in NFT markets, even as the regulatory perimeter was evolving.

In June 2022, the DOJ announced an arrest in a high-profile case of alleged market manipulation at the NFT industry's biggest trading platform, OpenSea. That month, a grand jury charged Nathaniel Chastain, a former product manager at OpenSea, with wire fraud and money laundering related to insider trading, alleging that he abused his position at the marketplace to obtain a trading advantage over OpenSea's users. Chastain's role at OpenSea involved selecting which NFTs would be featured on the site. In announcing the case, the DOJ claimed that Chastain used his knowledge of which NFTs would feature on OpenSea to buy those NFTs at low prices before they were featured, and then resold them later at substantially higher prices, sometimes earning five times his original purchase price.[26] The indictment charging Chastain also stated that he used peeling chain techniques to disguise the proceeds from the NFTs he sold, using "new Ethereum accounts without any prior transaction history in order to further conceal his involvement in the scheme."[27]

In May 2023, a jury in New York returned a verdict of guilty in Chastain's case, convinced by the government's argument that he had acted deliberately to commit fraud and money laundering.[28]

The case marked the first successful prosecution related to insider trading involving digital assets.

* * *

The froth in NFT markets that had bubbled up during the craze of 2021 and into early 2022 fizzled out just as dramatically, with NFT prices and trading volumes ultimately plummeting as broader crypto market prices declined as well. By late 2022, sales on Open-Sea were down more than 90% from their highs, and monthly sales across all NFT markets were down more than 60% – a drastic decline.[29] This led some critical observers to proclaim that NFTs were an overhyped fad – though NFT innovators saw the bursting bubble as an opportunity to weed out scammers and manipulators so that genuine and legitimate innovators could experiment further with the technology to unlock its true promise. Indeed, as of mid-2023, many corporate NFT projects continued apace, based on a belief that NFTs – however volatile in their early years – represented the future of content consumption and brand marketing.

When it came to crime, NFTs offered yet one more crypto-related innovation with which law enforcement agencies had to contend – and one that, like parallel developments in the DeFi space, tested the boundaries of regulation. The skills and capabilities that government watchdogs had obtained through the previous decade of investigating crypto-enabled crime were valuable when investigating the world of NFTs, but the rapidly changing technology continued to test the ability of governments to maintain pace with evolutions in the crypto ecosystem.

Perhaps just as importantly, the wave of NFT frauds, hacks, and market pumps across 2021 and 2022 offered a deeper glimpse into the future – a future that will feature as the final stop on our journey through the crypto laundering trail.

Chapter 10

Brave New World: The Metaverse, Web 3.0, and the Battle for the Future of Finance

Imagine this: The year is 2038. It's mid-morning, and you step outside, cup of coffee in hand. It's peaceful, calm, a beautiful day. The sky is an impossibly perfect blue. The only sound is the faint hum of a robotic lawnmower weaving a course through your overgrown, purple lawn. The lawnmower circles the base of a jagged magenta tree at the edge of your perfectly square property. It's the only tree remaining on this plot of land, which reminds you of what this plot looked like when you bought it three years ago. It was full of jagged magenta trees back then, vivid and lush, a sea of vibrant pink, but you had them felled to make room for the house where your family now lives.

Gazing back at your home, you're filled with pride. You designed it yourself: three stories of alternating blue and orange brick, with floor-to-ceiling windows, and topped with a red pagoda-style roof. You scrimped and saved to have it built from the ground up.

You made the downpayment with tokens you received from the DAO where you took a job a while back, and you put up a Bored Ape NFT as collateral to secure the remaining loan. You got a good deal on it, too – managed to get into the local property market just before the price boom of 2035. It took some settling into, but now it really feels like home – adorned with furniture you've accumulated over the years, like the Arhaus sofa that cost more gweis than you'd like to remember, the walls bedecked with NFTs, some of which you wish you hadn't spent so much ether on. You're still bitter about that one NFT that got stolen when your daughter clicked on the funny link in that email. . . but, hey, that's life.

Come to think of it, not only is your house decorated with NFTs – your house *is* an NFT. Your ownership of it is recorded on the blockchain, and someday, when you sell it, the transaction of that sale will be etched on the blockchain forever. Of course, at one point in time, those details would have been visible for anyone with prying eyes to see, but these days you can undertake private transactions that conceal the details using zero-knowledge proofs.

You love your neighborhood. It used to be an entire forest of magenta trees, but there's been more development recently. Some plots of land were going for huge figures at one point – there was even that plot down the street that sold for $1 million. One million dollars! At first you were sad to see the magenta trees go and worried that the area would become overdeveloped, but in truth, you're glad to have more neighbors around. It was getting lonely out here in the countryside.

Speaking of neighbors, here comes one now. It's Milo, who moved in last year. You've gotten to know him well since. You get beers occasionally at the bar in town, where you go to catch the latest NBA basketball games, and where you spend most of your time lamenting the plummeting value of your early Top Shot purchases. As Milo approaches, bedecked in neon green sunglasses, with his distinctive and matching green Mohawk, and wearing a puffy yellow adidas jacket that looks like a beehive on him, you can tell that something's wrong. He's normally laid back and chirpy, but he looks frazzled, distressed. He's mumbling something frantically and you can't understand a word.

Once Milo's calmed down, he explains. He just lost $250,000 worth of USDC in an exploit of a lending protocol he invested in a while back. The returns had been great for a while, so he kept investing. Thought the yields couldn't be beat. And then, one day. . . gone! Seems a hacker drained the whole lending pool. In addition to Milo's $250,000 that disappeared, the hackers made off with a stash of $45 million in tokens from other innocent investors. "And here's the thing," Milo says. You can see he's desperate, tears trickling down his cheeks from beneath his neon green glasses. "I never told my wife. That money was supposed to put our kids through college."

You tell him to relax. He's not the first person you know who's lost money this way. It's not uncommon, but it's not as dire a problem as it used to be. The police recover funds from a lot of these hacks now – he might get the money back. And investors have more protections now than they did years ago. The courts have issued numerous rulings holding that DAOs are liable for losses from hacks if a bug in the code of the smart contracts results in theft – so it may be worth talking to Jane, the attorney who owns the newly built house down the road, to see about getting compensated for the loss.

"Look," you tell Milo, "if it comes down to it, I can loan you some ether until you figure something out, and Marcy won't realize the money's gone."

Still flustered but looking somewhat reassured, Milo thanks you for the advice and walks back across the road to his house. As he disappears inside, you hear his bulldog, Sparky, the one with the blue and red eyes and a neon green streak in the shape of a lightning bolt running down his back, barking frantically – until the door shuts and all is quiet again.

Just as suddenly, the silence is broken and you hear the unmistakable blaring of police sirens. From down the road you can see a police car approaching. It comes to a screeching halt outside your house. An officer hops out and marches up to you.

"Morning," she says.

"Morning, officer."

She removes her sunglasses and eyes you suspiciously. She peeks over your shoulder and toward your house.

"You haven't seen anything unusual around here this morning, have you?"

You shake your head.

"You're sure?" She asks, still casting you a scrutinizing glance. "You haven't seen anyone suspicious come through this neighborhood at all?"

"Nope," you say with a shrug.

She puts her glasses back on and sighs.

"We're looking for an NFT thief who's on the run, we think he might be in the area."

"Let me know if you nab him," you say. "Might be the same guy who took my NFT last year."

The officer removes a business card from her pocket and hands it to you.

"Call me if you see anything out of the ordinary," she says, then returns to her car and speeds away.

You look at the card: DETECTIVE ZOE MURPHY, CRYPTOPIA POLICE DEPARTMENT, INVESTIGATIONS DIVISION.

You stick the card in your pocket and then gaze at your watch, one of the first wearables you bought a while back, a gold Rolex that didn't come cheap, but sure looks good. Nine o'clock. You walk back inside your house, where it's still quiet. Your family members are all asleep in their beds. Picking up the newspaper, *The DeFi Times*, you scan the headlines. The police busted another fentanyl storefront down by the riverside, seized a bunch of tokens in the process. A new Burger King is opening in town, offering Snoop Dogg NFTs to the first thousand customers. Snoop Dogg – is he still even a thing? What is he, about 65 now? Bank of America is closing a branch – seems their DEX project never took off, though you always liked their DeFi services. Speaking of DEXs, looks like the feds caught that guy who's been laundering funds through DEXs after stealing tokens from a bunch of bridges. North

Korean cybercriminal. No surprise. They've been at it for, what, two decades now?

You sigh. Nothing but the same old, depressing news stories every day.

You put the paper down and cast your eyes across the room. An NFT of an apathetic ape with long blonde hair and nose piercings stares back at you from the wall.

Just then, your daughter emerges from her bedroom.

"Morning sweetheart," you say.

"Morning," she yawns.

You give her a kiss.

"Can I get you some breakfa-"

You feel a tap on your shoulder.

"Take those stupid goggles off."

"Sorry?" You look around, but you can't see anyone other than your daughter, and the ape on the wall. "Who's there?"

"I said, take those stupid goggles off!"

You take your VR headset off and set it down on the table. You wince, as you always do when moving between worlds – needing a moment to orient yourself and transition from one universe to the next. Gazing up, you see your wife standing there, scowling.

"The kids need to be at school in half an hour. Why are you playing that stupid video game?"

"Hey. It's not 'a stupid video game.' It's an immersive virtual reality experi-"

"Oh, stop it, it's a stupid video game. And you, missy, you take your headset off, now. You need to get to school soon."

Taking her headset off, your daughter frowns. "Alright."

"Honestly, how much time will you two waste with those ridiculous goggles on? Get outside and get some fresh air or something. And get ready for school."

Your daughter runs upstairs to collect her things. Your wife gives you one last disapproving glance before leaving the room. You gaze back down at your headset, tempted to put it back on, tempted to return to the virtual world of impossibly blue skies and magenta trees and Bored Apes and colorful dogs – but you resist.

You go into the next room and grab your shoes – a beat-up old pair of Nikes that you've resigned yourself to wearing until your next paycheck lands in your bank account, the account that hardly pays any interest but deducts plenty in fees. You shout up the stairs.

"Kids, five minutes! Get your stuff together and let's go. I'm heading out to the car."

You step outside. It's a pleasant enough day. The sun is out, but tinted by a film of smog. Traffic's blaring and there's not a tree in sight amid the landscape of concrete and brick. You pull out your phone and scan the day's headlines: global warming, stock market slump, war raging, healthcare crisis, drought and wildfires, anti-bacterial resistance. . .

You sigh as you prepare to face the day.

You'd rather take your chances back in the metaverse.

The Metaverse and Web 3.0

Innovations such as decentralized autonomous organizations (DAOs), decentralized exchanges (DEXs), tokens, and non-fungible tokens (NFTs) are not isolated and unrelated developments. In the minds of visionary developers, they form the foundations of a complete reconceptualization of the Internet, and society at large.

These technologies are part of the larger evolution of Web 3.0 – a term that refers to the next iteration of online interaction. The Internet, so far, has been a largely centralized space: users have been able to create and consume content, information, and services, but access to those services has been controlled by gatekeepers, such as social media companies that control access to data, with ownership of the infrastructure underpinning online life concentrated in a relatively small number of hands. The Internet to date has been a place where users can participate in an increasingly wide array of interactions and space, but those same users do not own the actual architecture of the Web where they interact. But with the introduction of cryptocurrencies and blockchain technology, and related innovations, a new, decentralized online experience is imaginable:

one in which reliance on gatekeepers is substantially reduced; one in which users can own and generate income from content they distribute directly to their audience, through NFTs; where users can participate in the governance of new apps by holding a stake in DAOs; and where anyone, anywhere can access a range of disintermediated financial services. A world, in short, where the Web is not owned and controlled by intermediaries and centralized brokers, but is instead designed and owned by its users.

This notion of a new, decentralized type of Internet that is accessible to, and ultimately owned by, all is the basis of Web 3.0. This decentralized virtual architecture also underpins certain experimentations in the metaverse – or an emerging online ecosystem of self-contained virtual reality (VR) environments that has become a recent buzzword but that, in the minds of some in the crypto space at least, will ultimately converge to offer, from today's vantage point, unimaginable new digital experiences.

The metaverse is hardly a new concept. The term was coined in 1992 by novelist Neal Stephenson and refers to immersive, online gaming environments such as Second Life, World of Warcraft, and others where users engage in complex role-playing experiences and are represented as avatars of their real-life personas. What's new and more recent is the decentralization of some virtual worlds, and the potential for them to feature cryptocurrencies and blockchain-based apps interwoven into their design, as well as the potential fusion of these features with innovations in VR technology – including improvements in the quality of VR headsets, such as the thick white Oculus goggles users wear and that have become the defining image of the metaverse.

The first metaverse built with cryptocurrencies and blockchain at its core was Decentraland, a game created by Argentinian developers and released in February 2020. In Decentraland, users buy plots of land that are issued as NFTs and purchased using MANA, an ERC-20 token that operates as the native currency of the Decentraland ecosystem. Another popular metaverse is The Sandbox, which like Decentraland allows users to buy land and own virtual property as NFTs, but which uses its own native ERC-20 token known as SAND. Once in possession of land, users can rent it out, build virtual property on it, or license it for use by others. Within these environments, users access apps that mimic products and services available in the real world, and can even obtain employment to earn tokens – while the ecosystems are underpinned by smart contracts governed by a DAO. For example, the Decentraland DAO allows users to vote on policies, such as what wearables and NFTs should be permitted within Decentraland, when land should be auctioned, and membership of the Security Advisory Board, which is responsible for ensuring the safety of Decentraland's smart contracts. Land and property from these digital environments can be sold to users through NFT marketplaces such as OpenSea, where users can also buy wearables and other portable digital items that they can take with them into, and across, these virtual worlds. The open nature of the Ethereum blockchain allows developers to build and launch almost any conceivable virtual gaming environment, leveraging tokens they can create to act as a medium of exchange native to each new world. It's therefore perhaps more appropriate to speak not just of a single metaverse, but of a world of numerous and potentially interconnected metaverses that can be built upon blockchains and powered by cryptocurrencies.

User participation in the crypto-enabled metaverse remains relatively tiny. Decentraland and The Sandbox only receive a few thousand daily users.[1] Trends in broader crypto markets have tended to shape spikes and dips of activity in the metaverse. When the NFT craze of 2021 and 2022 was at its height, plots of land in Decentraland sold for as much as $100,000, with one sale made for an astounding $2.34 million. In February 2022, the rapper Snoop Dogg sold 10,000 avatars of his likeness as NFTs that fans could purchase and use in The Sandbox.[2] Only two months earlier, in December 2021, a plot of land in The Sandbox had sold for $450,000. The reason? It was next door to a virtual mansion Snoop had built.[3]

Some observers feel these developments show that a crypto-enabled, blockchain-based metaverse is nothing more than a passing fad. Others, however, anticipate that the metaverse could present the next great online commercial opportunity. The number of people interacting in metaverse experiences is expected to grow substantially. Research firm McKinsey anticipates that the average person will eventually spend several hours daily in metaverse environments.[4] Banking giant Citi estimates that the metaverse could generate up to $13 trillion in commercial and investment opportunities.[5] The governments of the United Arab Emirates and South Korea have announced metaverse development strategies to ensure their economies can take advantage of these emerging digital worlds. Japan's Digital Ministry announced in late 2022 its plan to launch an experimental DAO to explore how to make Web 3.0 and metaverse innovation part of Japan's long-term economic growth.[6]

In early 2022, J.P. Morgan became the first major bank to enter the metaverse, establishing a lounge in Decentraland. While the move was largely exploratory, the bank described the potential for mature financial services to appear someday in the metaverse, noting that "in time, the virtual real estate market could start seeing services much like in the physical world, including credit, mortgages and rental agreements. However, with the emergence of [DeFi], collateralized lending primitives and the composability of blockchain token-based digital assets, a next-generation financing company could potentially leverage digital clothing as collateral to underwrite virtual land and property mortgages. In fact, the financing company may not be a company at all, but instead, a selforganizing, mission-based community of people. . . ."[7] Other brands are exploring the metaverse, such as Atari and Samsung, both of which have purchased plots in Decentraland.[8]

It is not inevitable that cryptocurrencies will feature widely in the metaverse, or that these environments will all be built upon blockchains. The social media giant Facebook famously rebranded to Meta in late 2021, declaring its goal to be not just a platform for social posting and sharing, but a gateway for its two billion users to access an even more varied set of immersive digital experiences. Its metaverse, Meta Horizon Worlds, allows users to have a VR experience that includes playing games, attending comedy shows and concerts, engaging in exercise routines and sports, and participating in conferences and other collaborative work spaces.

Other tech giants such as Google, Apple, and Microsoft are exploring metaverse development. None of these corporate experiments involves the use of cryptocurrencies.

The believers in an open, crypto- and blockchain-enabled Web 3.0 feel these corporate attempts to develop the metaverse suffer from a fatal flaw, the same flaw that has been the weakness of most systems: they are centralized – owned by and for the benefit of the companies that create them. Crypto innovators believe that any metaverse that does emerge should be decentralized – not owned by corporations, but by the users of these environments, and therefore truly open and free to anyone who wishes to participate. The proponents of Web 3.0 aspire to create currently unimaginable forms of interaction that may elude corporate attempts to commoditize them easily, but which they believe will evolve organically through experimentation. As Vitalik Buterin tweeted in July 2022, "The 'metaverse' is going to happen but I don't think any of the existing corporate attempts to intentionally create the metaverse are going anywhere."[9]

The Future of Crypto Crime

Because the crypto-enabled metaverse is still in its infancy, crime there as of mid-2023 remains mostly a theoretical rather than a pressing problem. Nonetheless, there are already indications that criminals are exploring the metaverse, just as they have always explored and experimented with other innovations connected to cryptocurrencies. Should a decentralized, blockchain-based metaverse ever achieve the scale of financial and economic opportunity some believe is possible, it would be difficult to imagine a scenario where criminals did not attempt to exploit it.

In many respects, crime in the metaverse may simply resemble crime in other parts of the crypto ecosystem. In a report on *The Future of Financial Crime in the Metaverse*, Elliptic identified instances of NFTs representing land plots from Decentraland being stolen from users of OpenSea.[10] Other potential risks exist. The smart contracts underpinning Dapps deployed in the metaverse, such as DEXs and lending protocols, can be exploited and drained of funds – making them a target for hackers. Vendors of fentanyl and other deadly narcotics could begin to establish storefronts in the metaverse. There is also the prospect that terrorist and extremist organizations could disseminate propaganda and raise funds in these virtual environments. In late 2022 Europol issued a report, *Policing in the Metaverse: What Law Enforcement Needs to Know*, where it suggested that the expansion of digital environments in the metaverse will likely result in the creation of even more tokens to facilitate economic activity within these new environments, which in turn will require law enforcement agencies to obtain greater "knowledge of decentralised finance, the different blockchain implementations as well as familiarity with a range of different forms of digital currency."[11] The report also suggests that the use of NFTs in the metaverse could result in high levels of fraud if not controlled, and that users of metaverse apps may be attractive targets for ransomware attackers, who are already more than comfortable operating in crypto-enabled environments.

These issues, while serious and concerning, are not entirely new. Law enforcement agencies – though often stretched – have demonstrated impressive adaptability in their response to cryptocurrencies over the years. To have gone from the early days of the Silk Road, when investigators used the blockchain for the first time, to tracking down cybercriminal funds successfully through the complex plumbing of the DeFi ecosystem within a decade, is a truly impressive feat. Drawing on their experiences thus far, and leveraging capabilities such as blockchain analytics, law enforcement agencies may very well be able to identify crimes and seize funds used in the metaverse just as they have in other cases of crypto crime.

These new digital environments will unquestionably force law enforcement agencies to acquire new skills and knowledge to navigate them successfully. Law enforcement agencies are already taking steps to prepare themselves for a future of policing in the metaverse. In October 2022, INTERPOL launched an immersive training metaverse environment for law enforcement, allowing agents to "interact with other officers via their avatars, and even to take immersive training courses in forensic investigation and other policing capabilities"[12] (see Figures 10.1 and 10.2). One major challenge facing law enforcement is the potential, even if currently remote, for thousands upon thousands of metaverse environments to emerge over time, which would stretch the ability of agencies to police these environments. Jim Lee, the chief of the IRS's Criminal Investigations division, has worried about this possibility, noting: "Technology advancements are a great thing, but the Metaverse combined with Web 3.0 allows people to be more anonymous than ever."[13]

Of course, a key factor will be whether the cryptocurrency ecosystem retains a high level of traceability, or whether transactions become more highly anonymized. In theory, a finer balance between transparency and privacy should be more achievable than the highly polarized debate today suggests. Presumably, it should be

Figure 10.1 The avatar of a law enforcement agent at the virtual INTERPOL headquarters, in a metaverse environment that the global police organization created. @ INTERPOL. Reprinted with permission from INTERPOL.

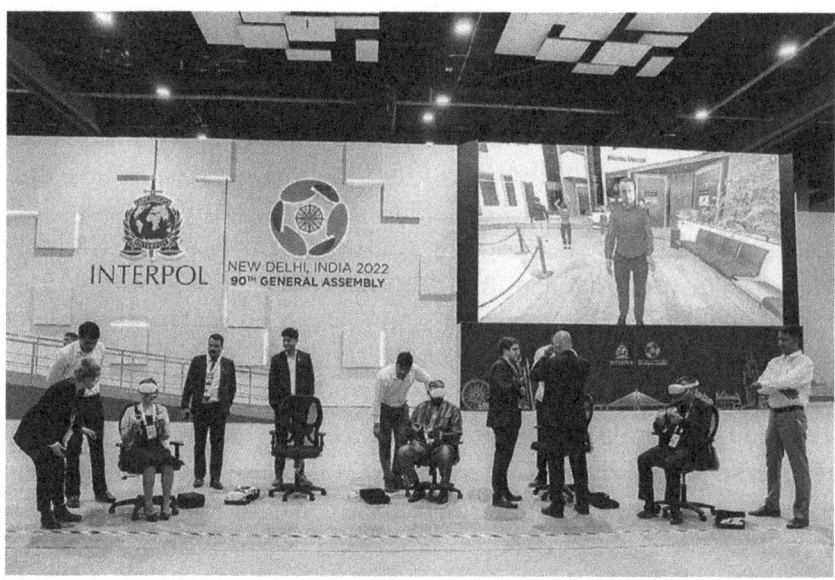

Figure 10.2   Law enforcement agents train with INTERPOL in an immersive metaverse. © INTERPOL. Reprinted with permission from INTERPOL.

possible for there to be a world where hackers', fraudsters', and rogue regimes' attempts to launder cryptocurrencies can be detected, but where legitimate users are not resigned to having so much of their transaction histories revealed for all to see. Attempts to enable greater privacy in the cryptocurrency space certainly will not abate. In January 2023, Buterin wrote a blog post describing the need for greater privacy in the Ethereum ecosystem, noting that "using the entire suite of Ethereum applications involves making a significant portion of your life public for anyone to see and analyze."[14] Continued innovations could make transactions in these future worlds less traceable than the current crypto ecosystem, if not necessarily entirely anonymous.

The metaverse also presents challenges for regulatory oversight and supervision. Which regulators have jurisdiction over financial transactions in a world of numerous, interconnected virtual environments populated by users from all over the globe? How can regulators monitor activities in these digital frontiers? Some policymakers are already grappling with these questions, and even adapting their legal frameworks in anticipation. The state of Wyoming and the Marshall Islands have both created legal frameworks providing for the incorporation of DAOs. The European Union had, as of late 2022, begun discussing how to bring DAOs, Dapps, and NFTs within the bloc's AML/CFT framework, noting in draft legislation that "The metaverse offers new opportunities for criminals who can convert cash acquired through illegal activities into non-traceable currencies to purchase and sell virtual real estate, virtual lands and other high-demand goods."[15] In August 2022, Owen Lock and Teresa Cascino, researchers from the Bank of England, recommended that regulators "address risks from cryptoassets' use in the metaverse before they reach systemic status."[16] One regulator has even gone so far as to immerse itself directly in the metaverse: in May 2022, the Dubai Virtual Assets Regulatory Authority (VARA), the first crypto-specific regulatory agency in the world, established a presence in The Sandbox, with the aim of using a metaverse headquarters to engage with the technology and its users.[17]

Law enforcement agencies and regulators are rushing to keep up, but an overarching problem remains: we simply do not know what the future will look like. The evolution of cryptocurrencies from Bitcoin to the frontiers of DeFi was hardly inevitable, and the line was not a straight one. The evolution of crypto crime from the Silk Road to the theft of cartoon apes was similarly unpredictable. We can speculate about what the metaverse may look like decades or even centuries from now, but we are left with more questions than answers.

Who governs this world, or worlds? What rules apply? Will governments manage to intervene? Will DAOs evolve to form sufficiently robust governance models to ensure these worlds can offer economic and financial freedom without devolving into anarchy? Or will the metaverse be primarily controlled by centralized corporations? Will crime in this future remain problematic, but ultimately addressable, as is the case with cryptocurrencies today? Or will it become a genuinely lawless and uncontrolled dystopia? Will a finer balance between privacy and traceability be achieved? Or will the vision of a fully decentralized future beyond the reach of government control finally prevail, offering nearly limitless freedom and preserving true anonymity for the well-intentioned, but providing boundless cover for the ill-intentioned as well?

Whatever the future holds, the reality will inevitably prove more complex than we can imagine.

Afterword: How Much Crime in Crypto?

ny treatment of cryptocurrencies and money laundering naturally leads to the question: "How much crime is there in cryptocurrencies?"

After all, there is far more to cryptocurrencies than crime. Satoshi Nakamoto's launch of Bitcoin nearly a decade and a half ago was a momentous event in the history of financial innovation. Terms such as *blockchain*, *DeFi*, *stablecoins*, and *NFTs* are becoming part of the lexicon of everyday finance and business. The ultimate impact these crypto-inspired innovations will have on the financial sector, and society at large, remains to be seen. Advocates of the technology feel ardently that the full promise of cryptocurrencies and blockchain has yet to be realized – and that continued iterations of the technology will create a radically different financial landscape of the future. Detractors believe the technology is nothing but a mirage that will fizzle out into oblivion – and that the various innovations Bitcoin has inspired are pure hype, or worse, outright fraud. These arguments for and against cryptocurrencies have been detailed thoroughly elsewhere, and the aim of this book has not been to revisit them.

So, why write a history of cryptocurrencies and crime? Simply because it is impossible to understand the impact of this technology on society without understanding *something* about its use in criminal activity. The story of cryptocurrencies writ large is much bigger than the story of their illicit use. But no one seeking to understand cryptocurrencies and their impact on our world could do so without understanding how illicit actors – whether fentanyl dealers, ransomware perpetrators, or a country such as North Korea – have utilized the technology, how they may seek to exploit the cryptocurrencies in the future, and how governments and the private sector are responding.

Crime has certainly been part of the story of cryptocurrencies from early in Bitcoin's history. Crypto-enabled crime has also evolved in lockstep with the launch of key innovations and iterations of the technology, from the creation of Bitcoin ATMs, to developments in privacy-enhancing services, to experiments in DeFi, to the emergence of NFTs – and crime will inevitably feature in the metaverse. While crime is just one part of the complex story of these innovations and their evolution, understanding how crime interacts with cryptocurrencies helps to illuminate where the technology is going, and what the implications for society may be.

Regarding the question of "how much" crime occurs in cryptocurrencies, some estimates exist. Most of these have been generated by blockchain analytics firms – the industry in which I work, and which is discussed in detail in Chapter 4. These estimates vary, depending on the methodology employed, but the typical approach is to use data from blockchains to calculate the total value of transactions identifiable as involving known criminal entities, and then to divide that figure by the total value of all transactions conducted in cryptocurrencies over time. Using this methodology, blockchain analytics firms such as Elliptic have estimated that illicit transactions account for less than 1% of all Bitcoin transactions – with figures across various studies ranging from approximately 0.12% to 0.5% for most years since

2017.[1] In absolute terms, this would place the overall value of criminal payments made in cryptocurrencies during 2022 at approximately $20–25 billion.

These figures should be treated as lower-bound estimates, for several reasons. Firstly, they only consider transactions sent to or from cryptocurrency wallets attributed to known criminal actors. They cannot account for transactions taking place through cryptocurrency wallets that may be controlled by criminal actors, but that have not yet been identified as such. Secondly, these estimates are based on blockchain data alone, and generally do not take account of linkages between illicit activity that originates in other parts of the economy – such as the cash economy – but where funds are ultimately laundered through the cryptocurrency ecosystem (a topic discussed in Chapter 5). Thirdly, these figures cannot take account of information that law enforcement agencies obtain through intelligence gathering methods that are not readily available to private firms.

The data do not, inevitably, provide a complete picture. Nonetheless, we can glean some trends. For example, available evidence suggests that crime now accounts for a substantially smaller component of overall cryptocurrency activity than during the early years of the technology. Using the methodology described above, Elliptic estimates that at least one-third of all Bitcoin transactions in 2012 related to illicit activity – primarily transactions conducted by users of the Silk Road dark web market (as described in Chapter 1). While the nominal value of criminal payments in cryptocurrencies has increased since then as the crypto space has grown, the proportion of all Bitcoin payments related to illicit activity today appears to be substantially smaller than a decade ago – even if figures citing less than 1% are a lower bound.

What accounts for the decline in the proportion of illicit activity among cryptocurrency transactions over time? The traceability of cryptocurrencies, and the substantial successes law enforcement agencies have achieved in disrupting cases of crypto-enabled crime, is certainly one major factor. The expanding regulatory perimeter around cryptocurrencies is likely another. And the adoption of the tech by a growing number of legitimate users seems to have made illicit use a relatively smaller slice of the overall cryptocurrency pie today versus a decade ago.

This trend may seem at odds with frequent news reports describing the use of cryptocurrencies in crime, and cases such as the implosion of the FTX cryptocurrency exchange that shook the industry in late 2022 and resulted in major losses to investors. Are we to conclude that crime in cryptocurrencies is not a problem? Certainly not. Another trend the evidence points to is that crime in cryptocurrencies, while diminishing as a proportion of overall crypto trading activity, has become more complex, with potentially more severe implications. In the first few years after Bitcoin's creation, criminal usage of the technology was primarily limited to operators of dark web markets selling drugs. Today, cryptocurrencies are used by a much wider array of criminal actors than a decade ago – including fraudsters, hackers, ransomware attackers, organized criminal networks engaged in human trafficking and prostitution, perpetrators of child sexual exploitation, nation states subject to international sanctions, and, occasionally, terrorist and extremist groups. Research conducted by Elliptic in mid-2023 found that Chinese companies have relied on cryptocurrencies to generate tens of millions of dollars in sales of precursor chemicals used to produce fentanyl – in quantities sufficient to earn billions of dollars in revenue for the drug gangs who sell fentanyl on the streets of the United States, with lethal consequences.[2] These and other illicit actors engage in money laundering through an increasingly complex, multi-layered ecosystem of cryptocurrency-related platforms and services that is far more varied and richer than existed a decade ago, and that, particularly with the emergence of DeFi, is creating substantial regulatory challenges. The severity of ransomware attacks and the presence of North Korea in cases of crypto-related cybercrime has also caused the public policy debate around cryptocurrencies to evolve from a law enforcement concern to one of international security. As of mid-2023, evidence had emerged that designated terrorist organizations including ISIS and al Qaeda were increasingly raising funds by soliciting donations using the Tether stablecoin on the TRON blockchain – another development likely to stoke concerns about the security implications of cryptocurrencies.[3]

These observations often lead to another question: "Is crime in cryptocurrencies worse than crime in the banking sector?"

Estimates of the scale of money laundering in the banking sector are famously imprecise. The United Nations Office of Drugs and Crime (UNODC) estimates the total annual value of money laundering globally at approximately $800 million to $2 trillion, but even the UNODC acknowledges significant limitations in estimating these figures.[4] Inevitably, a significant portion of this laundered money will, at some stage, have passed through the banking sector. In nominal terms, the scale of money laundering in the banking sector is unquestionably vastly higher than in cryptocurrencies, given the sheer size of the banking sector relative to the cryptocurrency space. But when speaking of which is "worse," what people really seem to be getting at is proportionality. The UNODC's figures suggest that money laundering globally accounts for between 2% and 5% of annual global GDP – a higher figure than the 0.12% to 0.5% rate of criminal activity often cited for cryptocurrencies. But the comparison is inevitably imperfect. Estimates of money laundering in the traditional financial sector do not – and cannot – use the same methodologies employed for estimating crime in cryptocurrencies, given the unique ability to draw on blockchains for open-source analysis of crypto activity. What we are left with, at best, is an uncertain picture.

Ultimately, the debate around whether crime in cryptocurrencies is "worse" than crime in the banking sector is unhelpful, particularly in terms of setting public policy. More useful to consider are the ways in which crime involving cryptocurrencies is *similar to* crime conducted in other parts of the financial sector, and the ways in which it is *different*. The cryptocurrency space is rife with Ponzi schemes – but these frauds have existed in the financial sector for a century; fraudsters will go on committing Ponzi schemes forever, with or without crypto. Ransomware, on the other hand, would likely not have emerged as an industrial-scale, global criminal enterprise with total revenues exceeding a billion dollars had it not been for the ability to harness the peer-to-peer nature of cryptocurrencies. It is also the case that the substantial successes law enforcement agencies have achieved in seizing cryptocurrencies used in crime would likely have been impossible were it not for the transparency of blockchains, which offer deeper insights into money laundering flows than is generally possible with bank payments.

It is these points of divergence and similarity, these paradoxes and their impact on the changing face of finance, that will continue to shape the trajectory of crime and cryptocurrencies.

Acknowledgements

This book is the product of a decade spent working at the crossroads of cryptocurrencies, financial crime, and regulatory policy. In that time, I've received guidance and support, and gained insight and knowledge, from more outstanding professionals and colleagues than I can possibly name here. Several, however, deserve special mention.

I'm extremely grateful to Simone Maini for taking time out of an incredibly busy schedule to pen the foreword – and, more generally, for being a source of consistent encouragement and mentorship.

I've learned more about crypto and crime from my colleague Tom Robinson than from anyone else, and I was fortunate to have him cast his expert and technical eye over a draft of this book.

Greg Kilminster, James Gillespie, and Allison Owen provided invaluable comments and feedback that helped to strengthen the final manuscript.

Thank you to Mira Samani for undertaking intrepid field research on my behalf, even if it did lead to a dead-end.

Tom Keatinge and the team at the Centre for Financial Crime and Security Studies at the Royal United Services Institute, where I am an associate fellow, have been a source of tremendous support in my professional endeavors. It was over beers at a pub in Westminster during the summer of 2016 that Tom and I came up with the idea to produce a report, *Virtual Currencies and Financial Crime: Challenges and Opportunities*, that really sent me plummeting down the crypto rabbit hole for good, and which allowed me to explore the ideas that eventually worked their way into this book, years later.

I'm grateful to Timon Molloy of *Money Laundering Bulletin*, who provided me an open forum for several years where I was able to write about many of the topics that I've explored here. I'm grateful as well to the team at Thomson Reuters Regulatory Intelligence, who have provided me a monthly forum for writing about these and related topics.

Gemma Valler, my acquiring editor at Wiley, deserves my enormous gratitude for the belief she had in this project from the outset, and for coaching me along the way in navigating the in-and-outs of publishing a book for the first time.

Thank you as well to Richard Samson of Wiley for his guidance throughout the production process, to Alice Hadaway for providing outstanding support, and to Sarah Lewis for her extremely thorough copy editing.

Finally, I'm hugely grateful to my wife, Juliette, not only for being a better and more scrutinizing editor than I could ever have imagined, but more importantly for providing me with constant support along the way, and for tolerating me as I worked on this book through some very late nights and very early, groggy mornings.

Glossary

AML/CFT: anti–money laundering and countering the financing of terrorism.

Anonymity-enhanced cryptocurrencies (AECs): cryptocurrencies that emphasize privacy as part of their design and conceal information about counterparties so that transactions cannot be traced, or where the ability to trace transactions is limited. AECs are also known as "privacy coins."

Application-specific integrated circuit (ASIC): specialized hardware used to mine Bitcoin.

Automated market maker (AMM): a protocol for facilitating peer-to-peer swaps of cryptocurrencies on decentralized exchanges (DEXs).

Big Game Hunting: a method of directing ransomware attacks at the largest and most high-profile targets, capable of paying very large ransoms.

Blockchain: a distributed public ledger that records information about transactions in a cryptocurrency network.

Bridge: an application that allows users to transfer value directly across blockchains, for example, across the Bitcoin and Ethereum blockchains.

Chain-hopping: a method of money laundering that involves moving funds between different cryptocurrencies with the aim of concealing the ultimate source of funds and frustrating the ability to trace across blockchains.

Cluster: a collection of cryptocurrency addresses that are controlled by a single individual or entity.

Coinjoin: a method for obfuscating the origin of Bitcoin transactions by combining funds from multiple users into a single transaction and then depositing funds for each user in an output address of the same value.

Cold storage: a method of safeguarding funds in a cryptocurrency wallet by maintaining the private keys to the wallet offline, for example on a USB drive or on paper.

Common spend analysis: a method of establishing that a given set of cryptocurrency addresses form a cluster by analyzing the connection between a user's unspent transaction outputs (UTXOs).

Crypto-jacking: a form of cybercrime in which a user's computing power is hijacked without their consent to mine cryptocurrencies.

Decentralized application (Dapp):   an application that operates in a decentralized finance (DeFi) network using smart contracts.

Decentralized autonomous organization (DAO):   an arrangement that uses smart contracts to set foundational rules for conducting various social, financial, or economic activities and that relies upon community-driven governance, with one's voting stake in the DAO determined by the allocation of blockchain-based tokens.

Decentralized exchange (DEX):   a DeFi application that allows users to swap cryptocurrencies without the presence of a centralized broker, generally by deploying an automated market maker (AMM).

Decentralized finance (DeFi): a term that refers to a variety of financial applications and services that can operate without reliance upon traditional, centralized intermediaries by deploying smart contracts on a blockchain.

Distributed ledger technology (DLT): a mechanism, such as the Bitcoin blockchain, that enables a disbursed group of participants to ensure the synchronized and shared recording of data without the presence of a central administrator.

ERC-20 standard: a standard that enables new tokens to be issued and utilized across the Ethereum network.

ERC-721 standard: a standard for representing unique tokens, or non-fungible tokens (NFTs), on the Ethereum blockchain.

Financial Action Task Force (FATF): an intergovernmental body that promotes global standards for combatting money laundering, terrorist financing, and the financing of the proliferation of weapons of mass destruction.

Financial Crimes Enforcement Network (FinCEN): a bureau of the US Department of the Treasury responsible for the administration of US AML/CFT requirements, and which is responsible for collecting and analyzing information about financial crime.

Hot storage: when a cryptocurrency wallet and the private keys that control the funds in it are maintained online.

Initial coin offering (ICO): a type of venture funding involving cryptocurrencies. In ICOs, newly minted blockchain-based tokens are sold to investors in return for a stake in an underlying project.

Know Your Customer (KYC): requirements under AML/CFT regulation that financial services firms must identify and verify information about their customers and avoid establishing anonymous accounts or business relationships.

Liquidity pools: collections of token pairs that counterparties can trade peer-to-peer on DEXs, with prices set based on the ratio of tokens in the pool.

Metaverse: an immersive, computer-generated environment in which users can interact in a shared digital space.

Mixer: a privacy-enhancing service that obscures the connection between the ultimate origin and destination of cryptocurrencies by co-mingling funds from numerous users.

Money service businesses (MSBs):   firms, including cryptocurrency exchanges, involved in activities such as currency dealing and exchange and that are regulated by FinCEN for AML/CFT purposes.

Multi-signature (multi-sig):   a type of cryptocurrency wallet that requires two or more users to provide the private keys needed to generate a transaction.

Non-fungible token (NFT):   a unique digital identifier recorded on the blockchain that can act as a representation of ownership in digital or physical assets.

Office of Foreign Assets Control (OFAC):   an office within the US Department of the Treasury responsible for the administration and enforcement of US economic and financial sanctions.

Peeling chain: a technique for attempting to obfuscate the source of cryptocurrencies by repeatedly drawing down the balance of funds in a cryptocurrency wallet and sending smaller amounts of funds into a series of previously unused intermediary addresses.

Privacy coins: another term for AECs.

Proof-of-work (PoW):   a method for achieving consensus about the accuracy of transactions on the blockchain by validating that miners have expended sufficient computational effort.

Ransomware-as-a-Service (RaaS):   a business model in the ransomware ecosystem in which operators develop and sell malware to affiliates, who then execute attacks. The model allows affiliates to launch ransomware attacks even if they lack the technical skill to develop malware.

Ring signature: a method for enabling a cryptocurrency transaction to be signed by any member of a group, which undermines common spend analysis.

Rug pull: a form of fraud in which scammers obtain funds from investors to purchase a purported token, NFT, or other similar offering but then disappear with the investors' funds.

Smart contract: an open-source protocol that defines the terms of interaction amongst counterparties in DeFi applications.

Specially Designated Nationals and Blocked Persons List (SDN List): a list of individuals and entities subject to financial sanctions measures administered by the US Treasury's OFAC.

Stablecoin: a cryptocurrency that aims to maintain a stable value by pegging its price to fiat currencies such as the US dollar, or to other assets.

Stealth address: a one-time address that conceals the ultimate destination of a transfer to all observers of the blockchain except the sender and recipient.

Suspicious activity reports (SARs): reports that regulated financial services firms must file where they identify transactions or activity that they suspect is reflective of money laundering, terrorist financing, or other illicit activity.

Travel Rule: a requirement of AML/CFT regulation that financial institutions collect, retain, and share complete information about the originators and beneficiaries of electronic funds transfers.

Unhosted wallet: a cryptocurrency wallet where the user retains control of her private keys and where a regulated institution does not maintain custody of the funds within the wallet (also commonly referred to as a private wallet, or self-hosted wallet).

Unspent Transaction Output (UTXO): any unused units of a cryptocurrency that remain after funds in an address have been spent, and which can be used as an input to generate a new transaction.

Virtual asset service provider (VASP): a business that conducts certain activities, including the exchange, transfer, or safekeeping of cryptoassets on behalf of clients.

Wearables: virtual clothing and accessories in the form of NFTs that can be used to dress an avatar in the metaverse.

Web 3.0: the concept that the next generation of the World Wide Web will be decentralized, with most user interaction occurring via applications built atop blockchains, and where users retain control of their data and content.

Zero-knowledge proofs: a cryptographic technique that allows two parties to verify data without disclosing that data. Zero-knowledge proofs are employed in some AECs to conceal information about counterparties and transactions.

List of Figures

Figure 1.1. Bitcoin payments Ross Ulbricht made to Carl Force, depicted in the US criminal complaint against Force. Source: US Department of Justice / Public Domain.

Figure 2.1. Bitcoin transfers Shaun Bridges made to Mt. Gox, depicted in the US criminal complaint against Bridges. Source: US Department of Justice / Public Domain.

Figure 3.1. Example of an unspent transaction output (UTXO) in a Bitcoin transaction.

Figure 3.2. Example of UTXOs used to generate a new Bitcoin transaction.

Figure 3.3. The Helix mixing service as it was advertised to users of the dark web.

Figure 4.1. An image of the Al Sadaqah fundraising campaign. Source: US Department of Justice.

Figure 5.1. A Bitcoin ATM the US government seized in the Herocoin case. Source: US Department of Justice.

Figure 6.1. Image of the WannaCry ransomware message.

Figure 7.1. Example of a peeling chain process, as illustrated in the criminal complaint against Tian Yinyin and Li Jaidong. Source: US Department of Justice / Public Domain.

Figure 8.1. The Lazarus Group's entry on the OFAC SDN List, showing the group's Ethereum addresses. Source: US Department of the Treasury / Public Domain.

Figure 9.1. Image from the Baller Ape Yacht Club NFT collection, which the US government alleges was a scam. Source: US Department of Justice.

Figure 10.1. The avatar of a law enforcement agent at the virtual INTERPOL headquarters, in a metaverse environment that the global police organization created. © INTERPOL. Reprinted with permission from INTERPOL.

Figure 10.2. Law enforcement agents train with INTERPOL in an immersive metaverse. © INTERPOL. Reprinted with permission from INTERPOL.

Bibliography

Bilton, N. (2017). *American Kingpin: The Epic Hunt for the Criminal Master-mind Behind the Silk Road.* London: Portfolio.

Buterin, V. (2014). *Ethereum: A Next-Generation Smart Contract and Decentralized Application Platform.* https://ethereum.org/en/whitepaper/

Carlisle, D. (2017). *Virtual Currencies and Financial Crime: Challenges and Opportunities.* Occasional Paper. Royal United Services Institute.

Carlisle, D. and Izenman, K. (2019). *Closing the Crypto Gap: Guidance for Countering North Korean Cryptocurrency Activity in Southeast Asia.* Occasional Paper. Royal United Services Institute.

Carlisle, D., Keatinge, T., and Keen, F. (2018). *Virtual Currencies and Terrorist Financing: Assessing the Risks and Evaluating Responses.* Report. European Parliament Think Thank.

Casey, M. and Vigna, P. (2016). *Cryptocurrency: The Future of Money?* London: Vintage.

Elliptic (2021). *DeFi: Risk, Regulation, and the Rise of DeCrime.*

Elliptic (2022). *Guide to Preventing Financial Crime in Cryptocurrencies.*

Elliptic (2022). *NFTs and Financial Crime.*

Elliptic (2022). *The Future of Financial Crime in the Metaverse.*

Financial Action Task Force (2021). *Updated Guidance for a Risk-Based Approach to Virtual Assets and Virtual Asset Service Providers.*

Institute for Security and Technology Ransomware Task Force (2021). *Combatting Ransomware: A Comprehensive Framework for Action.*

Leising, M. (2021). *Out of the Ether: The Amazing Story of Ethereum and the $55 Million Heist that Almost Destroyed It All.* Chichester, UK: Wiley.

Nakamoto, S. (2008). *Bitcoin: A Peer-to-Peer Electronic Cash System.* `https://bitcoin.org/bitcoin.pdf`

Narayanan, A., Bonneau, J., Miller, A., *et al.* (2016). *Bitcoin and Cryptocurrency Technologies.* Princeton, NJ: Princeton University Press.

Popper, N. (2016). *Digital Gold: The Untold Story of Bitcoin.* London: Penguin.

United States Department of Justice (2020). *Cryptocurrency Enforcement Framework.* Report of the Attorney General's Cyber Digital Task Force.

United States Department of the Treasury (2022). *Study of the Facilitation of Money Laundering and Terror Finance Through the Trade in Works of Art.*

United States Department of the Treasury (2023). *Illicit Finance Risk Assessment of Decentralized Finance.*

United States Government Accountability Office (2021). *Virtual Currencies: Additional Information Could Improve Federal Agency Efforts to Counter Human and Drug Trafficking.* Report to Congressional Requesters.

White, G. (2022). *The Lazarus Heist.* London: Penguin Business.

Notes

T his book draws from a wide array of sources, among them publicly available court documents, such as indictments and criminal complaints, related to cases of money laundering involving cryptocurrencies. In a few instances, these documents relate to cases that, as of the time this book went into production, had not been fully adjudicated. Where that is the case, any individuals who are the subject of outstanding allegations should, of course, be presumed innocent until proven guilty beyond reasonable doubt in a court of law.

1. The Dark Web: The Origins of Crypto Laundering

1. Joe Mullin, "'I have secrets': Ross Ulbricht's private journal shows the Silk Road's birth," *Ars Technica*, January 1, 2015. https://arstechnica.com/tech-policy/2015/01/silk-road-trial-fbi-reveals-whats-on-ross-ulbrichts-computer-in-open-court/ (accessed April 27, 2023).

2. Andy Greenberg, "Meet the Dread Pirate Roberts, the man behind boom-ing black market drug website Silk Road," *Forbes*, December 23, 2019. https://www.forbes.com/sites/forbesdigitalcovers/2019/12/23/meet-the-dread-pirate-roberts-the-man-behind-booming-black-market-drug-website-silk-road/?sh=3c3bb65f482a (accessed April 27, 2023).

3. Eric Hughes, "A Cypherpunk Manifesto," March 9, 1993. https://www.activism.net/cypherpunk/manifesto.html (accessed April 27, 2023).

4. Wei Dei, "B-Money." https://web.archive.org/web/2018032820 4908/http://www.weidai.com/bmoney.txt

5. See https://bitcointalk.org/index.php?topic=175.0 (accessed April 27, 2023).

6. See https://bitcointalk.org/index.php?topic=26350.msg329 190#msg329190 (accessed April 27, 2023).

7. Daniel Oberhaus, "Assassination markets for Jeff Bezos, Betty White, and Donald Trump are on the blockchain," *Vice*, July 25, 2018. https://www.vice.com/en/article/gy35mx/ethereum-assassination-market-augur (accessed April 27, 2023).

8. "Digital Currency Business E-Gold Pleads Guilty to Money Laundering and Illegal Money Transmitting Charges," United States Department of Justice press release, July 21, 2008. https://www.justice.gov/archive/opa/pr/2008/July/08-crm-635.html (accessed April 27, 2023).

9. *United States of America v. Liberty Reserve SA*, May 28, 2013. https://www.justice.gov/sites/default/files/usao-sdny/legacy/2015/03/25/Liberty Reserve, et al. Indictment - Redacted_0.pdf (accessed April 27, 2023).

10. "Treasury Identifies Virtual Currency Provider Liberty Reserve as Finan-cial Institution of Primary Money Laundering Concern under USA Patriot Act Section 311," United States Department of the Treasury press release, May 28, 2013. https://home.treasury.gov/news/press-releases/jl1956 (accessed April 27, 2023).

11. Satoshi Nakamoto post on P2P Foundation message board, Febru-ary 15, 2009. http://p2pfoundation.ning.com/forum/topics/bitcoin-open-source?commentId=2003008%3AComment%3A9493 (accessed April 27, 2023).

12. "US busts online drug ring Farmer's Market," *BBC*, April 17, 2012. https://www.bbc.co.uk/news/world-us-canada-17738207 (accessed April 27, 2023).

13. Mullin, "'I have secrets': Ross Ulbricht's private journal shows the Silk Road's birth."

14. Satoshi Nakamoto post on `bitcointalk.org`, February 6, 2010. `https://bitcointalk.org/index.php?topic=7.msg264#msg264` (accessed April 28, 2023).

15. Joshua Bearman and Tomer Hanuka, "The rise & fall of Silk Road," *Wired*, April 2015. `https://www.wired.com/2015/04/silk-road-1/` (accessed April 28, 2023).

16. Federal Bureau of Investigation, "Manhattan U.S. Attorney Announces Seizure of Additional $28 Million Worth of Bitcoins Belonging to Ross William Ulbricht, Alleged Owner and Operator of the 'Silk Road' Website," FBI New York Press Office, October 25, 2013. `https://archives.fbi.gov/archives/newyork/press-releases/2013/manhattan-u.s.-attorney-announces-seizure-of-additional-28-million-worth-of-bitcoins-belonging-to-ross-william-ulbricht-alleged-owner-and-operator-of-silk-road-website` (accessed April 28, 2023).

17. Post by user "silkroad" on `bitcointalk.org`, March 1, 2011. `https://bitcointalk.org/?topic=3984.0` (accessed April 28, 2023).

18. Sarah Meiklejohn et al., "A Fistful of Bitcoins: Characterizing Payments Among Men with No Names," October 23–25, 2013. `https://cseweb.ucsd.edu/~smeiklejohn/files/imc13.pdf` (accessed April 28, 2023).

19. Nick Bilton, *American Kingpin: The Epic Hunt for the Criminal Mastermind Behind the Silk Road*. London: Portfolio, 2017, p. 159.

20. Ibid., p. 121.

21. Andy Greenberg, "FBI says it's seized $28.5 million in bitcoins from Ross Ulbricht, alleged owner of Silk Road," *Forbes*, October 25, 2013. `https://www.forbes.com/sites/andygreenberg/2013/10/25/fbi-says-its-seized-20-million-in-bitcoins-from-ross-ulbricht-alleged-owner-of-silk-road/?sh=1cd4cbba2765` (accessed April 28, 2023).

22. Samuel Rubenfeld, "Silk Road mastermind's Bitcoin trail wasn't complicated," *Wall Street Journal*, February 24, 2015. `https://www.wsj.com/articles/BL-252B-6304` (accessed April 29, 2023).

23. See `https://www.blockchain.com/explorer/addresses/btc/1933phfhK3ZgFQNLGSDXvqCn32k2buXY8a` (accessed April 29, 2023).

24. Nathaniel Popper, "The tax sleuth who took down a drug lord," *New York Times*, December 27, 2015. `https://www.nytimes.com/2015/12/27/business/dealbook/the-unsung-tax-agent-who-put-a-face-on-the-silk-road.html` (accessed April 29, 2023). Joe Mulling, "The incredibly simple story of how the government Googled Ross Ulbricht,"

Ars Technica, January 26, 2015. https://arstechnica.com/tech-policy/2015/01/the-incredibly-simple-story-of-how-the-govt-googled-ross-ulbricht/ (accessed April 29, 2023).

25. *United States of America v. Ross William Ulbricht*, Indictment, United States District Court Southern District of New York, February 24, 2014. https://www.justice.gov/sites/default/files/usao-sdny/legacy/2015/03/25/US%20v.%20Ross%20Ulbricht%20Indictment.pdf (accessed April 29, 2023).

26. Andy Greenberg, "Prosecutors trace $13.4 million bitcoins from the Silk Road to Ulbricht's laptop," *Wired*, January 29, 2015. https://www.wired.com/2015/01/prosecutors-trace-13-4-million-bitcoins-silk-road-ulbrichts-laptop/ (accessed April 29, 2023).

27. *United States v. Ross Ulbricht*, Civil Forfeiture Complaint, October 24, 2013. https://www.justice.gov/sites/default/files/usao-sdny/legacy/2015/03/25/REDACTED%20-%20Application%20for%20Second%20Post-Complaint%20Protective%20Order%20-%20Silk%20Road.pdf (accessed April 29, 2023).

28. "Manhattan U.S. Attorney Announces Seizure of Additional $28 Million Worth of Bitcoins Belonging to Ross William Ulbricht, Alleged Owner and Operator of the 'Silk Road' Website," FBI New York Press Office.

29. Joshuah Bearman and Tomer Hanuka, "The rise and fall of the Silk Road, Part 2," *Wired*, May 2015. https://www.wired.com/2015/05/silk-road-2/ (accessed April 29, 2023).

30. "Manhattan U.S. Attorney Announces Seizure of Additional $28 Million Worth of Bitcoins Belonging to Ross William Ulbricht, Alleged Owner and Operator of the 'Silk Road' Website," FBI New York Press Office.

31. *United States of America v. Carl Mark Force IV, et al.*, United States District Court for the Northern District of California, March 25, 2015, p. 15. https://www.justice.gov/sites/default/files/opa/press-releases/attachments/2015/03/30/criminal_complaint_force.pdf (accessed April 29, 2023).

32. Ibid., p. 43.

33. "About US," United States Marshals Service webpage. https://www.usmarshals.gov/who-we-are/about-us (accessed April 29, 2023).

34. *United States of America v. Ross William Ulbricht*, Civil Forfeiture Complaint, p. 2.

35. United States Department of Justice Criminal Division, *Asset Forfeiture Policy Manual 2021*, pp. 28–29. https://www.justice.gov/criminal-afmls/file/839521/download (accessed April 29, 2023).

36. Brett Night and C. Alden Pelker, "Virtual currency: Investigative challenges and opportunities," *FBI Law Enforcement Bulletin*, United States Department of Justice, September 8, 2015. https://leb.fbi.gov/articles/featured-articles/virtual-currency-investigative-challenges-and-opportunities (accessed April 29, 2023).

37. Gertrude Chavez-Dreyfus, "Venture capitalist Draper wins U.S. bitcoin auction," *Reuters*, July 2, 2014. https://www.reuters.com/article/us-usa-bitcoin-idUSKBN0F719920140702 (accessed April 29, 2023).

38. United States Department of Justice Office of the Inspector General, *Audit of the United States Marshals Service's Management of Seized Cryptocurrency*, June 2022, p. i. https://oig.justice.gov/sites/default/files/reports/22-082.pdf (accessed April 29, 2023).

39. United States Department of Justice, "U.S. Attorney Announces Historical $3.36 Billion Cryptocurrency Seizure and Conviction in Connection with Silk Road Dark Web Fraud," press release, November 7, 2022. https://www.justice.gov/usao-sdny/pr/us-attorney-announces-historic-336-billion-cryptocurrency-seizure-and-conviction (accessed April 29, 2023).

40. "United States Files a Civil Action to Forfeit Cryptocurrency Valued at Over 1 Billion U.S. Dollars," United States Attorney's Office Northern District of California, November 5, 2020. https://www.justice.gov/usao-ndca/pr/united-states-files-civil-action-forfeit-cryptocurrency-valued-over-one-billion-us (accessed April 29, 2023).

41. Nicholas Weaver, "How I traced 20% of Ross Ulbricht's Bitcoin to the Silk Road," *Forbes*, January 20, 2015. https://www.forbes.com/sites/frontline/2015/01/20/bitcoin-silk-road-ulbricht/?sh=2ea2be156374 (accessed April 29, 2023).

2. Black Holes: The Rise of the Rogue Exchange

1. Paul Vigna and Michael Casey, *Cryptocurrency: The Future of Money?* London: Vintage, 2016, p. 67.

2. Ronan Manly, "Dawn of Bitcoin price discovery 2009–2011: The very early Bitcoin exchanges," *Bullionstar*, January 18, 2021. https://www.bullionstar.com/blogs/ronan-manly/dawn-of-bitcoin-price-discovery-2009-2011-the-very-early-bitcoin-exchanges/ (accessed April 29, 2023).

3. *United States of America v. Carl M. Force IV*, motion for pretrial detention. United States District Court for the District of Maryland, Baltimore Division, February 4, 2015, p. 6. https://cryptome.org/2015/04/force-md-011.pdf (accessed April 29, 2023).

4. *United States of America v. Carl Mark Force IV, et al.*, p. 18.

5. Ibid., p. 10.

6. Ibid., p. 8.

7. Ibid., p. 9.

8. Liesl Eicholz, "Mt. Gox, BTC-e, and the missing coins: A timeline of the greatest cyber crime ever," *ConsenSys Media*, August 10, 2017. https://media.consensys.net/mtgox-btc-e-and-the-missing-coins-a-living-timeline-of-the-greatest-cyber-crime-ever-f94fbb1eb42 (accessed April 29, 2023).

9. Abdelaziz Fathi, "Mt. Gox creditors to get their funds through Bitstamp, other exchanges," *Finance Feeds*, October 7, 2022. https://financefeeds.com/mt-gox-creditors-to-get-their-funds-through-bitstamp-other-exchanges/ (accessed April 29, 2023).

10. United States Department of the Treasury Financial Crimes Enforcement Network (FinCEN), "Application of FinCEN's Regulations to Persons Administering, Exchanging, or Using Virtual Currencies," March 18, 2013. https://www.fincen.gov/sites/default/files/shared/FIN-2013-G001.pdf (accessed April 29, 2023).

11. Financial Action Task Force, *Guide for a Risk Based Approach: Virtual Currencies*, June 2015. https://www.fatf-gafi.org/media/fatf/documents/reports/guidance-rba-virtual-currencies.pdf (accessed April 29, 2023).

12. Pete Rizzo, "FinCEN Director Jennifer Shasky Calavery: Full Interview," *CoinDesk*, September 30, 2014. https://www.coindesk.com/policy/2014/09/30/fincen-director-jennifer-shasky-calvery-full-coindesk-interview/ (accessed April 29, 2023).

13. Colleen Taylor, "With $1.5 million led by Winklevoss Capital, BitInstant aims to be the go-to site to buy and sell bitcoins," *TechCrunch*, May 17, 2013. https://techcrunch.com/2013/05/17/with-1-5m-led-by-winklevoss-capital-bitinstant-aims-to-be-the-go-to-site-to-buy-and-sell-bitcoins/ (accessed April 29, 2023).

14. United States Department of Justice, "Bitcoin Exchangers Plead Guilty in Manhattan Federal Court in Connection with the Sale of Approximately $1 Million in Bitcoins For Use on the Silk Road Website," press release,

September 4, 2014. https://www.justice.gov/usao-sdny/pr/bitcoin-exchangers-plead-guilty-manhattan-federal-court-connection-sale-approximately-1 (accessed April 29, 2023).

15. *United States of America v. Robert M. Faiella, a/k/a "BTCKing," and Charlie Shrem*, Indictment, United States District Court Southern District of New York, April 10, 2014. https://www.justice.gov/sites/default/files/usao-sdny/legacy/2015/03/25/Faiella%2C%20Robert%20and%20Shrem%20Charle%20Indictment.pdf (accessed April 29, 2023).

16. *United States of America v. Carl Mark Force IV, et al.*, p. 39.

17. United States Department of Justice, "Russian National and Bitcoin Exchange Charged in 21-Count Indictment for Operating Alleged International Money Laundering Scheme and Allegedly Laundering Funds from Hack of Mt. Gox," press release, July 26, 2017. https://www.justice.gov/usao-ndca/pr/russian-national-and-bitcoin-exchange-charged-21-count-indictment-operating-alleged (accessed April 29, 2023).

18. *United States of America v. BTC-e, a/k/a Canton Business Corporation, and Alexander Vinnik*, Superseding Indictment, United States District Court Northern District of California San Francisco Division, p. 5. https://www.justice.gov/d9/press-releases/attachments/2017/07/26/vinnik_superseding_indictment_redacted_0.pdf (accessed April 29, 2023).

19. Ibid., p. 11.

20. United States Department of the Treasury Financial Crimes Enforcement Network (FinCEN), "Assessment of Civil Monetary Penalty in the Matter of BTC-e a/k/a Canton Business Corporation and Alexander Vinnik," July 26, 2017, p. 2. https://www.fincen.gov/sites/default/files/enforcement_action/2017-07-26/Assessment%20for%20BTCeVinnik%20FINAL%20SignDate%2007.26.17.pdf (accessed April 29, 2023).

21. Francisco Memoria, "Greek police uncover plot to murder alleged Bitcoin launderer Alexander Vinnik," *CCN*, May 12, 2018. https://www.ccn.com/greek-police-uncover-plot-to-murder-alleged-bitcoin-launderer-alexander-vinnik/ (accessed April 29, 2023).

22. Anna Baydakova, "BTC-e operator Vinnik sentenced to 5 years in prison on money laundering charges," *CoinDesk*, December 7, 2020. https://www.coindesk.com/markets/2020/12/07/btc-e-operator-vinnik-sentenced-to-5-years-in-prison-on-money-laundering-charges/ (accessed April 29, 2023).

23. Sebastian Sinclair, "New Zealand police seize $90 million linked to alleged BTC-e exchange operator," *CoinDesk*, June 22, 2020. https://www .coindesk.com/policy/2020/06/22/new-zealand-police- seize-90m-linked-to-alleged-btc-e-exchange-operator/ (accessed April 29, 2023).

24. United States Department of Justice, "Alleged Russian Cryptocurrency Money Launderer Extradited to United States," press release, August 5, 2022. https://www.justice.gov/opa/pr/alleged-russian- cryptocurrency-money-launderer-extradited-united-states (accessed April 29, 2023).

25. United States Department of Justice, "Russian Nationals Charged with Hacking One Cryptocurrency Exchange and Illicitly Operating the Other," press release, June 9, 2023. https://www.justice.gov/opa/pr/russian- nationals-charged-hacking-one-cryptocurrency-exchange- and-illicitly-operating-another (accessed June 9, 2023).

26. "Shuttered bitcoin exchange BTC-e respawns as Singapore registered WEX," *CryptoNinjas*, September 18, 2017. https://www.cryptoninjas .net/2017/09/18/shuttered-bitcoin-exchange-btc-e- respawns-singapore-registered-wex/ (accessed April 29, 2023).

3. Mixers: Covering Up Their Tracks

1. United States Department of Justice, "Russian National and Bitcoin Exchange Charged in 21-Count Indictment for Operating Alleged International Money Laundering Scheme and Allegedly Laundering Funds from Hack of Mt. Gox."

2. Satoshi Nakamoto, "Bitcoin: A Peer-to-Peer Electronic Cash System," p. 6.

3. Samuel Rubenfeld, "Silk Road Mastermind's Bitcoin Trail Wasn't Complicated."

4. Andy Greenberg, "Prosecutors Trace $13.4 Million Bitcoins from the Silk Road to Ulbricht's Laptop."

5. "Why Are Billion-Dollar Darknet Markets Retiring?" https://www .elliptic.co/blog/why-are-the-operators-of-billion- dollar-darknet-markets-retiring (accessed April 30, 2023).

6. United States Department of Justice, "AlphaBay, the Largest Online 'Darknet Market,' Shut Down," press release, July 20, 2017. https:// www.justice.gov/opa/pr/alphabay-largest-online-dark- market-shut-down (accessed April 30, 2023).

7. See https://www.instagram.com/coinninja/?hl=en.

8. *United States of America v. Larry Dean Harmon*, United States District Court for the District of Columbia, August 10, 2021, p. 5. https://www.justice.gov/opa/press-release/file/1425346/download (accessed April 30, 2023).

9. Ibid.

10. Ibid.

11. United States Department of Justice, "Dark Web Narcotics Dealer 'Fentmaster,' Responsible for Overdose Death, Sentenced to Fifteen Years in Prison," press release, July 30, 2021. https://www.justice.gov/usao-sdny/pr/dark-web-narcotics-dealer-fentmaster-responsible-overdose-death-sentenced-15-years (accessed April 30, 2023).

12. Andrea Bellemare, "The secret life of Alexandre Cazes, alleged dark web mastermind," *CBC*, July 23, 2017. https://www.cbc.ca/news/canada/montreal/alexandre-cazes-millionaire-cars-property-alphabay-1.4215894#:~:text=He%20started%20AlphaBay%20in%20July,it%20publicly%20in%20December%202014.&text=U.S.%20authorities%20were%20able%20to,header%20of%20password%20recovery%20emails (accessed April 30, 2023).

13. United States Department of Justice, "AlphaBay, the Largest Online 'Darknet Market,' Shut Down."

14. "Bitcoin business man on trial in the U.S. owns property in Belize," *Channel 5 Belize*, February 14, 2020. https://edition.channel5belize.com/archives/198434 (accessed April 30, 2023).

15. *United States v. Sterlingov*, Statement of Fact, United States District Court for the District of Columbia, April 26, 2021, p. 4. https://www.courtlistener.com/docket/59856080/1/1/united-states-v-sterlingov/ (accessed April 30, 2023).

16. Europol, *Internet Organised Crime Threat Assessment (iOCTA)*, European Police Office, 2014, p. 42. https://www.europol.europa.eu/sites/default/files/documents/europol_iocta_web.pdf (accessed April 30, 2023).

17. Financial Action Task Force, *Guidance for Risk-Based Approach: Virtual Assets and Virtual Asset Services Providers*, June 2019, p. 28. https://www.fatf-gafi.org/media/fatf/documents/recommendations/rba-va-vasps.pdf (accessed April 30, 2023).

18. Europol, "Multi-Million Euro Cryptocurrency Laundering Service Bestmixer.io Taken Down," press release, May 22, 2019. https://www.europol.europa.eu/media-press/newsroom/news/multi-million-euro-cryptocurrency-laundering-service-bestmixerio-taken-down (accessed April 30, 2023).

19. United States Department of the Treasury Financial Crimes Enforcement Network (FinCEN), Assessment of Civil Monetary Penalty in the Matter of Larry Dean Harmon d/b/a Helix, October 19, 2020, p. 2. https://www.fincen.gov/sites/default/files/enforcement_action/2020-10-19/HarmonHelix%20Assessment%20and%20SoF_508_101920.pdf (accessed April 30, 2023).

20. United States Department of Justice, "Ohio Resident Charged with Operating Darknet-Based Bitcoin 'Mixer,' which Laundered Over $300 Million," press release, February 13, 2020. https://www.justice.gov/opa/pr/ohio-resident-charged-operating-darknet-based-bitcoin-mixer-which-laundered-over-300-million (accessed April 30, 2023).

21. United States Department of the Treasury Financial Crimes Enforcement Network (FinCEN), Assessment of Civil Monetary Penalty in the Matter of Larry Dean Harmon d/b/a Helix, pp. 7–11.

22. United States Department of Justice, "Ohio Man Pleads Guilty for Unlawfully Stealing Over 712 Seized Bitcoin Subject to Forfeiture in Brother's Pending Criminal Case," press release, January 6, 2023. https://www.justice.gov/usao-dc/pr/ohio-man-pleads-guilty-unlawfully-stealing-over-712-seized-bitcoin-subject-forfeiture#:~:text=According%20to%20court%20documents%2C%20in,over%20%24300%20million%20at%20the. Cheyenne Ligon, "Brother of criminal Bitcoin mixing CEO pleads guilty to stealing 712 bitcoins from IRS," *CoinDesk*, January 6, 2023. https://www.coindesk.com/policy/2023/01/06/brother-of-criminal-bitcoin-mixing-ceo-pleads-guilty-to-stealing-712-bitcoins-from-irs/ (accessed April 30, 2023).

23. *United States v. Sterlingov*, Statement of Facts, p. 8.

24. Andy Greenberg and Lily Hay Newman, "Bitcoin fog case could put cryptocurrency tracing on trial," *Wired*, August 2, 2022. https://www.wired.com/story/bitcoin-fog-roman-sterlingov-blockchain-analysis/ (accessed April 30, 2023).

25. See https://wasabiwallet.io/ (accessed April 30, 2023).

26. See https://bitcointalk.org/?topic=279249 (accessed April 30, 2023).

27. Europol EC3 Cybercrime Centre, *Wasabi Wallet Report*, April 2020. https://www.tbstat.com/wp/uploads/2020/06/Europol-Wasabi-Wallet-Report.pdf (accessed April 30, 2023).

28. Dr. Tom Robinson, "Over 13% of all proceeds of crime in Bitcoin are now laundered through privacy wallets," December 9, 2020. https://

www.elliptic.co/blog/13-bitcoin-crime-laundered-through-privacy-wallet (accessed April 30, 2023).

29. Ibid.

30. Dr. Tom Robinson, "Over 50% of the #TwitterHack bitcoins have now been sent through mixers – What does that mean for crypto AML?," July 31, 2020. https://www.elliptic.co/blog/what-does-the-twitterhack-mean-for-crypto-aml (accessed April 30, 2023).

31. United States Department of the Treasury Financial Crimes Enforcement Network (FinCEN), "FinCEN Alerts Financial Institutions to Convertible Virtual Currency Scam Involving Twitter," FinCEN Alert, July 16, 2020. https://www.fincen.gov/sites/default/files/2020-07/FinCEN%20Alert%20Twitter_508%20FINAL.pdf (accessed April 30, 2023).

32. *United States of America v. Nima Fazeli*, Criminal Complaint, United States District Court for the Northern District of California, July 15, 2020. https://www.justice.gov/d9/press-releases/attachments/2020/07/31/fazeli_complaint_0.pdf (accessed April 30, 2023).

33. Makena Kelly, "Coinbase says it halted more than $280,000 in bitcoin transactions during Twitter hack," *The Verge*, July 20, 2020. https://www.theverge.com/2020/7/20/21331499/coinbase-twitter-hack-elon-musk-bill-gates-joe-biden-bitcoin-scam (accessed April 30, 2023).

34. Elizabeth Napolitano, "2020 Twitter Hacker Sentenced to 5 Years on Crypto Theft, SIM Swapping Scheme," *CoinDesk*, June 23, 2023. https://www.coindesk.com/policy/2023/06/23/2020-twitter-hacker-sentence-to-5-years-on-crypto-theft-sim-swapping-scheme/ (accessed June 23, 2023).

35. Namcios, "Wasabi Wallet parent company explains decision to censor Bitcoin transactions," *Bitcoin Magazine*, March 28, 2022. https://bitcoinmagazine.com/business/wasabi-wallet-explains-new-bitcoin-censorship (accessed April 30, 2023).

4. Privacy Coins: Going Underground

1. Drew Angerer, "Senator calls for total ban of 'dangerous' Bitcoin," February 27, 2014. https://www.nbcnews.com/tech/innovation/senator-calls-total-ban-dangerous-bitcoin-n39541 (accessed May 1, 2023).

2. "The largest ICO scams swindled $687.4 million," *Finance Monthly*, October 2018, https://www.finance-monthly.com/2018/10/the-10-biggest-ico-scams-swindled-687-4-million/ (accessed May 1, 2023).

3. United States Securities and Exchange Commission, "SEC Charges Latvian Citizen with Digital Asset Fraud," press release, December 2, 2021. https://www.sec.gov/news/press-release/2021-248 (accessed May 1, 2023).

4. Office of the United States Attorney Southern District of California, "Almost $57 Million in Seized Cryptocurrency Sold for Victims of BitConnect Fraud," press release, November 16, 2021. https://www.justice.gov/media/1175886/dl?inline (accessed May 1, 2023). Office of the United States Attorney Southern District of California, "U.S. Promoter of Foreign Cryptocurrency Company Sentenced to Prison for Role in Fraud Scheme," press release, September 16, 2022. https://www.justice.gov/media/1248056/dl?inline (accessed May 1, 2023).

5. Office of the United States Attorney Southern District of California, "Almost $57 Million in Seized Cryptocurrency Sold for Victims of BitConnect Fraud."

6. Amitoj Singh, "BitConnect founder, indicted in US over missing Bitcoin, is now wanted in India, too," *CoinDesk*, August 17, 2022. https://www.coindesk.com/policy/2022/08/17/fugitive-bitconnect-founder-kumbhani-indicted-in-us-is-now-wanted-in-india-too/ (accessed May 1, 2023).

7. United States Department of Justice, "BitConnect Founder Indicted in Global $2.4 Billion Cryptocurrency Scheme," press release, February 25, 2022. https://www.justice.gov/opa/pr/bitconnect-founder-indicted-global-24-billion-cryptocurrency-scheme (accessed May 1, 2023).

8. Fergal Reid and Martin Harrigan, "An Analysis of Anonymity in the Bitcoin System," arXiv:1107.4524 [physics.soc-ph]. Last revised May 7, 2012. https://doi.org/10.48550/arXiv.1107.4524 (accessed May 1, 2023).

9. Sarah Meiklejohn *et al.*, "A Fistful of Bitcoins: Characterizing Payments Among Men with No Names," IMC'13, October 23–25, 2013, Barcelona, Spain. https://cseweb.ucsd.edu/~smeiklejohn/files/imc13.pdf (accessed May 1, 2023).

10. M. Möser, R. Böhme, and D. Breuker, "An inquiry into money laundering tools in the Bitcoin ecosystem," 2013 APWG eCrime Researchers Summit, 2013, pp. 1–14. https://ieeexplore.ieee.org/document/6805780 (accessed May 1, 2023).

11. Financial Action Task Force, "Second 12-Month Review of the Revised FATF Standards on Virtual Assets and Virtual Asset Service Providers," June 2021, p. 30. https://www.fatf-gafi.org/media/fatf/documents/recommendations/Second-12-Month-Review-Revised-FATF-Standards-Virtual-Assets-VASPS.pdf (accessed May 1, 2023).

12. New York Department of Financial Services, "RE: Guidance on Use of Blockchain Analytics," April 28, 2022. https://www.dfs.ny.gov/industry_guidance/industry_letters/il20220428_guidance_use_blockchain_analytics (accessed May 1, 2023).

13. United States Senate Committee on Banking, Housing, and Urban Affairs, "Toomey: Misconduct, Not Crypto, to Blame for FTX Collapse," December 14, 2022. https://www.banking.senate.gov/newsroom/minority/toomey-misconduct-not-crypto-to-blame-for-ftx-collapse (accessed May 1, 2023).

14. Nicolas Van Saberhagen, "CryptoNote v 2.0," October 17, 2013, p. 1. https://bytecoin.org/old/whitepaper.pdf (accessed May 1, 2023).

15. Ibid.

16. I. Miers, C. Garman, M. Green and A. D. Rubin, "Zerocoin: Anonymous distributed e-cash from Bitcoin," 2013 IEEE Symposium on Security and Privacy, pp. 397–411. https://ieeexplore.ieee.org/document/6547123 (accessed May 1, 2023).

17. Evan Duffield and Daniel Diaz, "Dash: A Payments-Focused Cryptocurrency," January 18, 2014. https://github.com/dashpay/dash/wiki/Whitepaper (accessed May 1, 2023).

18. "How It Works." https://z.cash/technology/ (accessed May 1, 2023).

19. Naomi Brockwell, "Edward Snowden played key role in Zcash privacy coin's creation," *CoinDesk*, April 27, 2022. https://www.coindesk.com/tech/2022/04/27/edward-snowden-played-key-role-in-zcash-privacy-coins-creation/ (accessed May 1, 2023).

20. Tobias Kaiser, "About privacy on Monero and Lightning: Interview with Riccardo Spagni," *BeInCrypto*, October 27, 2020. https://beincrypto.com/about-privacy-on-monero-and-lightning-interview-with-riccardo-spagni/ (accessed May 1, 2023).

21. Europol, *IOCTA 2016: Internet Organized Threat Assessment*, The Hague, 2016, pp. 43–44. https://www.europol.europa.eu/cms/sites/default/files/documents/europol_iocta_web_2016.pdf (accessed May 1, 2023).

22. Europol, *IOCTA 2017: Internet Organized Threat Assessment*, The Hague, 2017, p. 61. https://www.europol.europa.eu/cms/sites/default/files/documents/iocta2017.pdf (accessed May 1, 2023).

23. Mark Hunter, "How AlphaBay made Monero," *Fully Crypto*, September 6, 2020. https://fullycrypto.com/how-alphabay-made-monero (accessed May 1, 2023).

24. Europol, "Double Blow to Dark Web Marketplaces," press release, May 3, 2019. https://www.europol.europa.eu/media-press/newsroom/news/double-blow-to-dark-web-marketplaces (accessed May 1, 2023).

25. Mohar Chatterjee, "The demise of White House market will shake up the dark web," *Wired*, November 1, 2021. https://www.wired.com/story/white-house-market-dark-web-drugs-goes-down/ (accessed May 1, 2023).

26. Ibid.

27. Andy Greenberg, "AlphaBay is taking over the dark web – again," *Wired*, June 6, 2022. https://www.wired.com/story/alphabay-dark-web-market-ranking/ (accessed May 1, 2023).

28. Brigid O'Gorman, "Cryptojacking: A Modern Cash Cow," October 2, 2018. https://symantec-enterprise-blogs.security.com/blogs/threat-intelligence/cryptojacking-modern-cash-cow (accessed May 1, 2023).

29. Ibid.

30. *United States of America v. 155 Virtual Assets*, Verified Compliant for Forfeiture In Rem, August 13, 2020, p. 15. https://extremism.gwu.edu/sites/g/files/zaxdzs2191/f/Criminal%20Complaint_Al-Ikhwa%20Accounts.pdf (accessed May 1, 2023).

31. United States Department of Justice, "Global Disruption of Three Terror Finance Cyber-Enabled Campaigns," press release, August 13, 2020. https://www.justice.gov/opa/pr/global-disruption-three-terror-finance-cyber-enabled-campaigns (accessed May 1, 2023).

32. Dr. Tom Robinson, "The US takedown of crypto-linked terrorist financing," August 14, 2020. https://www.elliptic.co/blog/the-us-takedown-of-crypto-linked-terrorist-financing (accessed May 1, 2023).

33. Silfversten, Erik, Marina Favaro, Linda Slapakova, Sascha Ishikawa, James Liu, and Adrian Salas, *Exploring the Use of Zcash Cryptocurrency for Illicit or Criminal Purposes*. Santa Monica, CA: RAND Corporation, 2020, pp. vii–viii. https://www.rand.org/pubs/research_reports/RR4418.html (accessed May 2, 2023).

34. Dr. Tom Robinson, "Lower risk than bitcoin? Achieving AML and sanctions compliance with privacy coins," June 30, 2020. https://www.elliptic.co/blog/achieving-aml-and-sanctions-compliance-with-privacy-coins (accessed May 2, 2023).

35. Christine Vasileva, "Europol: Monero payments cannot be traced," *Bitcoinist*, December 30, 2019. `https://bitcoinist.com/europol-monero-payments-cannot-be-traced/` (accessed May 2, 2023).

36. *United States v Alexandre Cazes*, pp. 20–21. `https://www.justice.gov/opa/press-release/file/982821/download` (accessed May 2, 2023).

37. United States Department of Justice, "Global Disruption of Three Terror Finance Cyber-Enabled Campaigns."

38. *United States of America v. Paul Engstrom, Vincent Cuomo, Abraham Elliot, and Joseph Krieger*, Criminal Complaint, June 22, 2021, p. 10. `https://www.justice.gov/opa/page/file/1444546/download` (accessed May 2, 2023).

39. Ibid., p. 8.

40. Malte Möser, Kyle Soska, Ethan Heilman, Kevin Lee, Henry Heffan, Shashvat Srivastava, Kyle Hogan, Jason Hennessey, Andrew Miller, Arvind Narayanan, and Nicolas Christin: "An empirical analysis of traceability in the Monero blockchain," *Proceedings on Privacy Enhancing Technologies*, 2018(3): 143–163. `http://www.contrib.andrew.cmu.edu/~nicolasc/publications/Moeser-PETS18.pdf` (accessed May 2, 2023).

41. Vitalik Buterin, "Privacy on the blockchain," January 15, 2016. `https://blog.ethereum.org/2016/01/15/privacy-on-the-blockchain` (accessed May 2, 2023).

42. Financial Action Task Force, *Updated Guidance on a Risk Based Approach for Virtual Assets and Virtual Asset Service Providers*, October 2021, p. 72. `https://www.fatf-gafi.org/media/fatf/documents/recommendations/Updated-Guidance-VA-VASP.pdf` (accessed May 2, 2023).

43. Financial Action Task Force, *Virtual Asset Red Flag Indicators of Money Laundering and Terrorist Financing*, September 2020, p. 9. `https://www.fatf-gafi.org/media/fatf/documents/recommendations/Virtual-Assets-Red-Flag-Indicators.pdf` (accessed May 2, 2023).

44. United States Department of the Treasury Financial Crimes Enforcement Network (FinCEN), "Application of FinCEN's regulations to certain business models involving convertible virtual currencies," *FinCEN Guidance*, May 9, 2019, pp. 19–20. `https://www.fincen.gov/sites/default/files/2019-05/FinCEN%20Guidance%20CVC%20FINAL%20508.pdf` (accessed May 2, 2023).

45. United States Department of the Treasury Financial Crimes Enforcement Network (FinCEN), Consent Order Imposing Civil Monetary Penalty in

the Matter of Bittrex, Inc., October 11, 2022. https://www.fincen.gov/sites/default/files/enforcement_action/2022-10-11/Bittrex%20Consent%20Order%2010.11.2022.pdf (accessed May 2, 2023).

46. Robert Viglione, "Japan's ban is a wake-up call to defend privacy coins," *CoinDesk*, May 29, 2018. https://www.coindesk.com/markets/2018/05/29/japans-ban-is-a-wake-up-call-to-defend-privacy-coins/ (accessed May 2, 2023).

47. New York State Department of Financial Services, "Guidance regarding adoption of listing of virtual currencies," *Virtual Currency Business Guidance*, June 24, 2020. https://www.dfs.ny.gov/industry_guidance/industry_letters/il20200624_adoption_listing_vc (accessed May 2, 2023).

48. Gemini, "Gemini is now the world's first licensed Zcash exchange!," May 14, 2018. https://www.gemini.com/blog/gemini-is-now-the-worlds-first-licensed-zcash-exchange (accessed May 2, 2023).

49. Elliptic, *Coinswap Services Briefing Note*, November 2022, p. 2. https://hub.elliptic.co/reports/coin-swap-services-briefing-note/ (accessed May 2, 2023).

50. Europol, *Cryptocurrencies: Tracing the Evolution of Criminal Finances*, December 2021, p. 7. https://www.europol.europa.eu/cms/sites/default/files/documents/Europol%20Spotlight%20-%20Cryptocurrencies%20-%20Tracing%20the%20evolution%20of%20criminal%20finances.pdf (accessed May 2, 2023).

51. Zooko Wilcox and Paige Peterson, "Press Release: Zero-knowledge Security Layer to be Added to Quorum Blockchain Platform," Electric Coin Company, May 22, 2017. https://electriccoin.co/blog/zsl-quorum/ (accessed May 2, 2023).

5. Bitcoin ATMs: Crypto Hits the Streets

1. Paul Vigna, "Crypto and its many fees: What to know about the hidden costs of digital currency," *The Wall Street Journal*, December 18, 2021. https://www.wsj.com/articles/crypto-and-its-many-fees-what-to-know-about-the-hidden-costs-of-digital-currency-11639825202 (accessed May 2, 2023).

2. David Carlisle, *Virtual Currencies and Financial Crime: Challenges and Opportunities*. Royal United Services Institute, Occasional Paper, p. 2. https://static.rusi.org/rusi_op_virtual_currencies_and_financial_crime.pdf (accessed May 2, 2023).

3. CoinATM Radar. www.coinatmradar.com (accessed May 2, 2023).

4. United States Department of Justice, "'Bitcoin Maven' Sentenced to One Year in Federal Prison in Money Laundering Case," press release, July 9, 2018. https://www.justice.gov/usao-cdca/pr/bitcoin-maven-sentenced-one-year-federal-prison-bitcoin-money-laundering-case (accessed May 2, 2023).

5. *United States of America v. Theresa Tetley, aka "Bitcoin Maven."* http://www.courtcasedocs.com/Case%20Files/17-CR-00585-GMS/pdf/224-1-20180720.pdf (accessed May 2, 2023).

6. Cyrus Farivar, "After years of investigation, feds bust one of AlphaBay's largest drug rings," *Ars Technica*, August 22, 2017. https://arstechnica.com/tech-policy/2017/08/after-years-of-investigation-feds-bust-one-of-alphabays-largest-drug-rings/ (accessed May 2, 2023).

7. *United States of America v. Theresa Tetley, aka "Bitcoin Maven,"* p. 11. https://www.documentcloud.org/documents/4501475-adec1f54-3bfa-47dd-bca9-4588f16da0a8.html#document/p15/a436845 (accessed May 2, 2023).

8. Ibid., p. 13.

9. Dr. Tom Robinson, "Buried treasure – How tightening regulation is forcing criminals to go to extreme lengths to cash-out their cryptoassets," March 22, 2021. https://www.elliptic.co/blog/buried-treasure-criminals-to-go-to-extreme-lengths-to-cash-out-crypto (accessed May 2, 2023).

10. Koos Couvee, "European Traffickers Pay Colombian Cartels Through Bitcoin ATMs: Europol Official," February 28, 2018. https://www.moneylaundering.com/news/european-traffickers-pay-colombian-cartels-through-bitcoin-atms-europol-official/ (accessed May 2, 2023).

11. Europol, "Cryptocurrency Laundering as a Service: Members of Criminal Organisation Arrested in Spain," press release, May 8, 2019. https://www.europol.europa.eu/media-press/newsroom/news/cryptocurrency-laundering-service-members-of-criminal-organisation-arrested-in-spain (accessed May 2, 2023).

12. Ibid.

13. Kieran Corcoran, "Drug dealers are laundering cash at Bitcoin ATMs, London police say," December 4, 2017. https://www.businessinsider.com/drug-dealers-laundering-their-money-at-bitcoin-atms-london-police-say-2017-12?r=US&IR=T (accessed May 2, 2023).

14. United States Government Accountability Office, *Virtual Currencies: Additional Information Could Improve Federal Agency Efforts to Counter Human and Drug Trafficking*, December 2021, p. 26. https://www.gao.gov/assets/gao-22-105462.pdf (accessed May 2, 2023).

15. Financial Action Task Force Report, *Financial Flows From Human Trafficking*, July 2018, p. 67. https://www.fatf-gafi.org/media/fatf/content/images/human-trafficking-2018.pdf (accessed May 2, 2023).

16. United States Department of Justice, "Justice Department Leads Effort to Seize Backpage.com, the Internet's Leading Forum for Prostitution Ads, and Obtains a 93-Count Federal Indictment," press release, April 9, 2018. https://www.justice.gov/opa/pr/justice-department-leads-effort-seize-backpagecom-internet-s-leading-forum-prostitution-ads (accessed May 2, 2023).

17. *United States of America v. Michael Lacey, et al.*, Indictment, March 28, 2018, pp. 4–5. https://www.justice.gov/file/1050276/download (accessed May 2, 2023).

18. Luke Parker, "Backpage goes Bitcoin-only," *Brave New Coin*, July 8, 2015. https://bravenewcoin.com/insights/backpage-goes-bitcoin-only (accessed May 2, 2023).

19. Cryptocurrency Compliance Cooperative, "Post-Super Bowl Bitcoin ATM Red Flags." https://crypto3c.org/blog/post-super-bowl-bitcoin-atm-red-flags/ (accessed May 2, 2023).

20. Hawaiian Electric, "New Twist on Old Scam: Crooks Now Demanding Payments for 'Overdue' Utility Bills," press release, August 14, 2018. https://www.hawaiianelectric.com/new-twist-on-old-scam-crooks-now-demanding-payments-for-overdue-utility-bills-in-bitcoin (accessed May 2, 2023).

21. Charlie Coe, "New cryptocurrency scam is fleecing victims out of tens of thousands of dollars by tricking them into using a Bitcoin ATM," *Daily Mail*, October 5, 2018. https://www.dailymail.co.uk/news/article-6242365/New-cryptocurrency-scam-fleecing-victims-ten-thousands-dollars-Bitcoin-ATM.html (accessed May 2, 2023).

22. Michael Schwartz, "Buffalo woman loses retirement savings in Bitcoin ATM scam," April 12, 2022. https://www.wkbw.com/7problemsolvers/buffalo-woman-loses-retirement-savings-in-bitcoin-atm-scam (accessed May 2, 2023).

23. State of New Jersey Commission of Investigation, *Bitcoin ATMs: Scams, Suspicious Transactions and Questionable Practices at Cryptocurrency*

Kiosks, February 2021, p. 10. https://www.nj.gov/sci/pdf/SCI%20 Bitcoin%20Report.pdf (accessed May 2, 2023).

24. Federal Bureau of Investigation, "The FBI Warns of Fraudulent Schemes Leveraging Cryptocurrency ATMs and QR Codes to Facilitate Payment," November 4, 2021. https://www.ic3.gov/Media/Y2021/PSA211104 (accessed May 2, 2023).

25. Christina Miranda, Division of Consumer and Business Education, "New cryptocurrency payment scam alert," Federal Consumer Trade Commission, January 10, 2022. https://consumer.ftc.gov/ consumer-alerts/2022/01/new-crypto-payment-scam-alert (accessed May 2, 2023).

26. State of New Jersey Department of Law and Public Safety, "Bureau of Securities Orders Three Website Operators to Stop Offering Fraudulent Cryptocurrency Investment Opportunities, Urges NJ Residents to Beware of 'Pig Butchering' Scams," press release, February 3, 2023. https:// www.njoag.gov/bureau-of-securities-orders-three- website-operators-to-stop-offering-fraudulent-crypto currency-investment-opportunities-urges-nj-residents- to-beware-of-pig-butchering-scams/ (accessed May 2, 2023).

27. Federal Bureau of Investigation, "Cryptocurrency Investment Schemes," October 3, 2022. https://www.ic3.gov/Media/Y2022/PSA221003 (accessed May 2, 2023).

28. Alastair McCready, "From industrial-scale scam centers, trafficking victims are being forced to steal billions," *Vice*, July 13, 2022. https://www .vice.com/en/article/n7zb5d/pig-butchering-scam- cambodia-trafficking (accessed May 2, 2023).

29. United States Department of the Treasury Financial Crimes Enforcement Network (FinCEN), "Application of FinCEN's regulations to certain business models involving convertible virtual currencies," *FinCEN Guidance*, May 9, 2019, pp. 17–18.

30. Coinsource, "Bitcoin ATMs, Regulation and Compliance," November 9, 2018.https://blog.coinsource.net/bitcoin-atms-regulations- and-compliance/ (accessed May 2, 2023).

31. Coinsource, "Coinsource First Ever Bitcoin ATM Operator to Receive License from NYDFS," November 1, 2018. https://blog.coinsource. net/coinsource-first-ever-bitcoin-atm-operator-to- receive-license-from-nydfs/ (accessed May 2, 2023).

32. Cryptocurrency Compliance Cooperative, "About." https:// crypto3c.org/about/.

33. United States Department of Justice, "O.C. Man Admits Operating Unlicensed ATM Network that Laundered Millions of Dollars of Bitcoin and Cash for Criminals' Benefit," press release, July 22, 2020. https://www.justice.gov/usao-cdca/pr/oc-man-admits-operating-unlicensed-atm-network-laundered-millions-dollars-bitcoin-and (accessed May 2, 2023).

34. Ibid.

35. Manhattan District Attorney's Office, "D.A. Bragg Announces Indictment in Citywide Illegal Bitcoin ATM Operation," press release, April 13, 2022. https://www.manhattanda.org/d-a-bragg-announces-indictment-in-citywide-illegal-bitcoin-atm-operation/ (accessed May 2, 2023).

36. Martin Young, "Bitcoin ATM frim allegedly profited from crypto scam via unlicensed kiosks: prosecutor," *Cointelegraph*, March 6, 2023. https://cointelegraph.com/news/bitcoin-atm-firm-profited-from-crypto-scams-via-unlicensed-kiosks-secret-service (accessed May 2, 2023).

37. Monetary Authority of Singapore, "MAS Issues Guidelines to Discourage Cryptocurrency Trading by General Public," press release, January 17, 2022. https://www.mas.gov.sg/news/media-releases/2022/mas-issues-guidelines-to-discourage-cryptocurrency-trading-by-general-public (accessed May 2, 2023).

38. Financial Conduct Authority, "Warning on Illegal Crypto ATMs Operating in the UK," press release, March 11, 2022. https://www.fca.org.uk/news/news-stories/warning-illegal-crypto-atms-operating-uk (accessed May 2, 2023).

6. Ransomware: Cybercrime Goes Industrial

1. Marlesse Lessing, "Case Study: AIDS Trojan Ransomware," June 3, 2020. https://www.sdxcentral.com/security/definitions/what-is-ransomware/case-study-aids-trojan-ransomware/ (accessed May 3, 2023).

2. "Ransomware," https://www.malwarebytes.com/blog/threats/ransomware

3. Marlesse Lessing, "Case Study: Reveton Ransomware," June 17, 2020. https://www.sdxcentral.com/security/definitions/what-is-ransomware/case-study-reveton-ransomware/ (accessed May 3, 2023).

4. Ibid.

5. "CryptoLocker Ransomware." https://www.knowbe4.com/crypto locker-ransomware (accessed May 3, 2023).

6. Ibid.

7. Violet Blue, "CryptoLocker's Crime Wave: A Trail of Millions Laundered in Bitcoin," December 22, 2013. https://www.zdnet.com/article/cryptolockers-crimewave-a-trail-of-millions-in-laundered-bitcoin/ (accessed May 3, 2023).

8. Michael Daniel, "Cyber Threat Alliance Cracks the Code on CryptoWall Crimeware Associated with $325 Million in Payments," October 28, 2015. https://cyberthreatalliance.org/cyber-threat-alliance-cracks-code-cryptowall-crimeware-associated-325-million-payments/ (accessed May 3, 2023).

9. *United States of America v. BTC-e, a/k/a Canton Business Corporation, and Alexander Vinnik*, p. 12.

10. FinCEN, Assessment of Civil Monetary Penalty in the Matter of Larry Dean Harmon d/b/a Helix, p. 6.

11. "WannaCry Cyber-Attack Cost the NHS £92m After 19,000 Appointments were Cancelled," October 12, 2018. https://www.nationalhealth executive.com/articles/wannacry-cyber-attack-cost-nhs-ps92m-after-19000-appointments-were-cancelled (accessed May 3, 2023).

12. Charles Cooper, "WannaCry: Lessons Learned One Year Later," May 16, 2018. https://symantec-enterprise-blogs.security.com/blogs/feature-stories/wannacry-lessons-learned-1-year-later (accessed May 3, 2023).

13. Thomas Brewster, "WannaCry hackers are using this Swiss company to launder $142,000 Bitcoin ransoms," *Forbes*, August 3, 2017. https://www.forbes.com/sites/thomasbrewster/2017/08/03/wannacry-hackers-use-shapeshift-to-launder-bitcoin/?sh=e0520b93d0d2 (accessed May 3, 2023).

14. Olivia Solon, "WannaCry ransomware has links to North Korea, cybersecurity experts say," May 15, 2017. https://www.theguardian.com/technology/2017/may/15/wannacry-ransomware-north-korea-lazarus-group (accessed May 3, 2023).

15. "Press Briefing on the Attribution of the WannaCry Malware Attack to North Korea," White House press briefing, December 19, 2017. https://trumpwhitehouse.archives.gov/briefings-statements/press-briefing-on-the-attribution-of-the-wannacry-malware-attack-to-north-korea-121917/ (accessed May 3, 2023).

16. United States Department of Justice, "North Korean-Backed Programmer Charged with Conspiracy to Conduct Multiple Cyber Attacks and Intrusions," press release, September 6, 2018. https://www.justice.gov/opa/pr/north-korean-regime-backed-programmer-charged-conspiracy-conduct-multiple-cyber-attacks-and (accessed May 3, 2023).

17. United States Department of the Treasury, "Treasury Designated Iran-Based Financial Facilitators of Malicious Cyber Activity and for the First Time Identifies Associated Digital Currency Addresses," press release, November 28, 2018. https://home.treasury.gov/news/press-releases/sm556 (accessed May 3, 2023).

18. Ibid.

19. United States Department of the Treasury, "Treasury Sanctions North Korean State-Sponsored Malicious Cyber Groups," press release, September 3, 2019. https://home.treasury.gov/news/press-releases/sm774 (accessed May 3, 2023).

20. Kurt Baker, "Ransomware as a Service (RaaS) Explained," February 7, 2022. https://www.crowdstrike.com/cybersecurity-101/ransomware/ransomware-as-a-service-raas/ (accessed May 3, 2023).

21. "Estimated average ransom amount demanded by ransomware attackers worldwide from 2014 to H1 2017," Statista. https://www.statista.com/statistics/696048/ransomware-demanded-payments-world/ (accessed May 3, 2023).

22. Jamie Crawley, "Anatomy of a ransomware attack: Chat support, a discount and a surcharge for Bitcoin," *CoinDesk*, July 19, 2021. https://www.coindesk.com/markets/2021/07/19/anatomy-of-ransomware-attack-chat-support-a-discount-and-a-surcharge-for-bitcoin/ (accessed May 3, 2023).

23. Eric Loui, Karl Sheuerman, and Aaron Pickett, "Targeted Dharma Ransomware Intrusions Exhibit Consistent Techniques," April 16, 2020. https://www.crowdstrike.com/blog/targeted-dharma-ransomware-intrusions-exhibit-consistent-techniques/ (accessed May 3, 2023).

24. Ionut Arghire, "Financially-motivated Iranian hackers adopt Dharma ransomware," *Security Week*, August 24, 2020. https://www.securityweek.com/financially-motivated-iranian-hackers-adopt-dharma-ransomware (accessed May 3, 2023).

25. "Over Half of Ransomware Victims Pay the Ransom, But Only a Quarter See Their Full Data Returned," March 30, 2021. https://www

.kaspersky.com/about/press-releases/2021_over-half-of-ransomware-victims-pay-the-ransom-but-only-a-quarter-see-their-full-data-returned (accessed May 10, 2023).

26. Alexander Hanel, "Big Game Hunting with Ryuk: Another Lucrative Targeted Ransomware," January 10, 2019. https://www.crowdstrike.com/blog/big-game-hunting-with-ryuk-another-lucrative-targeted-ransomware/ (accessed May 3, 2023).

27. United States Department of State, "DarkSide Ransomware as a Service (RaaS)," Transnational Organized Crime Rewards Program, November 4, 2021. https://www.state.gov/darkside-ransomware-as-a-service-raas/. Dr. Tom Robinson, "DarkSide ransomware has netted over $90 million in Bitcoin," May 18, 2021. https://www.elliptic.co/blog/darkside-ransomware-has-netted-over-90-million-in-bitcoin (accessed May 4, 2023).

28. Dr. Tom Robinson, "Elliptic follows the Bitcoin ransoms paid by Colonial Pipeline and other DarkSide ransomware victims," May 14, 2021. https://www.elliptic.co/blog/elliptic-follows-bitcoin-ransoms-paid-by-darkside-ransomware-victims (accessed May 4, 2023).

29. United States Department of Justice, "Department of Justice Seizes $23 Million in Cryptocurrency Paid to the Ransomware Extortionists Darkside," press release, June 7, 2021. https://www.justice.gov/opa/pr/department-justice-seizes-23-million-cryptocurrency-paid-ransomware-extortionists-darkside (accessed May 4, 2023).

30. Ibid.

31. United States Department of the Treasury, "Treasury Sanctions IRGC-Affiliated Cyber Actors for Roles in Ransomware Activity," press activity, September 14, 2022. https://home.treasury.gov/news/press-releases/jy0948 (accessed May 4, 2023).

32. Matt Burgess, "Conti's attack against Costa Rica sparks new ransomware era," *Wired*, June 12, 2022. https://www.wired.co.uk/article/costa-rica-ransomware-conti (accessed May 4, 2023).

33. "Ransomware Annex to G7 Statement," October 13, 2022. https://home.treasury.gov/system/files/136/G7-Ransomware-Annex-10132020_Final.pdf (accessed May 4, 2023).

34. Financial Action Task Force, "Regulation of Virtual Assets," October 19, 2018. https://www.fatf-gafi.org/publications/fatfrecommendations/documents/regulation-virtual-assets.html (accessed May 4, 2023).

35. Thomas Frank, "Mnuchin says Treasury will ensure Bitcoin doesn't become 'Swiss numbered bank accounts," *CNBC*, July 18, 2019. https://www.cnbc.com/2019/07/18/mnuchin-says-us-will-ensure-bitcoin-doesnt-become-like-anonymous.html (accessed May 4, 2023).

36. United States Department of the Treasury Financial Crimes Enforcement Network (FinCEN), "Requirements for Certain Transactions Involving Convertible Virtual Currency or Digital Assets," Notice of Proposed Rulemaking, Federal Register 31 CFR Parts 1010, 1020, and 1022, December 23, 2020. https://public-inspection.federalregister.gov/2020-28437.pdf (accessed May 4, 2023).

37. CoinCenter, "Comments to the Financial Crimes Enforcement Network on Requirements for Certain Transactions Involving Convertible Virtual Currency or Digital Assets," December 22, 2020. https://www.coincenter.org/app/uploads/2020/12/2020-12-22-comments-to-fincen.pdf (accessed May 4, 2023).

38. Karen Painter Randall and Joseph McNelis III, "Two States Now Prohibit Public Entities from Paying Ransoms," August 18, 2022. https://www.connellfoley.com/blog/Two-States-Prohibit-Public-Entities-Paying-Ransoms (accessed May 4, 2023).

39. David Carlisle, "OFAC ransomware crackdown targets SUEX crypto exchange that has received more than $909 million," September 21, 2021. https://www.elliptic.co/blog/ofac-ransomware-crackdown-targets-suex-crypto-exchange-that-has-received-more-than-900-million (accessed May 4, 2023).

40. United States Department of the Treasury, "Treasury Takes Robust Actions to Counter Ransomware," press release, September 21, 2021. https://home.treasury.gov/news/press-releases/jy0364 (accessed May 4, 2023).

41. Michael Kan, "US Sanctions Russian Cryptocurrency Exchange for Facilitating Ransomware Payments," *PCMag*, September 21, 2021. https://uk.pcmag.com/security/135781/us-sanctions-russian-cryptocurrency-exchange-for-facilitating-ransomware-payments (accessed May 4, 2023).

42. United States Department of the Treasury, "Treasury Continues to Counter Ransomware as Part of Whole-of-Government Effort; Sanctions Ransomware Operators and Virtual Currency Exchange," November 8, 2021. https://home.treasury.gov/news/press-releases/jy0471 (accessed May 4, 2023).

43. https://home.treasury.gov/news/press-releases/jy0701 (accessed May 4, 2023).

44. United States Department of the Treasury, "Treasury Sanctions Russia-Based Hydra, World's Largest Dark Market, and Ransomware-Enabling Virtual Currency Exchange Garantex," press release, April 5, 2022. `https://home.treasury.gov/news/press-releases/jy0701` (accessed May 4, 2023).

45. United States Department of the Treasury Financial Crimes Enforcement Network (FinCEN), "FinCEN Identifies Virtual Currency Exchange Bitzlato as 'Primary Money Laundering Concern' in Connection with Russian Illicit Finance," press release, January 18, 2023. `https://www.fincen.gov/news/news-releases/fincen-identifies-virtual-currency-exchange-bitzlato-primary-money-laundering` (accessed May 4, 2023).

46. United States Department of the Treasury, "Treasury Sanctions IRGC-Affiliated Cyber Actors for Roles in Ransomware Activity," press release, September 14, 2022. `https://home.treasury.gov/news/press-releases/jy0948` (accessed May 4, 2023).

47. Rashmi Ramesh, "Ransomware payments on pace to set new record in 2023," *Bank Info Security*, July 12, 2023. `https://www.bankinfosecurity.com/ransomware-crypto-payments-poised-to-set-new-record-in-2023-a-22529` (accessed July 31, 2023).

7. Hacked: Crypto Exchange Heists

1. "51 Crypto Exchange Hacks: A History that'd Blow Your Mind!," April 22, 2022. `https://coinsutra.com/crypto-exchange-hacks/#1inde-bitcoinica` (accessed May 7, 2023).

2. See `https://www.xapobank.com/security` (accessed July 30, 2023).

3. David Z. Morris, "4 Unanswered Questions About the Bitfinex Hack," February 9, 2022. `https://www.coindesk.com/layer2/2022/02/09/4-unanswered-questions-about-the-bitfinex-hack/` (accessed May 7, 2023).

4. Kai Sedgwick, "54% of exchanges have security holes," October 2, 2018. `https://news.bitcoin.com/54-of-cryptocurrency-exchanges-have-security-holes/` (accessed May 7, 2023).

5. David Carlisle, *Preventing Financial Crime in Cryptoassets: The Definitive Practical Guide for Governance, Risk, and Compliance Professionals*, Elliptic, 2022, p. 25. Arnold Kirimi, "Report: Scammers Are Buying Dark Web KYC Identities for Crypto Theft," *Daily Coin*, November 18, 2022.

https://dailycoin.com/report-scammers-are-buying-dark-web-kyc-identities-for-crypto-theft/ (accessed May 7, 2023).

6. United States Department of the Treasury, "Treasury Sanctions Russian Cyber Actors for Virtual Currency Theft," press release, September 16, 2020. https://home.treasury.gov/news/press-releases/sm1123 (accessed May 7, 2023).

7. Sam Kim, "North Korean hackers hijack computers to mine cryptocurrencies," *Bloomberg*, January 2, 2018. https://www.bloomberg.com/news/articles/2018-01-02/north-korean-hackers-hijack-computers-to-mine-cryptocurrencies?leadSource=uverify%20wall (accessed May 7, 2023).

8. David Carlisle and Kayla Izenman, *Closing the Crypto Gap: Guidance for Countering North Korean Cryptocurrency Activity in Southeast Asia*, Royal United Services Institute, April 2019, pp. 13–14. https://static.rusi.org/20190412_closing_the_crypto_gap_web.pdf (accessed May 7, 2023).

9. Aaron Wood, "World's Sixth Largest Exchange Bithumb Hacked, Loses $30 Mln," *Cointelegraph*, June 20, 2018. https://cointelegraph.com/news/world-s-sixth-largest-crypto-exchange-by-trade-volume-bithumb-hacked (accessed May 7, 2023).

10. Dr. Tom Robinson, "Elliptic software follows the money from the Bithumb hack," October 9, 2018. https://www.elliptic.co/blog/following-money-from-bithumb-hack (accessed May 7, 2023).

11. Chris Doman, Fernando Martinez, and Jaime Blasco, "Malicious documents from Lazarus Group targeting South Korea," June 22, 2018. https://cybersecurity.att.com/blogs/labs-research/malicious-documents-from-lazarus-group-targeting-south-korea (accessed May 7, 2023).

12. *United States of America v. 113 Virtual Currency Accounts*, United States District Court for the District of Columbia, Verified Complaint for Forfeiture In Rem, March 2, 2020, p. 8. https://www.justice.gov/opa/press-release/file/1253491/download (accessed May 7, 2023).

13. Ibid., pp. 10–11.

14. Ibid., p. 14.

15. Ibid., p. 17.

16. United States Department of the Treasury, "Treasury Sanctions Individuals Laundering Cryptocurrency for the Lazarus Group," press release, March 2, 2020. https://home.treasury.gov/news/press-releases/sm924 (accessed May 7, 2023).

17. "Guidance on the Democratic People's Republic of Korea Information Technology Workers," May 16, 2022. https://home.treasury.gov/system/files/126/20220516_dprk_it_worker_advisory.pdf (accessed May 7, 2023).

18. United Nations Security Council, "Final Report of the Panel of Experts Submitted Pursuant to Resolution 2569," March 1, 2022, p. 4. https://documents-dds-ny.un.org/doc/UNDOC/GEN/N22/252/09/PDF/N2225209.pdf?OpenElement (accessed May 7, 2023).

19. United Nations Security Council, "Midterm Report of the Panel of Experts Submitted Pursuant to Resolution 2627," September 7, 2022, p. 75. https://documents-dds-ny.un.org/doc/UNDOC/GEN/N22/608/53/PDF/N2260853.pdf?OpenElement (accessed May 7, 2023).

20. Elliptic, "The $100 Million Horizon Hack: Following the Trail Through Tornado Cash to North Korea," June 29, 2022. https://hub.elliptic.co/analysis/the-100-million-horizon-hack-following-the-trail-through-tornado-cash-to-north-korea/ (accessed May 7, 2023).

21. United States Department of the Treasury, "Treasury Targets Actors Facilitating DPRK Financial Activity in Support of Weapons Programs," press release, 24 April 2023. https://home.treasury.gov/news/press-releases/jy1435 (accessed May 1, 2023).

22. US Department of Justice, "Two Arrested for Alleged Conspiracy to Launder $4.5 Billion in Stolen Cryptocurrency," press release, February 8, 2022. https://www.justice.gov/opa/pr/two-arrested-alleged-conspiracy-launder-45-billion-stolen-cryptocurrency (accessed May 7, 2023).

23. Heather R. Morgan, "Experts share tips to protect your business from cybercriminals," *Forbes*, June 18, 2020. https://www.forbes.com/sites/heathermorgan/2020/06/18/protect-your-business-from-cybercriminals/?sh=3ecedee52f27 (accessed May 7, 2023).

24. Nick Bilton, "The Ballad of Razzlekhan and Dutch, Bitcoin's Bonnie and Clyde," *Vanity Fair*, August 18, 2022. https://www.vanityfair.com/news/2022/08/the-ballad-of-razzlekhan-and-dutch-bitcoins-bonnie-and-clyde (accessed May 7, 2023).

25. *United States of America v. Ilya Lichtenstein and Heather Rhiannon Morgan*, Statement of Facts, February 7, 2022, p. 5. https://www.justice.gov/opa/press-release/file/1470211/download (accessed May 7, 2023).

26. Ibid., p. 7.

27. Dr. Tom Robinson, "Elliptic follows the $7 billion in Bitcoin stolen from Bitfinex in 2016," May 13, 2021. https://www.elliptic.co/blog/elliptic-analysis-bitcoin-bitfinex-theft (accessed May 7, 2023).

28. Ibid.

29. *United States of America v. Ilya Lichtenstein and Heather Rhiannon Morgan*, p. 8.

30. Nick Bilton, "The Ballad of Razzlekhan and Dutch, Bitcoin's Bonnie and Clyde."

31. US Department of Justice, "Two Arrested for Alleged Conspiracy to Launder $4.5 Billion in Stolen Cryptocurrency."

33. US Department of Justice, "Bitfinex Hacker and Wife Plead Guilty to Money Laundering Conspiracy Involving Billions in Cryptocurrency," August 3, 2023. https://www.justice.gov/opa/pr/bitfinex-hacker-and-wife-plead-guilty-money-laundering-conspiracy-involving-billions (accessed August 3, 2023).

33. Luc Cohen, "Buried gold, burning trash: US admits to hiding hacked crypto," *Reuters*, August 3, 2023. https://www.reuters.com/world/us/us-man-pleads-guilty-laundering-crypto-stolen-bitfinex-hack-2023-08-03/ (accessed August 3, 2023).

34. Helen Partz, "Report: Blockchain-related hacks have declined in 2020," *Cointelegraph*, November 2, 2020. https://cointelegraph.com/news/report-blockchain-related-hacks-have-declined-in-2020 (accessed May 7, 2023).

8. DeFi: Tornadoes, Bridges, and the Frontiers of Regulation

1. Michelle Nichols and Rafael Satter, "U.N. experts point finger at North Korea for $281 million cyber theft," *Reuters*, February 10, 2021. https://www.reuters.com/article/us-northkorea-sanctions-cyber-idUSKBN2AA00Q (accessed May 9, 2023).

2. Vitalik Buterin, "Ethereum: A Next-Generation Smart Contract and Decentralized Application Platform," Ethereum Foundation, January 2014. https://ethereum.org/669c9e2e2027310b6b3cdce6e1c52962/Ethereum_Whitepaper_-_Buterin_2014.pdf (accessed May 9, 2023).

3. Ibid., p. 1.

4. Ibid., p. 13.

5. Michelle Lim, "74% of stablecoins are issued on Ethereum, according to new report," *Forkast*, January 28, 2021. https://forkast.news/stablecoin-ethereum-consensys-defi-usdt-nft/ (accessed May 9, 2023).

6. See https://github.com/tornadocash (accessed May 9, 2023).

7. Tornado Cash Community Twitter account. `https://twitter.com/TornadoCashOrg`.

8. Wolfie Zhao, "KuCoin has recovered 84% of affected funds in $280M hack, co-founder says," *The Block*, November 11, 2020. `https://www.theblock.co/linked/84248/kucoin-280m-stolen-recovered` (accessed May 9, 2023).

9. Arda Akartuna, "Cross-chain crime: How "coin swap" services have laundered $1.2 billion in high-risk crypto," *Elliptic Connect*, November 21, 2022. `https://hub.elliptic.co/analysis/cross-chain-crime-how-coin-swap-services-have-laundered-1-2-billion-in-high-risk-crypto/` (accessed May 9, 2023).

10. Elliptic, "DeFi: Risk, Regulation, and the Rise of DeCrime," November 18, 2021. `https://www.elliptic.co/resources/defi-risk-regulation-and-the-rise-of-decrime` (accessed May 9, 2023).

11. Laura Shin, "Exclusive: Austrian programmer and ex-crypto CEO likely stole $11 billion of ether," *Forbes*, February 22, 2022. `https://www.forbes.com/sites/laurashin/2022/02/22/exclusive-austrian-programmer-and-ex-crypto-ceo-likely-stole-11-billion-of-ether/?sh=73f11c3a7f58` (accessed May 9, 2023).

12. Catalin Cimpanu, "Hackers steal $130 million from Cream Finance; the company's 3rd hack this year," *The Record*, October 27, 2021. `https://therecord.media/hackers-steal-130-million-from-cream-finance-the-companys-3rd-hack-this-year/` (accessed May 9, 2023).

13. Arda Akartuna, "Top five DeFi crime trends of 2022," *Elliptic Connect*, December 15, 2022. `https://hub.elliptic.co/analysis/top-five-defi-crime-trends-of-2022/` (accessed May 9, 2023).

14. Bill Toulas, "Hackers stole $620 million from Axie Infinity via fake job interviews," *Bleeping Computer*, July 12, 2022. `https://www.bleepingcomputer.com/news/security/hackers-stole-620-million-from-axie-infinity-via-fake-job-interviews/` (accessed May 9, 2023).

15. Adi Robertson and Corin Faife, "A hacker stole $625 million from the blockchain behind NFT game Axie Infinity," *The Verge*, March 29, 2022. `https://www.theverge.com/2022/3/29/23001620/sky-mavis-axie-infinity-ronin-blockchain-validation-defi-hack-nft` (accessed May 9, 2023).

16. Nikhilesh De and Danny Nelson, "US government recovers $30m from crypto game Axie Infinity hack," *CoinDesk*, September 8, 2022. `https://www.coindesk.com/policy/2022/09/08/us-government-recovers-30m-from-crypto-game-axie-infinity-hack/` (accessed May 9, 2023).

17. Financial Action Task Force, *Guidance on a Risk Based Approach: Virtual Assets and Virtual Asset Service Providers*, October 2021, p. 36.

18. United States Department of the Treasury, "Treasury Designates DPRK Weapons Representatives," press release, November 8, 2022. https:// home.treasury.gov/news/press-releases/jy1087#:~:text= Tornado%20Cash%2C%20an%20entity%20that,virtual%20 currency%20heist%20to%20date (accessed May 9, 2023).

19. United States Department of the Treasury, "U.S. Treasury Sanctions Notorious Virtual Currency Mixer Tornado Cash," press release, August 8, 2022. https://home.treasury.gov/news/press-releases/jy0916 (accessed May 9, 2023).

20. Rahul Nambiampurath, "Tornado Cash Monthly Users Fall by Over 50% Post-US Sanctions," October 3, 2022. https://beincrypto-com .webpkgcache.com/doc/-/s/beincrypto.com/tornado-cash- monthly-users-fall-50-us-sanctions/ (accessed May 9, 2023).

21. Jerry Brito and Peter Van Valkenburgh, "Analysis: What is and what is not a sanctionable entity in the Tornado Cash case," August 15, 2022. https://www.coincenter.org/analysis-what-is-and-what- is-not-a-sanctionable-entity-in-the-tornado-cash-case/ (accessed May 9, 2023).

22. Zac Colbert, "OFAC backtracks but Tornado Cash sanctions already set a terrifying precedent," *CoinDesk*, September 15, 2022. https:// www.coindesk.com/layer2/2022/09/15/ofac-backtracks- but-tornado-cash-sanctions-already-set-a-terrifying- precedent/ (accessed May 9, 2023).

23. Lachlan Keller, "Vitalik Buterin says he used Tornado Cash to donate to Ukraine," August 10, 2022. https://forkast.news/vitalik-buterin- says-used-tornado-cash-donate-ukraine/ (accessed May 9, 2023). Elliptic, "Crypto Donations to Ukraine and Russia: Breaking Down the Numbers," March 3, 2023. https://hub.elliptic.co/analysis/ crypto-donations-to-ukraine-and-russia-breaking-down-the- numbers/ (accessed August 29, 2023).

24. Brian Armstrong, "Defending privacy in crypto," September 8, 2022. https://www.coinbase.com/blog/defending-privacy-in- crypto (accessed May 9, 2023).

25. FIOD Belastingdienst, "Arrest of suspected developer of Tornado Cash," August 12, 2022. https://www.fiod.nl/arrest-of-suspected- developer-of-tornado-cash/ (accessed May 9, 2023).

26. United States Department of the Treasury, "Remarks by Assistant Secretary Elizabeth Rosenberg at the Crypto Council for Innovation," press release,

November 18, 2022. `https://home.treasury.gov/news/press-releases/jy1119` (accessed May 9, 2023).

27. Ryan Browne, "Cryptocurrency exchange FTX hits $32 billion valuation despite bear market fears," *CNBC*, January 31, 2022. `https://www.cnbc.com/2022/01/31/crypto-exchange-ftx-valued-at-32-billion-amid-bitcoin-price-plunge.html` (accessed May 9, 2023).

28. United States Department of Justice, "United States Attorney Announces Charges Against FTX Founder Samuel Bankman-Fried," press release, December 13, 2022. `https://www.justice.gov/usao-sdny/pr/united-states-attorney-announces-charges-against-ftx-founder-samuel-bankman-fried` (accessed May 9, 2023).

29. United States Securities and Exchange Commission, "SEC Charges Samuel Bankman-Fried with Defrauding Investors in Crypto Asset Trading Platform FTX," press release, December 13, 2022. `https://www.sec.gov/news/press-release/2022-219` (accessed May 9, 2023). United States Commodity Futures Trading Commission, "CFTC Charges Sam Bankman-Fried, FTX Trading and Alameda with Fraud and Material Misrepresentation," press release, December 13, 2022. `https://www.cftc.gov/PressRoom/PressReleases/8638-22` (accessed May 9, 2023).

30. Dr. Tom Robinson, "$477 Million in 'unauthorized transfers' from FTX," *Elliptic Connect*, November 20, 2022. `https://hub.elliptic.co/analysis/477-million-in-unauthorized-transfers-from-ftx/` (accessed May 9, 2023).

31. "Moving on from Alameda," November 18, 2022. `https://medium.com/renproject/moving-on-from-alameda-da62a823ce93` (accessed May 9, 2023).

32. Ava Benny-Morrison, "US probes how $372 million vanished in hack after US bankruptcy," *Bloomberg*, December 27, 2022. `https://www.bloomberg.com/news/articles/2022-12-27/us-probes-how-372-million-vanished-in-hack-after-ftx-bankruptcy?leadSource=uverify%20wall` (accessed May 9, 2023).

9. NFTs: Virtual Art, Virtual Crime

1. Yoni Assia, Vitalik Buterin, Lior Hakim, Meni Rosenfeld, and Rotem Lev, "Colored Coins White Paper," 2013. `https://www.etoro.com/wp-content/uploads/2022/03/Colored-Coins-white-paper-Digital-Assets.pdf` (accessed May 9, 2023).

2. "ERC-721 Non-Fungible Token Standard," Ethereum Foundation, August 15, 2022. https://ethereum.org/en/developers/docs/standards/tokens/erc-721/ (accessed May 9, 2023).

3. "CryptoKitties: A pioneer in Ethereum gaming and NFTs," March 10, 2022. https://www.gemini.com/cryptopedia/cryptokitties-nft-crypto-ethereum-token (accessed May 9, 2023).

4. "CryptoKitties: Getting in the flow." https://www.cryptokitties.co/blog/post/cryptokitties-on-flow/#:~:text=At%20nearly%20100%2C000%20Kitty%20owners,used%20smart%20contracts%20on%20Ethereum (accessed May 9, 2023).

5. United States Department of the Treasury, *Study of the Facilitation of Money Laundering and Terrorist Financing Through the Trade in Works of Art*, February 2022, p. 26. https://home.treasury.gov/system/files/136/Treasury_Study_WoA.pdf (accessed May 9, 2023).

6. "Non Fungible Token Market, by Category (Collectibles, Utility, Art, Metaverse, Game), by Application (Real Estate, Medical, Academic, Gaming), and by Region Forecast to 2030," Emergen Research, December 2022. https://www.emergenresearch.com/industry-report/non-fungible-token-market (accessed May 9, 2023).

7. Yashu Gola, "OpenSea trading volume explodes 76,240% YTD amid NFT boom," *CoinTelegraph*, August 13, 2021. https://cointelegraph.com/news/opensea-trading-volume-explodes-76-240-ytd-amid-nft-boom (accessed May 9, 2023).

8. Isabelle Lee, "Sales of Bored Ape Yacht Club NFTs jump past $1 billion amid heightened interest from collectors," *Business Insider*, January 4, 2022. https://markets.businessinsider.com/news/currencies/bored-ape-yacht-club-nft-sales-1-billion-opensea-bayc-2022-1 (accessed May 12, 2023).

9. Scott Reyburn, "JPG file sells for $69 million, as 'NFT mania' gathers pace," *The New York Times*, March 11, 2021. https://www.nytimes.com/2021/03/11/arts/design/nft-auction-christies-beeple.html (accessed May 12, 2023).

10. "TIME releases 3 special magazine covers for auction," *TIME Magazine*, March 22, 2021. https://time.com/5948741/time-nft-covers/ (accessed May 12, 2023).

11. See the Adidas Genesis collection on OpenSea: https://opensea.io/collection/adidas-virtual-gear (accessed May 12, 2023).

12. Annabelle Liang, "Former US President Donald Trump sells out NFT trading cards," *BBCNews*, December 16, 2022. https://www.bbc.co.uk/news/business-63995563 (accessed May 12, 2023).

13. Isabelle Lee, "NFT scammers made off with $1.3 million in solana after a 'rug pull' despite the project creators being vetted," *Business Insider*, January 21, 2022. https://markets.businessinsider.com/news/currencies/nft-scam-solana-big-daddy-ape-club-rug-pull-civic-2022-1 (accessed May 12, 2023).

14. Vittoria Benzine, "French authorities say they have nabbed a youth cyber-gang that stole $2.5 million in NFTs," *ArtNet*, October 13, 2022. https://news.artnet.com/art-world/nft-phishing-bored-apes-2191685 (accessed May 12, 2023).

15. Arda Akartuna and Chris DePow, *NFTs and Financial Crime: Money Laundering, Market Manipulation, and Scams & Sanctions Risks in Non-Fungible Tokens*, Elliptic NFT Report 2022 Edition, August 2022, p. 4. https://www.elliptic.co/resources/nfts-financial-crime (accessed May 12, 2023).

16. "Slow Mist: Investigation of North Korean APT's Large-Scale Phishing Attack on NFT Users," https://slowmist.medium.com/slowmist-our-in-depth-investigation-of-north-korean-apts-large-scale-phishing-attack-on-nft-users-362117600519 (accessed May 12, 2023).

17. United States Department of the Treasury, *Study of the Facilitation of Money Laundering and Terrorist Financing Through the Trade in Works of Art*, p. 27.

18. Financial Action Task Force, *Targeted Update on the Implementation of the FATF Standards on Virtual Assets and Virtual Asset Service Providers*, p. 25.

19. Arda Akartuna and Chris DePow, *NFTs and Financial Crime: Money Laundering, Market Manipulation, and Scams & Sanctions Risks in Non-Fungible Tokens*, p. 4.

20. Rupert Neate, "HMRC seizes NFTs for the first time amid fraud inquiry," *The Guardian*, February 14, 2022. https://www.theguardian.com/technology/2022/feb/14/hmrc-seizes-nfts-for-first-time-amid-fraud-inquiry (accessed May 12, 2023).

21. United States Department of Justice, "Justice Department Announces Enforcement Action Charing Six Individuals with Cryptocurrency Fraud Offences in Cases Involving Over $100 Million in Intended Loses," press release, June 30, 2022. https://www.justice.gov/opa/pr/justice-department-announces-enforcement-action-charging-six-individuals-cryptocurrency-fraud (accessed May 12, 2023).

22. *United States of America v. Le Ahn Tuan*, Grand Jury Indictment, United States District Court for the Central District of California, March 2022, p. 10.

https://www.justice.gov/criminal-vns/case/file/1516756/ download (accessed May 12, 2023).

23. United States Department of Justice, "Non-Fungible Token (NFT) Developer Charted in Multi-Million Dollar International Fraud Scheme," press release, January 5, 2023. https://www.justice.gov/usao-ednv/pr/ non-fungible-token-nft-developer-charged-multi-million- dollar-international-fraud (accessed May 12, 2023).

24. *United States of America v. Aurelein Michel*, United States District Court Eastern District of New York, January 4, 2023, pp. 13–15. https://www .justice.gov/usao-ednv/press-release/file/1560886/ download (accessed May 12, 2023).

25. "Almost $23.7B NFTs minted in 2022, while wash trading scams rise," *Crypto News*, December 26, 2022. https://cryptonews.net/news/ nft/18317217/ (accessed May 12, 2023).

26. Ibid.

27. *United States of America v. Nathaniel Chastain*, United States District Court Southern District of New York, Grand Jury Indictment, June 2022, p. 5. https://www.justice.gov/usao-sdnv/press-release/ file/1509701/download (accessed May 12, 2023).

28. Luc Cohen, "Ex-OpenSea Manager convicted in NFT insider trading case," *Reuters*, May 2, 2023. https://www.reuters.com/legal/ex- opensea-manager-convicted-nft-insider-trading-case-2023- 05-03/ (accessed May 4, 2023).

29. Vittoria Benzine, "OpenSea, one of the top NFT platforms, has seen trading volume fall by more than 90 percent since January," *Artnet*, August 31, 2022. https://news.artnet.com/market/openseas-sales-are- down-future-2168369 (accessed May 12, 2023). Elizabeth Howcroft, "NFT sales plunge in Q3, down by 60% from Q2," *Reuters*, October 3, 2022. https://www.reuters.com/technology/nft-sales-plunge-q3- down-by-60-q2-2022-10-03/ (accessed May 12, 2023).

10. Brave New World: The Metaverse, Web 3.0, and the Battle for the Future of Finance

1. Cam Thompson, "It's lonely in the metaverse: Dapp radar data suggests Decentraland has 38 'daily active' users in $1.3B ecosystem," *CoinDesk*, October 7, 2022. https://www.coindesk.com/web3/2022/10/07/ its-lonely-in-the-metaverse-decentralands-38-daily- active-users-in-a-13b-ecosystem/ (accessed May 14, 2023).

2. See `https://www.sandbox.game/en/snoopdogg/` (accessed May 14, 2023).

3. Jamie Redman, "Virtual land adjacent to Snoop Dogg's Sandbox estate sells for $450,000," December 4, 2021. `https://news.bitcoin.com/virtual-land-adjacent-to-snoop-doggs-sandbox-estate-sells-for-450k-in-ethereum/` (accessed May 14, 2023).

4. Adario Strange, "People expect to spend at least 4 hours a day in the metaverse," *Quartz*, August 15, 2022. `https://qz.com/people-expect-to-spend-at-least-4-hours-a-day-in-the-me-1849406012#:~:text=A%20new%20study%20indicates%20that,2022` (accessed May 14, 2023).

5. Will Canny, "Metaverse-related economy could be as much as $13T: Citi," *CoinDesk*, June 7, 2022. `https://www.coindesk.com/business/2022/06/07/metaverse-related-economy-could-be-as-much-as-13-trillion-citi/` (accessed May 14, 2023).

6. Jamie Crawley, "Japan Digital Ministry to create DAO for Web3," *Coin-Desk*, November 3, 2022. `https://www.coindesk.com/policy/2022/11/03/japanese-digital-ministry-to-create-dao-for-web3-exploration/` (accessed May 14, 2023).

7. Christine Moy and Adit Gadgil, *Opportunities in the Metaverse*, J.P. Morgan, 2022, p. 8. `https://www.jpmorgan.com/content/dam/jpm/treasury-services/documents/opportunities-in-the-metaverse.pdf` (accessed May 14, 2023).

8. Kristi Waterworth, "6 Businesses that have bought land in the metaverse," *The Motley Fool*, February 11, 2022. `https://www.fool.com/investing/2022/02/11/7-businesses-that-have-bought-land-in-the-metavers/` (accessed May 14, 2023).

9. See `https://twitter.com/VitalikButerin/status/1553526863783657472?ref_src=twsrc%5Etfw%7Ctwcamp%5Etweetembed%7Ctwterm%5E1553526863783657472%7Ctwgr%5E96275ed76bb73434aaf18071c4a2e9bef391f1c1%7Ctwcon%5Es1_&ref_url=https%3A%2F%2Fen.cryptonomist.ch%2F2022%2F08%2F01%2Fvitalik-buterin-speaks-future-metaverse%2F` (accessed May 14, 2023).

10. Tara Annison, *The Future of Financial Crime in the Metaverse*, Elliptic Metaverse Report 2022, June 2022, pp. 15–16. `https://www.elliptic.co/resources/crime-in-the-metaverse` (accessed May 14, 2023).

11. Europol, *Policing in the Metaverse: What Law Enforcement Needs to Know*, Europol Innovation Lab, October 2022, p. 15. `https://www.europol.europa.eu/cms/sites/default/files/documents/Policing%20in%20the%20metaverse%20-%20what%20law%20enforcement%20needs%20to%20know.pdf` (accessed May 14, 2023).

12. INTERPOL, "INTERPOL launches first global police Metaverse," October 20, 2022. `https://www.interpol.int/en/News-and-Events/News/2022/INTERPOL-launches-first-global-police-Metaverse` (accessed May 14, 2023).

13. Tad Simons, "ACAMS: Fighting financial crime in the metaverse," *Thomson Reuters*, December 5, 2022. `https://www.thomsonreuters.com/en-us/posts/investigation-fraud-and-risk/acams-2022-financial-crime-metaverse/` (accessed May 14, 2023).

14. Vitalik Buterin, "An incomplete guide to stealth addresses," January 20, 2023. `https://vitalik.ca/general/2023/01/20/stealth.html` (accessed May 14, 2023).

15. Jack Shickler, "Money laundering via metaverse, DeFi, NFTs targeted by EU lawmakers' latest draft," *CoinDesk*, September 29, 2022. `https://www.coindesk.com/policy/2022/09/29/money-laundering-via-metaverse-defi-nfts-targeted-by-eu-lawmakers-latest-draft/` (accessed May 14, 2023).

16. Owen Lock and Teresa Cascino, "Cryptoassets, the metaverse, and systemic risk," *BankUnderground*, August 9, 2022. `https://bankunderground.co.uk/2022/08/09/cryptoassets-the-metaverse-and-systemic-risk/` (accessed May 14, 2023).

17. Government of Dubai Media Office, "Dubai Virtual Assets Regulatory Authority becomes world's first regulator to make its debut in the Metaverse," May 3, 2022. `https://mediaoffice.ae/en/news/2022/May/03-05/Dubai-Virtual-Assets-Regulatory-Authority-becomes-world-first` (accessed May 14, 2023).

Afterword: How Much Crime in Cryptocurrencies?

1. David Carlisle, "Treasury's unhosted wallet proposal: Unnecessary, ineffective, and counterproductive," December 31, 2020. `https://www.elliptic.co/blog/us-treasury-unhosted-wallet-proposal-unnecessary-ineffective-counterproductive-says-elliptic` (accessed May 14, 2023). Chainalysis, "2023 Crypto crime trends: Illicit cryptocurrency volumes reach all-time high amid surge in sanctions designations and hacking," January 12, 2023. `https://blog.chainalysis.com/reports/2023-crypto-crime-report-introduction/` (accessed May 14, 2023).

2. Elliptic, "Chinese Businesses Fueling the Fentanyl Epidemic Receive Tens of Millions in Crypto Payments." https://www.elliptic.co/blog/chinese-businesses-fueling-the-fentanyl-epidemic-receive-millions-in-cryptocurrency-payments (accessed August 1, 2023).

3. Elliptic, "US Sanctions Target Terrorist Cryptoassets Linked to the Islamic State in Afghanistan." https://hub.elliptic.co/analysis/us-sanctions-target-terrorist-cryptoassets-linked-to-the-islamic-state-in-afghanistan/ (accessed August 1, 2023).

4. United Nations Office on Drugs and Crime, "Money Laundering." https://www.unodc.org/unodc/en/money-laundering/overview.html (accessed May 14, 2023).

Index

Page numbers followed by *f* refer to figures.

A

Adams, Hayden, 144
AECs (anonymity-enhanced
    cryptocurrencies), 78
Agora (dark web market), 44, 46
AIDS Trojan Horse, 99
Alameda Research, 158–161
Alford, Gary, 13
AlphaBay, 45–48, 72, 76,
    86, 120, 135
Al Qaeda, 74, 105, 196
Al Sadaqah, 73–74, 75*f,* 76
AML/CFT, *see* Anti-money
    laundering and
    countering the
    financing of terrorism

AMM (automated market
    making), 143
Amsterdam, Netherlands, 157
Anonymity, 3–5, 31, 34, 39–45,
    41*f,* 48, 67–70, 76, 78,
    79, 81, 82, 87, 95, 114,
    136, 158, 191
Anonymity-enhanced
    cryptocurrencies
    (AECs), 78
Anonymity set, 43
Anti-money laundering and
    countering the
    financing of terrorism
    (AML/CFT), xi, 30–31
Apple iTunes, 131

249

Application-specific integrated circuits (ASICs), 73
Arcaro, Glenn, 62
Armstrong, Brian, 156–157
ASICs (application-specific integrated circuits), 73
Assassination markets, 7
Asset forfeiture, 18–20
Assia, Yoni, 164
Atari, 185
ATM networks, 103. *See also* Bitcoin ATMs
Augur blockchain, 7
Australia, 66, 104
Austria, 149
Automated market making (AMM), 143
Auzins, Ivars, 61
Axie Infinity, xiii, 150, 151, 154

B
backpage.com, 89–90
Bahamas, 160, 161
Balancer Protocol, 144
Baller Ape Club NFT fraud scheme, xiv, 172, 173*f*
Bangladeshi Central Bank, 103
Bankman-Fried, Sam, 158–160
Bank of England, 190
Banksy, 170
Beeple, 168. *See also* Winkelman, Mike
Bestmixer mixing service, xiii, 50–51, 54, 59
Bezos, Jeff, 54
Biden, Joe, 54, 110

Big Daddy Ape Club, 169
Big Game Hunting, 109–112
Bilyuchenko, Alexy, xiv, 36, 37
Binance, 24, 55, 167
Bitcoin (bitcoins), 193–196. *See also* Bitcoin ATMs
  attempts to ban, 60
  and BitConnect, 61–62
  and Bitfinex, xii–xiv, 133–137
  and colored coins, 164
  Ethereum vs., 140–141, 161
  exchanges, 23–26, 27*f*, 28–38
  and hacking, 123–131, 133–137
  limitations of, 140–141, 144
  and mixers, 46–52
  origins of, 3–10
  price of, 60, 167
  privacy/anonymity of, 39–45, 41*f*, 64, 67
  and ransomware, 97–104, 106–112, 114, 115, 119, 120
  and rise of DeFi laundering, 144–148
  and rise of privacy coins, 67–77, 81
  and Silk Road, xii, 1–16, 17*f*, 18–22
  and Twitter, xiii
  2016 hack and crash of, xv–xviii
  wallets, xvi, 6, 12–16, 19–20, 22, 29, 40, 41, 41*f*, 44, 46, 51, 84, 90, 100, 111
  and Wasabi Wallet, 53, 54, 56

Bitcoin: A Peer-to-Peer Electronic Cash System (white paper), xi, 3–4, 23, 40
Bitcoin7 (exchange), 124, 127
Bitcoin ATMs, 83–96, 94*f*, 114, 135, 194
  as bridge between cash and crypto underworlds, 85–93
  first, xi, 84
  fraud involving, 91–92
  functioning of, 84
  government crack-down on, 93–96
Bitcoin Cash, 50
Bitcoin Fog mixing service, xi, xiii, 48–52, 59, 63, 139
Bitcoin Foundation, 32
Bitcoin Magazine, 56, 140
Bitcoin Market, 24
"Bitcoin Maven," 85–86
Bitcoin of America, 95
bitcointalk.org, 6, 10, 13, 48, 53, 69
BitConnect, 61–62
BitConnect Coin (BCC), 61
Bitfinex exchange, xii, xiii, xiv, xv–xviii, 123, 124, 127–138, 146
Bitfloor, 124
BitGold, 5
Bithumb, 128, 129–130
BitInstant, 32–33
BitLicense framework, 79, 93
Bittrex, 78
Bitzlato, xiv, 121

Black Market Peso Exchange, 88
Blockchain(s), 5–7, 11–14, 16, 22, 24–26, 35, 161, 178
  and Bitcoin ATMs, 86, 93
  and Bitfinex, 133, 135–138
  Ethereum, 24, 77, 139–152, 161
  and mixers, 37–45, 49, 50, 52–55
  and NFTs, 163–167, 169–172
  and peeling chains, 129
  and privacy coins, 59, 62–67, 69, 70, 75–78, 80, 81
  and ransomware, 102, 103, 107, 109, 111, 112, 118, 119
  sidechains, 150
  TRON, 197
  and Web 3.0, 182–185
Blockchain analytics firms, 63–67, 160, 194
Blockchain Intelligence Group, 65
B-Money, 5
Bored Ape NFT, 178
Bored Ape Yacht Club, 166–167, 169, 170
Botnets, 100
Bots, data-extracting, 64–65
Brady, Tom, 159
Bridges (DeFi), 150–151
Bridges, Shaun, 15, 16, 25, 26, 27*f*, 28, 29
British Virgin Islands, 34

BTC-e cryptocurrency
     exchange, xi, xii, xiv,
     33–39, 48, 59, 63, 80, 101
BTCKing cash-for-crypto
     swapping service, 85
Budovsky, Author, 7–8
Bundchen, Gisele, 159
"Buried treasure" service, 86
Buterin, Vitalik, xi, 77,
          140–144, 156, 163, 164,
          168, 186, 189

C
Calavery, Jennifer Shasky, 32
California, 85, 94, 137
Cambodia, 93
CampBX, 25–26
Canada, 45, 104, 140, 166
Canton Business Corporation,
          34, 36
Cash transactions, 87
Cazes, Alexandre, 45, 47,
          50, 76, 77
CFTC (Commodity Futures
     Trading Commission),
     160
Chainalysis, 64, 65
Chain-hopping, 135, 172
Chainlink, 139, 148
Changelly, 103
Chastain, Nathaniel, xiv,
          174–175
Chatex, 120
Chaum, David, 4
China, xiii, 130, 131, 133

China Guangfa Bank, 131
Chinese yuan, 131
ChipMixer, 139
Christie's, 168
Ciphertrace, 65
Circle, 145
Citi, 185
Civil forfeiture, 18
"Clarissa," xvii, 134
Cloud 9 (dark web market),
          44, 46
Clusters and clustering,
          41–42, 45, 49, 64, 65
Coinbase, 24, 32, 37, 55, 146,
          156–157, 167
CoinCenter, 117–118, 156
CoinDesk, 156
Coinfirm, 65
CoinJoin, 53–54, 56, 67
CoinMKT, 26
Coin Ninja, 50
Coinsource, 93
Coinswaps (coinswap services),
          80, 103, 114, 126
Cold storage, 19–20, 124–125
Colombia, 88, 89, 105
Colonial Pipeline attack, xiii,
          110–112
Colored coins, 164
Combating Russian Money
          Laundering Act,
          xiv, 121
Commodity Futures Trading
          Commission
          (CFTC), 160

Common spend analysis, 42, 64, 65, 68

Comprehensive Crime Control Act (1984), 18

Conti RaaS gang, 120

Conti ransomware attack, 112, 120, 121

Costa Rica, 7, 112, 120

Counterfeiting, 5, 165

Cream Finance, 150

Criminal forfeiture, 18, 51, 76

"Crocodile of Wall Street," 134

Crowdfunding, 76

Crypto.com, 167

Cryptocurrency Compliance Cooperative, 90, 93

Crypto-jacking, 73, 80, 127

CryptoKitties, 166

CryptoLocker, 100–101, 103, 104

CryptoNote White Paper (Saberhagen), 68, 69

CryptoWall, 101, 103, 104

CTRs (currency transaction reports), 117

Cuba, 105

Currency transaction reports (CTRs), 117

Curve, 144, 146, 148, 149

Cypherpunks, 4–6, 8, 31, 42, 67, 70

A Cypherpunk's Manifesto (Hughes), 4

Cyprus, 34

Czech Republic, 103, 119

D

DAOs, see Decentralized autonomous organizations

Dapper Labs, 166, 168

Dapps, see Decentralized applications

DarkSide ransomware gang, xiii, 111, 120

Dark web, xi, 21, 23, 44, 48, 66, 71–72. See also Silk Road

Dash, 69–71, 74, 75, 84

Dash White Paper (Duffield), 69

DEA, see US Drug Enforcement Administration

Decentraland, 183–186

Decentralized applications (Dapps), 141, 142, 144–146, 149–151, 153, 154, 163, 165, 166, 187, 190

Decentralized autonomous organizations (DAOs), 142–145, 147, 149, 153, 154, 163, 165, 178, 179, 182–185, 190

Decentralized exchanges (DEXs), 143–149, 151–153, 161, 163, 172, 182, 187

Decentralized finance (DeFi), xiv, 139–163, 171, 175, 185, 187, 190, 193, 194, 196

Decentralized finance (DeFi)
    (*continued*)
  Ethereum, 140–143
  and FTX, 158–162
  hacking, 149–152
  regulation of, 152–158
  and rise of DeFi laundering,
    143–149
DeFi, *see* Decentralized
    finance
Dei, Wei, 5
De-mixing, 43
DEXs, *see* Decentralized
    exchanges
Dharma ransomware strain,
    109–110
DigiCash, 4
Digital images (digital art),
    165–168
Digital Mint, 85, 93
Distributed ledger technology
    (DLT), 5–6
DODO, 144
DOJ, *see* US Department of
    Justice
Double-spend, 5
Draper, Tim, 20
"Dread Pirate Roberts,"
    see Ulbricht, Ross
Dream Market, 44, 46
DropBit, 50
Drug sales (drug trade), xii,
    1–3, 7, 9–11, 13, 23,
    33, 44, 47–48, 77,
    87–88, 187, 196
Dubai, 190

Duffield, Evan, 69
"Dutch," xvii, 134
dYdX, 144

E
eBay, 3, 169
e-Gold, 7, 8, 30
Electric Coin Company,
    70, 74, 81–82
Elliptic, 54, 63–65, 80, 86, 111,
    119, 128, 133, 135,
    149, 161, 170, 172,
    186, 194–196
Eminem, 167
Engstrom, Paul, 77
ERC-20 standard, xii, 144–145,
    147–148, 151, 159–161,
    163, 183–184
ERC-721 standard, xii,
    164, 166
Estonia, 120
Ether, 84, 139, 144, 145,
    147–149, 151, 152, 156,
    161, 164, 166–168, 170,
    172, 178, 179
Ethereum, xi, xii, 24, 77,
    139–151, 154, 155*f*,
    157, 161–167, 170,
    174, 184, 189
Ethereum Classic, 149
Ethereum White Paper
    (Buterin), 140–142
eToro, 164
European Union (European
    Commission), 45, 47, 50,
    52, 59, 66, 113, 118, 190

Europol, xii–xiii, 45, 49, 50,
    54, 59, 71, 72, 76,
    80–81, 88, 187
Everydays - The First 5000 Days
    (Beeple), 168
Evolution (dark web market),
    44, 46
Exchanges, cryptocurrency,
    22–26, 28–38. *See also*
    specific exchanges

F
Facebook, 32, 185
Faiella, Robert, xii, 33, 85
Farber, William, 86
Farmer's Market, 9
FATF, *see* Financial Action
    Task Force
FBI, *see* US Federal Bureau of
    Investigation
FCA (Financial Conduct
    Authority), 95
Federal Trade Commission, 91
Fentanyl, 47–48, 180, 187, 196
Fiat currencies, 23, 25, 30,
    31, 37, 38, 47, 79, 80,
    101, 115, 119, 128–131,
    144, 145, 148. *See*
    also US dollar
Fidelity Investments, 26
Financial Action Task Force
    (FATF), xiii, 31, 49, 50,
    65, 78, 80, 89, 112–119,
    152, 153, 171
Financial Conduct Authority
    (FCA), 95

Financial Crimes Enforcement
    Network (FinCEN), xi,
    xiv, 30–33, 35–38, 47, 50,
    51, 54–55, 63, 78, 93, 94,
    101, 117, 121, 152
The Financial Flows of Human
    Trafficking (report), 89
FinCEN, *see* Financial Crimes
    Enforcement Network
FIOD (Dutch anti-money
    laundering agency), 157
First Amendment, 117
"Fluffypony," 70
Forbes magazine, 2, 134
Force, Carl, 14–16, 17*f*,
    25–26, 33–34, 43
Forks, 69, 149
France, 34, 36, 170
Fraud, 60–62, 90–93, 95, 134,
    137, 160, 169–175, 187,
    194, 197. *See also* Money
    laundering
"French Maid," 15, 16, 17*f*
FTT, 159
FTX cryptocurrency exchange,
    xiv, 158–162, 196
Fungibility, concept of, 164

G
G7 countries, 112–113
G20, 31
Gambling, 23
GameOver Zeus, 100
Gaming platforms, online,
    28, 141, 150–151, 166,
    168–169, 183–185

Garantex, 120
Gemini, 24, 32, 37, 79
Germany, 64, 120
Ghorbaniyan, Mohammad, 106
Gibraltar, 53
Global Financial Crisis
        (2008), 3
Google, 104, 186
Grams, 46
Great Redistribution of the
        Climate Change Disaster
        (NFT image), 170
Greece, 35
Green, Curtis, 16
Green, Matthew, 68–70
Grens, Mark, 85
Guidance for a Risk-Based
        Approach to Virtual
        Assets and Virtual
        Asset Service Providers
        (FATF), xiii, 114
Gulf Cooperation Council, 113
Gweis, 164

H
Hacking, 123–138
    of Bitfinex, 127–138
    crypto-jacking, 73
    exchanges as target
        of, 123–126
    North Korea's role
        in, 127–133
Hamas, 76
Hardware Security Modules
        (HSM), 124
Harmat, Bálint, 56

Harmon, Gary, 51
Harmon, Larry Dean, xii, xiii,
        45–48, 50–51, 56
Harrigan, Martin, 64
Harvard University, 99
Helix mixing service, xii,
        xiii, 46–48, 46*f*, 50–52,
        54, 59, 63, 101, 139, 147
Hess, Amy, 39
Hilton, Paris, 169
Hoenisch, Toby, 149
Hong Kong, xv, 38, 121, 133, 158
Hot storage, 124, 125
Hot wallets, 125, 128
HSM (Hardware Security
        Modules), 124
Hughes, Eric, 4
Human trafficking, 89–90, 93
Hutchins, Marcus, 102
Hydra, 86, 111, 120, 121, 135
Hyok, Park Jin, 104

I
Identity theft, 35, 91, 126, 130
India, xvii, 61, 62
Initial coin offerings (ICOs),
        60–61, 145
"Insta," 77
Internal Revenue Service (IRS),
        11, 13, 16, 26, 49, 59, 188
Internet, 3, 49, 87, 165, 182–183.
        See also Dark web
Internet Organised Crime
        Threat Assessment
        (IOCTA), 71
Internet Protocol (IP), 1

INTERPOL, xiv, 187–188, 188*f*–189*f*
IOCTA *(Internet Organised Crime Threat Assessment)*, 71
IP addresses, 50, 77
Iran, xii, 105, 106, 109, 121
IRS, *see* Internal Revenue Service
Islamic Revolutionary Guard Corp (IRGC), 121
Islamic State (ISIS), 105, 196

J
James, LeBron, 168
Japan, xii, 26, 28, 29, 66, 78–79, 104, 161, 185
Japan Financial Services Agency (JFSA), 78–79
Jones, Tommy Lee, 18
J.P. Morgan, 81–82, 185

K
Karasavidi, Dimitrii, 127
Kardashian, Kim, 54
Karpeles, Mark, 28, 29
Kaspersky, 104
Kazakhstan, 137
"Khaleesi," 131
Khorashadizadeh, Ali, 106
Know Your Customer (KYC), 30
Korner, Ryan, 62
Kraken, 24, 32
KuCoin exchange, 139–140, 147, 148, 151
Kumbhani, Satish, 61–62

L
Laos, 93
Latvia, 61, 120
Lazarus Group, xii, xiii, xiv, 103–104, 107, 111, 127, 130–134, 138–140, 147, 148, 150–152, 154, 155, 155*f,* 161
Lee, Jim, 188
Libertarianism, 4, 9
Liberty Reserve, 7–8, 30, 34, 48, 52, 121
Lichtenstein, Ilya, xiii, xiv, 134–137
Li Jaidong, xiii, 129*f,* 130–132
Liquid, 161
Liquidity pools, 143–144, 149
Litecoin, 24, 34, 50, 84
Lobbying groups, 117–118, 156
LocalBitcoins, 86
London Metropolitan Police, 88–89

M
Madonna, 167
Magic: The Gathering Online, 28
Malware, 2, 99, 100, 102, 104, 107–108, 120, 125, 130, 150
MANA, 183
Manchin, Joe, 60, 66
Manhattan District Attorney's Office, 94–95
Market manipulation, 173
Marshall Islands, 190

MAS (Monetary Authority of
　　Singapore), 95
Mbappé, Kylian, 168
McCaleb, Jeb, 28
McDonald's, 169
McKinsey and Associates,
　　185
Meiklejohn, Sarah, 64, 65
Melbourne, Australia, 91
Merkle Science, 65
Messi, Lionel, 168
Meta, 185
Meta Horizon Worlds, 185
Metaverse, 177–182
　　origin of term, 183
　　and Web 3.0, 182–186
Mexico, 89
Michel, Aurelien, 172
Microsoft Windows,
　　102, 186
Miners, 5
Mining farms, 73
Mixers, 43–57, 67, 126
　　government investigation
　　　　of, 49–52
　　Helix, 45–49
　　and privacy, 56–57
　　Wasabi Wallet, 52–56
MLATs (mutual legal assistance
　　treaties), 12
Mnuchin, Steve, 116–117, 132
Mohammad, Kaish, 94
Monaco, Lisa, 136
Monero, xii, 69–78, 80–81, 84,
　　103, 109, 127, 135
Monetary Authority of
　　Singapore (MAS), 95

Money laundering, xii, xiii, xiv,
　　12, 13, 16, 19, 25, 31,
　　34–39, 44, 47, 51, 54, 56,
　　59, 62, 80, 85, 87–91,
　　101, 113, 119–121, 126,
　　128–129, 131, 134, 144,
　　146–148, 157, 160, 161,
　　174, 196, 197. *See also*
　　Anti-money laundering
　　and countering the
　　financing of terrorism
　　(AML/CFT)
Money mules, 126, 137
Money service businesses
　　(MSBs), 30
Morgan, Heather, xiii, xiv,
　　134–137
Moscow, Russia, 119
Möser, Malte, 64
Mt. Gox cryptocurrency
　　exchange, xii, xiv–xvi,
　　26, 27*f*, 28–30, 34–37, 48,
　　52, 64, 123, 124, 160
MPC (Multi-Party
　　Computing), 124
MSBs (money service
　　businesses), 30
Mujahidin, 73–74, 75*f*
Multi-Party Computing
　　(MPC), 124
Multi-signature ("multi-sig")
　　hot wallets, 125
Musk, Elon, xiii, 54
Mutant Ape Planet, 172
Mutual legal assistance
　　treaties (MLATs), 12
Myanmar, 105

N

Nakamoto, Satoshi, xi, 3–6,
    8, 9, 23, 40, 42, 43, 52,
    70, 83, 129, 141, 193
National Basketball Association,
    168
National Health Service, 102
Nelson, Brian, 155
Netherlands, xiv, 50, 157
New Jersey, 91
New Liberty Standard, 24
New York City, 13, 32, 47,
    94–95, 136, 174–175
New York Department of
    Financial Services
    (NYDFS), 65–66, 79, 93
New York state, 79, 93, 110
New Zealand, 34, 36, 104
NFTs, *see* Non-fungible tokens
Nike, 169
"Nob," 15, 16
Non-fungible tokens (NFTs),
    xii, xiv, 163–175, 182,
    187, 190, 194
  law enforcement's response
    to, 171–175
  minting, 165
  origin of, 164–169
  as vehicle for fraud, 169–170
North Korea, xii, xiii, xiv,
    xvii, 103–105, 107,
    113–114, 127–133,
    138–139, 150, 153, 154,
    170, 180–181, 194, 196
NYDFS, *see* New York Depart-
    ment of Financial
    Services

O

Obama, Barack, xiii,
    54, 105–106
Ocean Protocol, 140
O'Connor, John, 55
OFAC, *see* Office of Foreign
    Assets Control
"Off-chain" recording, 35
Office of Foreign Assets
    Control (OFAC), xii,
    xiv, 104–107, 119–121,
    127, 132, 133, 154,
    155*f,* 156–157
Okparaeke, Chukwuemeka,
    47–48
Onion Router network, 1
OpenSea, 167–170, 174–175,
    184, 186
Operation Guatuzo, 88, 95
Operation Onymous, 45
Organized criminal networks,
    87–88

P

Palestine, 76
Panama, 33–34
Pancake Swap, 144
PayPal, 24, 30
PC Cyborg Corporation, 99
Peeling chain technique,
    128–131, 129*f,*
    134–136, 174
Peer-to-peer exchangers, 85, 86
Peer-to-peer transactions,
    4, 5, 21, 100, 115–116,
    140–143, 153, 167, 198
Pertsev, Alexey, xiv, 146, 157

Phishing, 99, 125–126
Pig butchering, 92–93, 95
Policing in the Metaverse:
    What Law Enforcement
    Needs to Know (Europol
    report), 187
Ponzi, Charles, 61
Ponzi schemes, 61, 197
Popp, Joseph, 99, 100
Potekhin, Danil, 127
PoW (proof-of-work)
    algorithm, 5
Privacy coins, 59–82
  birth of, 67–71
  illicit activity
      involving, 71–74
  regulation of, 78–82
  and rise of blockchain
      analytics industry,
      63–67
Privacy concerns, 4–5, 9,
    56–57. *See also*
    Anonymity
Private keys, 14, 19–20, 29,
    40–41, 51, 68, 76, 116,
    124–125, 130, 170
PrivateSend technique, 69
Proof-of-work (PoW)
    algorithm, 5
Prostitution, 89–90
Pump and dump schemes, 173

Q
Quantum International
    Investments LLC, 26

R
RaaS (ransomware-as-a-service),
    107–112
RAND Corporation, 74
Ransomware, xiii, 97–122, 98*f,*
    196, 197–198
  involving Bitcoin, 99–104
  Office of Foreign Assets
      Control's response to,
      104–107, 112–119
  RaaS and Big Game Hunting
      attacks, 104–107
  recent trends, 122
  sanctions as weapon
      against, 119–121
Ransomware-as-a-service
    (RaaS), 107–112
Ray, John J., III, 160
"Razzlekhan," xvii, 134
Regulatory arbitrage, 38
Reid, Fergal, 64
RenBridge, 161
RenBTC, 161
Requirements for Certain
    Transactions Involving
    Convertible Virtual
    Currency or Digital
    Assets (FinCEN), 117
Retirement fraud, 91
Reveton, 99–101
REvil ransomware attack, 112
Ring signatures, 68
Ripple, 24
Role playing, 28, 183
Ronin Bridge, xiii, 150–151, 154

Rosenberg, Elizabeth, 158
Rug pulls, 61, 172
Russia, 7, 34, 36, 37, 48, 80, 86,
    98–100, 109–112,
    119–121, 127, 130, 134,
    137, 140, 146, 156
Ryuk ransomware, 110, 120

S
Saberhagen, Nicolas van, 68
St. Vincent and the Grenadines,
    120
SamSam ransomware
    scheme, 106
Samsung, 185
SAND, 184
The Sandbox, 183–184, 190
SARs (suspicious activity
    reports), 30
Scams, 90–93. *See also specific*
    scams, e.g.: Phishing
SEC (US Securities and
    Exchange Commission),
    61, 160
Second Life, 183
Semenov, Roman, 146
September 11, 2001 terrorist
    attacks, 114
1718 Sanctions Committee, 132
Sex trade, 89–90
Seychelles, 34
ShapeShift, 103
Shin, Laura, 149
Shopify, 169
Shrem, Charlie, xii, 32–33, 85

Shroomery, 13
Sidechains, 150
Silk Road, xi, xii, 1–3, 9–16,
    18–22, 25, 26, 27f, 28, 33,
    35, 42–45, 48, 49, 56, 60,
    63, 85, 187, 190, 195
Silk Road 2.0, 22
Singapore, 34, 66, 95, 139, 159
Sky Mavis, 150, 151
Smart contracts, 141–151,
    153–155, 165, 171–172,
    179, 184
Smurfing, 25, 88
Snoop Dogg, 169, 180, 184
Snowden, Edward, 71
Social engineering cam-
    paigns, 125–126
Software-as-a-service
    (SaaS), 108
Solana, 167, 169, 170, 172
Sorare, 168
Sotheby's, 168
South Africa, 70
South America, 88
South Korea, 127–128, 130, 185
Spagni, Riccardo, 70, 71
Spain, xii, 7, 88, 95
Specially Designated Nationals
    and Blocked Persons List
    (SDN List), xii, 105–107,
    154, 155f
Stablecoins, xii, 145, 151,
    159, 196–197
Stealth addresses, 68
Stephenson, Neal, 183

Sterlingov, Roman,
	xiii, 48, 51–52
"Stipulation for interlocutory
	sale," 20
Storm, Roman, 146
*Study of the Facilitation of
	Money Laundering and
	Terror Finance Through
	the Trade in Works
	of Art* (US Treasury
	report), 171
SUEX, 119–120
Sushiswap, 144
Suspicious activity reports
	(SARs), 30
Sweden, 48
Swiss bank accounts, 114–116
Swiss franc, 115
Switzerland, 103
Symantec, 73, 102, 104
Syria, 73–74, 75*f*
Szabo, Nick, 4–5

T
Taylor, Robert, 95
Telegram, 74
Terra USD, 159
Terrorist organizations,
	73–74, 75*f*, 76, 105,
	121, 196–197
Tether, 84, 139, 145, 196–197
Tetley, Theresa Lynn, 85–86
Texas, 110
Thailand, 48
Three Arrows Capital (3AC),
	159

Tian Yinyin, xiii, 129*f*, 130–132
TIME magazine, 168
Tokenization, 165
Tokens, 182
Toomey, Pat, 66
TopShot, 168
TORN, 147
Tornado Cash mixer, xiv,
	146–148, 151–152,
	154–158, 172
Tor network, 1, 6, 8–10, 15, 46,
	50, 51, 77
Total value locked
	(TVL), 149, 150
Travel Rule, 114–115
TRM Labs, 65
TRON, 167, 197
Trump, Donald, and
	administration, 118, 169
Tuan, Le Ahn, xiv, 172
Turing-complete scripts, 141
"Turkish Martha Stewart," 134
TVL (total value
	locked), 149, 150
Twitter, xiii, 48, 51, 54, 55, 59,
	60, 74, 128, 169

U
UK, *see* United Kingdom
Ukraine, 7, 121, 137, 156
Ulbricht, Ross, xi, 1–3, 8–16,
	17*f*, 19–22, 25–26, 43, 44,
	48–50, 71, 77
Underground Brokers, 9
Unhosted wallets, 116–118,
	134, 152, 156

UniCC, 44
Uniswap, 144–146, 148, 149, 151
United Arab Emirates, 172, 185
United Kingdom (UK), 55,
    63–64, 66, 88–89, 95, 99,
    102, 104, 172
United Nations Office of
    Drugs and Crime
    (UNODC), 197
United Nations Security
    Council (UNSC), 132
UNI token, 145
UNODC (United Nations
    Office of Drugs and
    Crime), 197
UNSC (United Nations Security
    Council), 132
UN Security Council, 139
Unspent transaction outputs
    (UTXOs), 40, 41*f*, 42, 64
Unstoppable privacy
    protocols, 147
USA PATRIOT Act, 8
USDC (stablecoin),
    145, 151, 179
US Department of Homeland
    Security, 29
US Department of Justice
    (DOJ), xiii, xiv, 18, 33, 35,
    51–52, 62, 74, 76, 94, 101,
    104, 111–112, 130–133,
    137, 162, 172, 174
US Department of State,
    110, 132
US Department of the Treasury,
    xi, xii, 8, 30, 104–105,
    116–117, 121, 132,
    154–156, 155*f*, 158,
    171–172
US dollar, 9, 23–26, 29, 31,
    33, 34, 47, 80, 83, 115,
    133, 145, 159
US Drug Enforcement
    Administration (DEA),
    9, 11, 14–15, 26, 86
US Federal Bureau of Investiga-
    tion (FBI), xi, 11, 13–14,
    19, 20, 22, 39, 44, 45,
    59, 92, 99
US Federal Trade Commission
    (FTC), 92
US Government Accountability
    Office (GAO), 89
US Marshals Service (USMS),
    xii, 18–21
US Secret Service, 15, 26, 95
US Securities and Exchange
    Commission
    (SEC), 61, 160
Utility fraud, 91
UTXOs, *see* Unspent
    transaction outputs

V
Valhalla Marketplace, 72
VARA (Virtual Assets
    Regulatory Authority),
    190
VASPs (virtual asset service
    providers), 114–116
Venture capital, 20, 158–159
Verge, 74

Verner, Aleksandr, xiv, 36
Vietnam, 150
Vinnik, Alexander, xi, xii,
    xiv, 34–38
Virtual assets, 113
Virtual asset service providers
    (VASPs), 114–116
Virtual Assets Regulatory
    Authority (VARA), 190
Virtual reality (VR), 183, 185
Virtual worlds, 183–184
Voorhees, Erik, 103

W
Wallets:
    Bitcoin, xvi, 6, 12–16, 19–20,
        22, 29, 40, 41, 41*f,* 44, 46,
        51, 84, 90, 100, 111
    hot, 125, 128
    unhosted, 116–118,
        134, 152, 156
Wall Street Market, 72
Walmart, 136
WannaCry ransomware
    attack, xii, 98–99, 98*f,*
    101–107, 111, 127
War on Drugs, 1–2, 44
Wasabi Wallet, xiii,
    52–56, 135, 139
Washington, George, 18
Wash trading, 173–174
Wearables, 168–169, 180, 184
Weaver, Nicholas, 22
Web 3.0, 182–186
Web-scraping, 64–65
Western Union, 30

White House Market, 72, 77
White paper, bitcoin, 42, 53
Wilcox-O'Hearn, Zooko, 70
Winkelman, Mike "Beeple,"
    168
Winklevoss, Cameron, 32
Winklevoss, Tyler, 32
WinLock, 99, 100
Wire fraud, 174
Wizard Spider, 110
World Health Organization, 99
World of Warcraft, 183
World Wide Web, 3
Wyoming, 190

X
Xapo, 124
XCoin, 69

Y
YoBit, 130
YouBit, 127–128
Yuga Labs, 166–167
Yum, Ilhwan, 11

Z
Zcash, 70–71, 74–76, 79, 84
Zerocash Electric Coin
    Company, 70
Zerocoin White Paper
    (Green), 68–69
Zero-knowledge proofs, 69, 70,
    81–82, 147, 178
Zhong, James, 21
zkSNACKs, 53–56
Zuckerberg, Mark, 32